IMAGES
of America

PLANT CITY

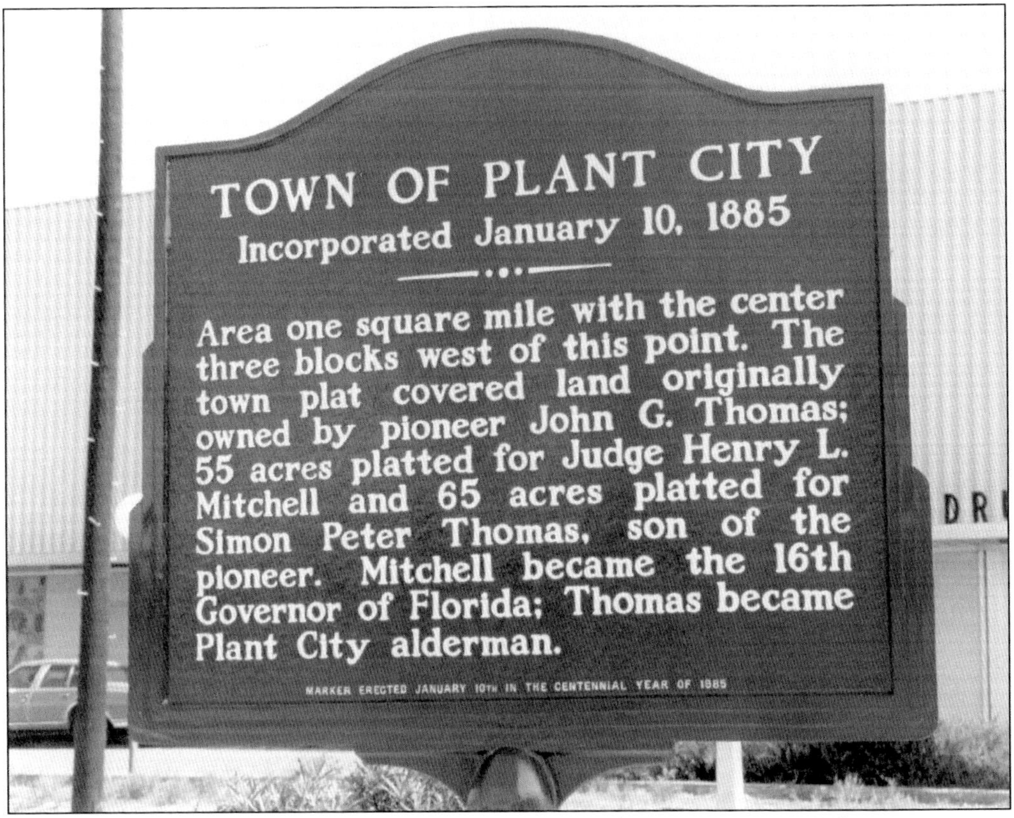

INCORPORATION. The town of Plant City was incorporated on January 10, 1885.

IMAGES
of America

PLANT CITY

East Hillsborough Historical Society

ARCADIA
PUBLISHING

ISBN 978-0-7385-1738-4

Published by Arcadia Publishing
Charleston, South Carolina

Printed in the United States of America

Library of Congress Catalog Card Number: 2004113868

For all general information contact Arcadia Publishing at:
Telephone 843-853-2070
Fax 843-853-0044
E-mail sales@arcadiapublishing.com
For customer service and orders:
Toll-Free 1-888-313-2665

Visit us on the Internet at www.arcadiapublishing.com

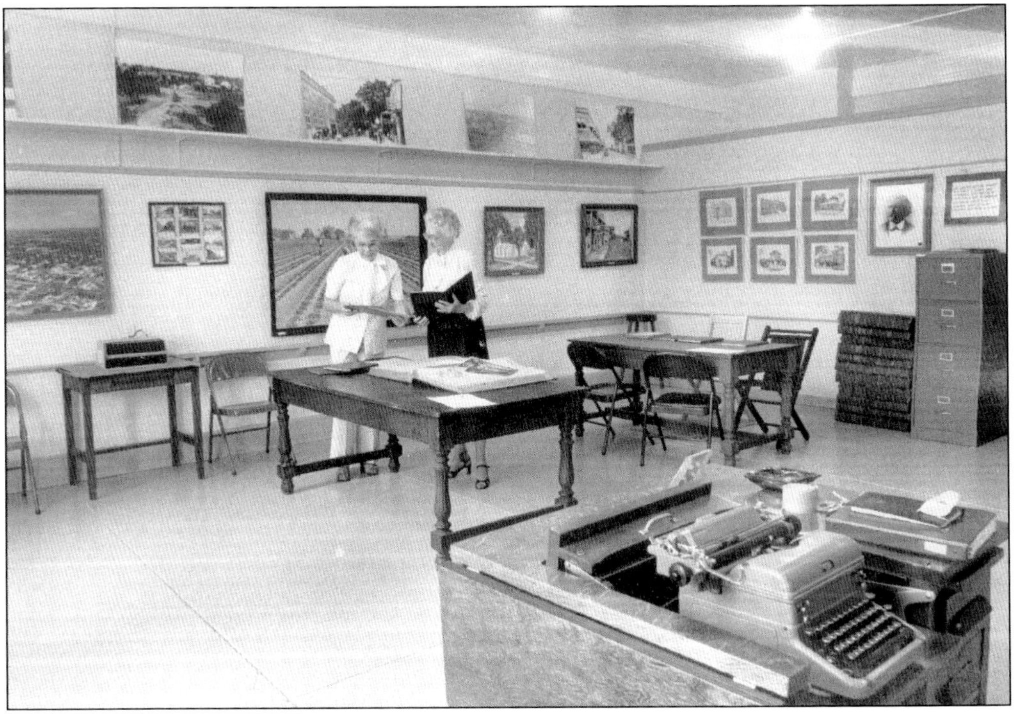

The Quintilla Geer Bruton Archives Center in its Early Days. Pictured from left to right are Quintilla Geer Bruton and Virginia Jordan Hull, the "pioneers" of the archives center. The Quintilla Geer Bruton Archives Center contains holdings of more than 4,000 books covering many genealogy-related topics. The focus of this collection, however, is on the Plant City area, Hillsborough County, and Florida. The archives center collection also includes microforms of such items as census records, newspapers, CD-ROMs, family history, and genealogy files, as well as historic photographs; it is staffed entirely by volunteers.

Contents

ACKNOWLEDGMENTS

The East Hillsborough Historical Society, formed in 1974, is a 501(C)3 non-profit organization dedicated to the preservation of the historical and cultural heritage of Plant City and Eastern Hillsborough County. The offices of the society are located in the 1914 Plant City High School (see below), a National Register of Historic Places Site, owned by the City of Plant City and operated under partnership with the East Hillsborough Historical Society. The general purpose of this society, as set forth in Article II of the Articles of Incorporation, is to foster and encourage interest in historic inquiry and study generally, but especially among its members; to collect, preserve, and house historic documents and objects, especially those pertaining to eastern Hillsborough County and the state of Florida; to collect, preserve, and house genealogical books and materials to aid genealogical research; and further, to encourage and participate in historic preservation.

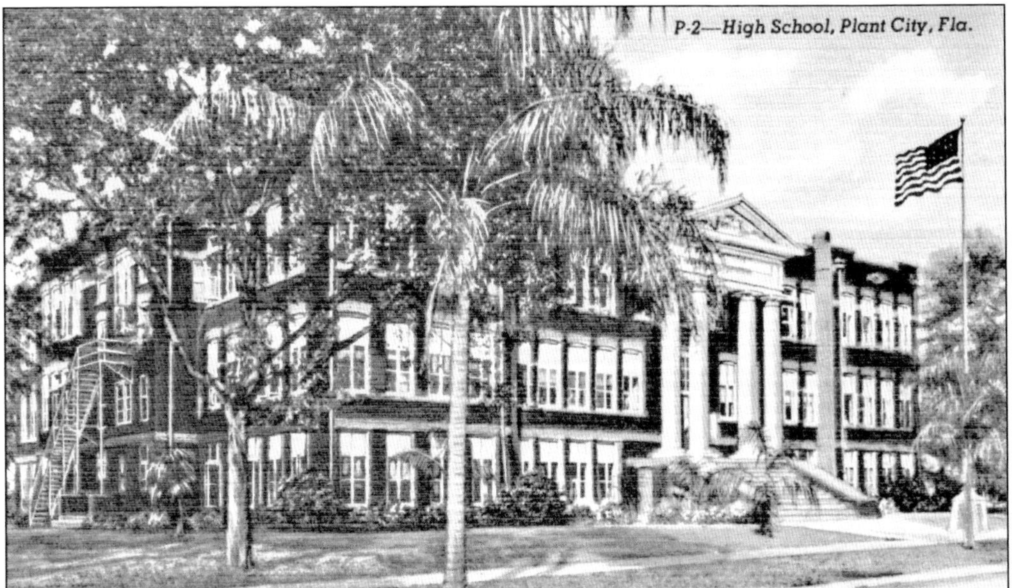

Introduction

We can attribute Plant City's development to Henry B. Plant's 1883 extension of his South Florida Railroad into the Central Florida area, known as Ichepuckesassa. We knew the peninsula of Florida as Kanyuksaw, or "point of land." Our agricultural industries changed to include citrus, strawberries, and vegetable crops. Constantine Shannon brought strawberries to the area in the early 1880s from Shannon, Mississippi. In Plant City, known as the Winter Strawberry Capital of the World, strawberries are a multimillion-dollar industry.

Earlier settlers in the area, both Native American and white, inhabited the area north of town known as Hichipucksassa. Central Florida had many forts that provided shelter and safety to the settlers who were trying to tame the new territory. The first white settlers came into the area in the late 1830s. Rev. Daniel Simmons, a Baptist minister from Savannah, came to establish a mission in the known Indian territory. Other correspondence of this era refers to Chief Billy Bowlegs having a camp near the Lake Thonotosassa area. Early Florida was quite different. Vast amounts of land were open prairies.

As the settlers began to make their way to the area, every aspect of life as we see it today came with them. Religion was one priority of the inhabitants. Early family names that are still prominent in Plant City are Sparkman, Thomas, Evers, Collins, Knight, Platt, Wilder, Mitchell, Howell, and Futch.

By 1880, the population of Hillsborough County had reached more than 5,000. Manatee and Polk Counties had been created and were beginning their development. The railroads were expanding, and life would never be the same. Locally, our communities of Cork, Shiloh, Collinstown, Knights, and Wilder would see changes. Cork now had its own doctor and post office, and citrus was its leading crop. Shiloh had a sawmill and several general merchandise stores. Farming crops was not only for sustenance but for cash business. Vegetables and cattle were a big part of this area's early agricultural economy. Alafia, Turkey Creek, and Springhead were thriving with merchants and farmers. Education had become a priority. By 1885, Plant City, with a population of 300, had 13 stores, 2 churches (Baptist and Methodist), and an academy known as Shiloh.

Plant City incorporated as a town on January 10, 1885. Land was selling at prices between $10 and $75 per acre. Cotton and lumber had joined vegetables, fruits, and cattle as the principal shipments, which rail now moved. By 1900, many changes had occurred and Plant City had suffered many losses, including the malaria epidemic of 1887 and the winter of 1894–1895, the coldest on record to date. The loss of crops was more than anyone could imagine.

The historic residential neighborhoods began to be built. Home styles varied from the simple vernaculars and bungalows to the ornate elegance of Queen Anne and Colonial and classical revivals.

Mr. F.W. Merrin started Plant City's first newspaper, the *Plant City Courier*, on September 24, 1884. He had brought his printing press here from Mississippi. Along with banking, the telephone came to town in 1902, having 34 subscribers. Cars were on the streets. The 1911 telephone directory listed 250 names. Downtown had the Roselawn Hotel (the former Tropical Hotel) and Olivette Hotel.

The women of Plant City had sewing parties at their Thimble Club and took action at their Woman's Christian Temperance Union and the School Improvement Association. The 1910s brought many changes to the community. World War I left its mark and was quickly followed by the troubling years of the 1920s and 1930s. Many families and businesses would never recover from either of these times of sorrow. On January 15, 1914, they laid the first brick streets in Plant City. Phosphate mining had become a big part of the economy. The Coronet mine was in full production, and the interest had spanned to include Hopewell, Alafia, and Turkey Creek. They ratified the 19th Amendment in 1920, giving women the right to vote. Dial phone service came to Plant City in 1923.

The $500,000 Hotel Plant opened its doors in 1926. Five thousand people attended this gala event. Demolished for progress in the 1970s, it is now the site of the former Sun Trust Bank building, recently acquired by the First United Methodist Church. In 1929, the Woman's Club of Plant City formed what later became the public library of Plant City.

Social activity was on the rise, and Plant City saw its first Strawberry Festival in 1930. In 1932, there were no Sunday movies in Plant City. Postage rates were raised from 2¢ to 3¢. With the 1940s came new change, and Plant City was back on the road to recovery. Service had become the new business in town. Plant City had eight or more grocery stores, all of them offering customer service, including fresh meats and vegetables delivered to your door. Automobile dealerships were downtown. Other social amenities—including parks and recreation—were added, rounding out Plant City's social offerings.

Plant City, proud of its history and heritage, has listed the Downtown Commercial, North Plant City Residential, and Downtown Residential Historic Districts on the local and National Register of Historic Places. The 1914 Plant City High School, Union Station Railroad Depot, Hillsboro Bank Building, Amoco Gas Station, and Bing-Washington Rooming House are individual listings on the National Register of Historic Places.

Welcome to Plant City!

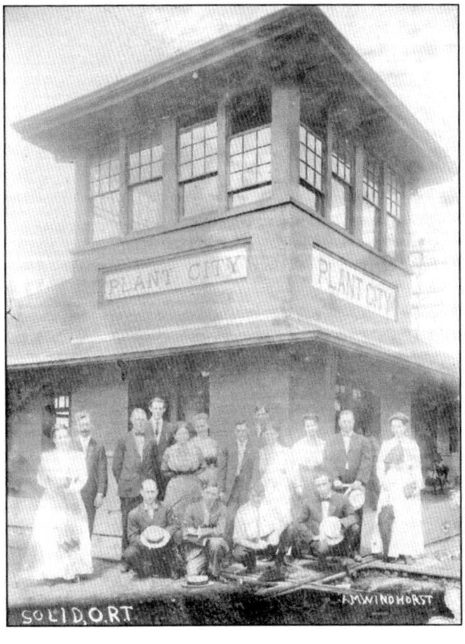

ORDER OF RAILROAD TELEGRAPHERS GROUP, ATLANTIC COAST LINE AND SEABOARD AIR LINES RAILWAYS, PLANT CITY. Pictured from left to right are (front row) C.B. Marsh; C.V. Franklin; H.J. Marshall; and J.M. McCaskill; (back row) Mrs. and Mr. T.J. Tedder, local chairman, Order of Railroad Telegraphers; J.S. Nickels; C.T. Neuner; Mrs. J.S. Nickels; Mrs. C.T. Neuner; R.M. Morgan; Mr. and Mrs. J.R. Tedder; Mrs. and Mr. A.W. Smith; and Mrs. S.V. Anders. According to R.M. Morgan, Union Station was built in 1908 and occupied in 1909.

One

Plant City's Beginnings

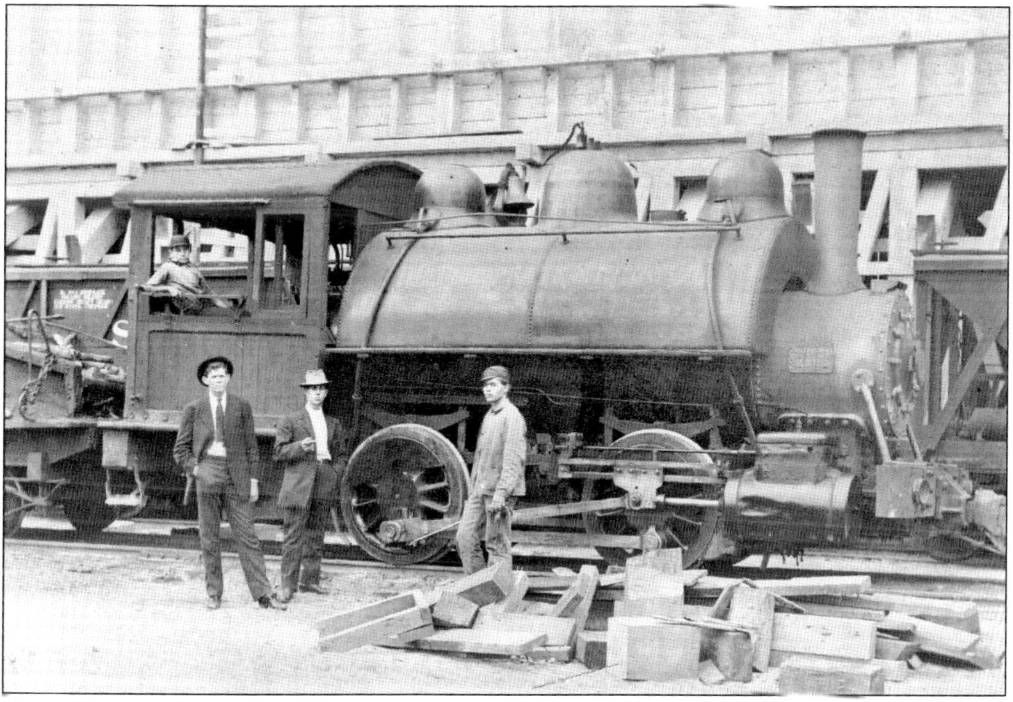

Early Days in Plant City Depended on the Railroad. According to the 1886–1887 *Florida State Gazetteer and Business Directory*, the population of Plant City was 600. E.S. Tyner was postmaster, and cotton, lumber, fruits, vegetables, and cattle were the principal crops. Plant City had an express and telegraph office, 13 general stores, 4 hotels, a carriage maker, 2 lodge organizations, 3 steam sawmills, and a grist mill run by water power. The *South Florida Courier* was the weekly newspaper. The Methodist, Baptist, and Presbyterian churches were present. The price of land ranged from $10 to $75 per acre.

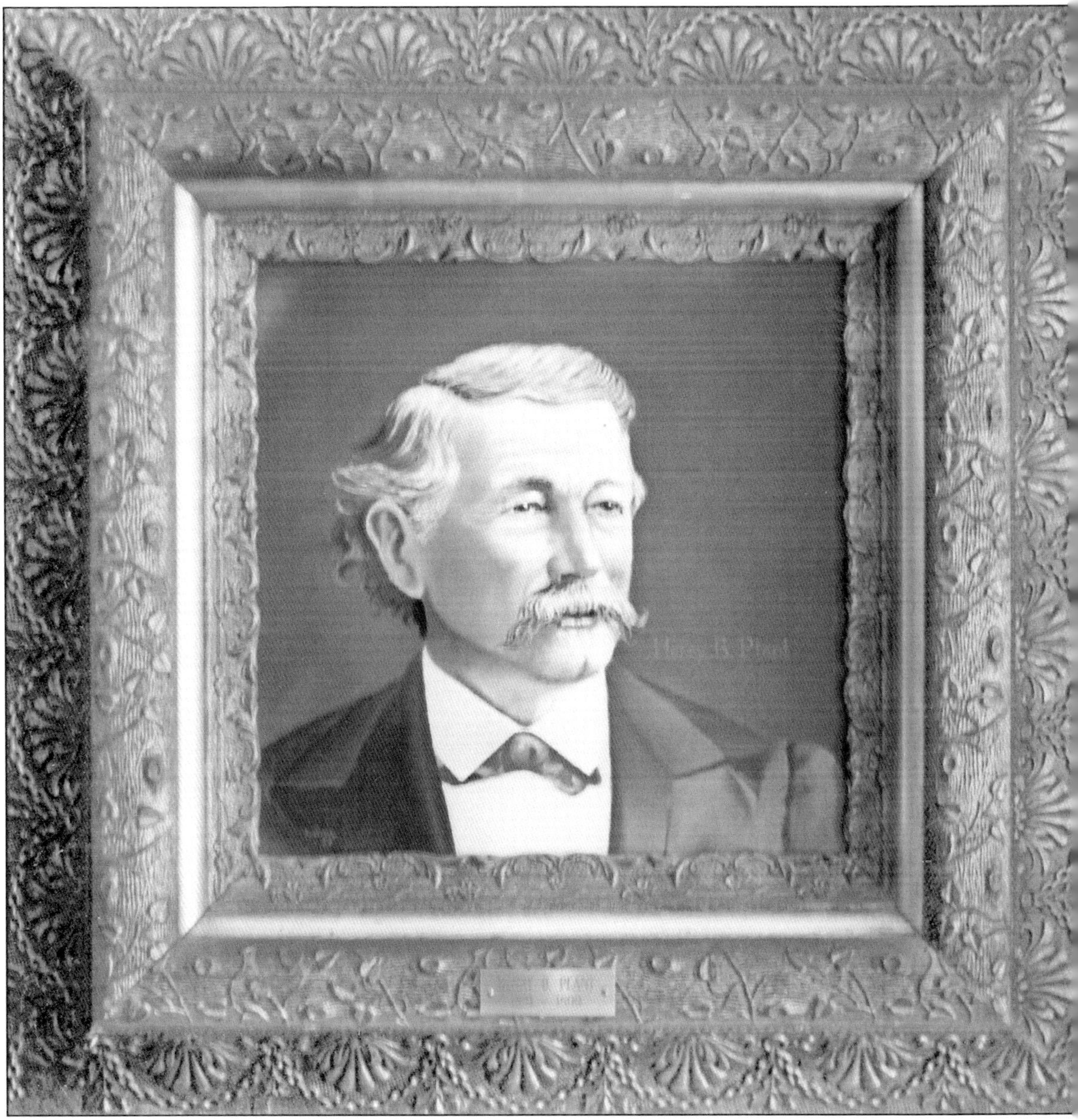

Henry Bradley Plant. This oil portrait of Henry Bradley Plant, for whom Plant City was named, is by artist John Briggs. Henry B. Plant, of Connecticut, came to the South during the winters for his wife's health. He became one of the organizers of the Southern Express Company. Adams Express Company merged with Southern Express Company and became part of the American Railway Express Company, changing to Railway Express Agency in 1929. Plant acquired the Atlantic & Gulf Railroad, and the name changed to the Savannah, Florida, and Western Railway. He continued to enlarge his railway holdings to more than 2,200 miles. The Plant Steamship Line was established in Tampa, Florida, in 1886. The Plant system hotels became the winter resorts on the west coast of Florida. The famous Tampa Bay Hotel is on the banks of the Hillsborough River at the mouth of Tampa Bay. His development and promotion brought rapid growth and expansion to Florida and the areas that were served by his railways. (Courtesy of John Briggs.)

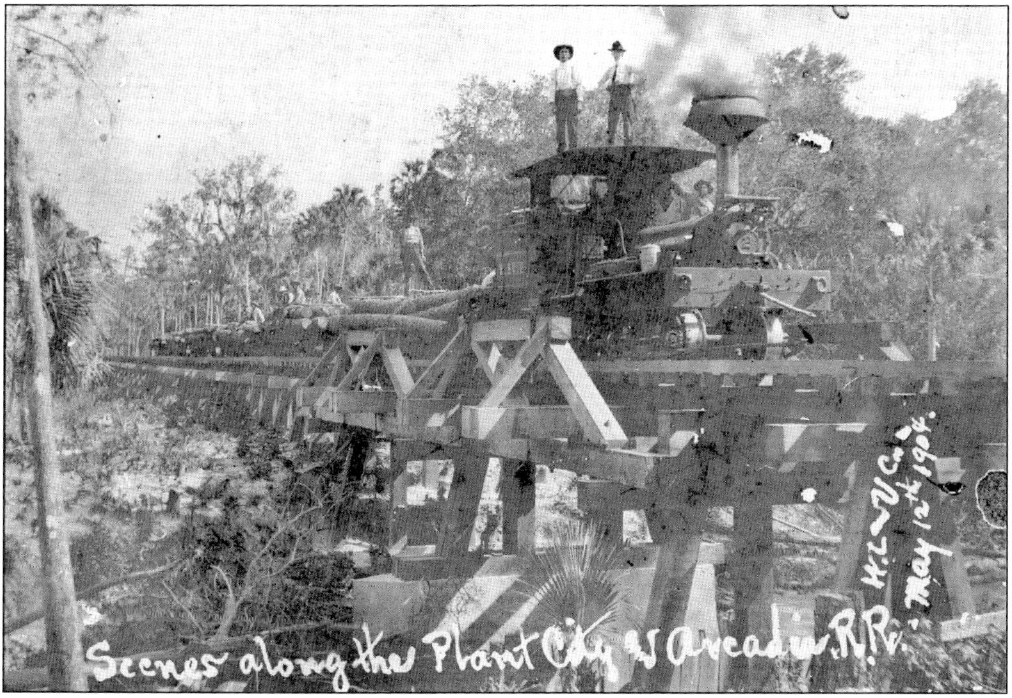

SCENES ALONG THE PLANT CITY AND ARCADIA R.R. Log trains like this one, crossing the trestle on the Plant City and Arcadia Railroad in 1904, were a familiar sight at the turn of the century. Written sideways on the photo is "W.L. and V. Ca. May 12, 1904."

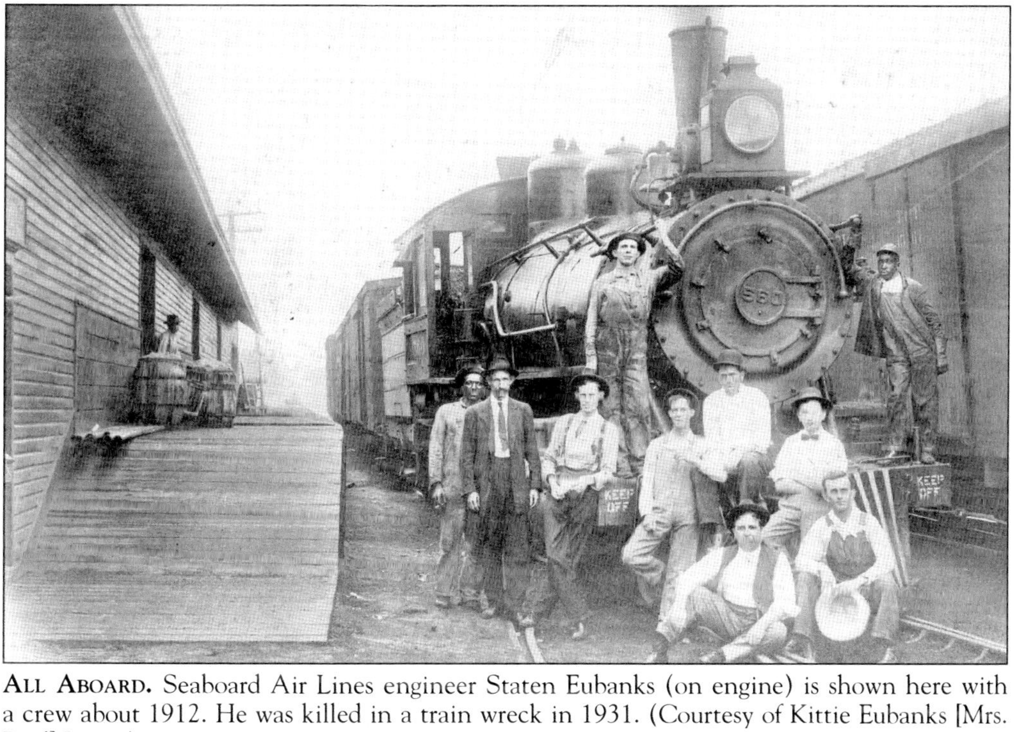

ALL ABOARD. Seaboard Air Lines engineer Staten Eubanks (on engine) is shown here with a crew about 1912. He was killed in a train wreck in 1931. (Courtesy of Kittie Eubanks [Mrs. Paul] Jones.)

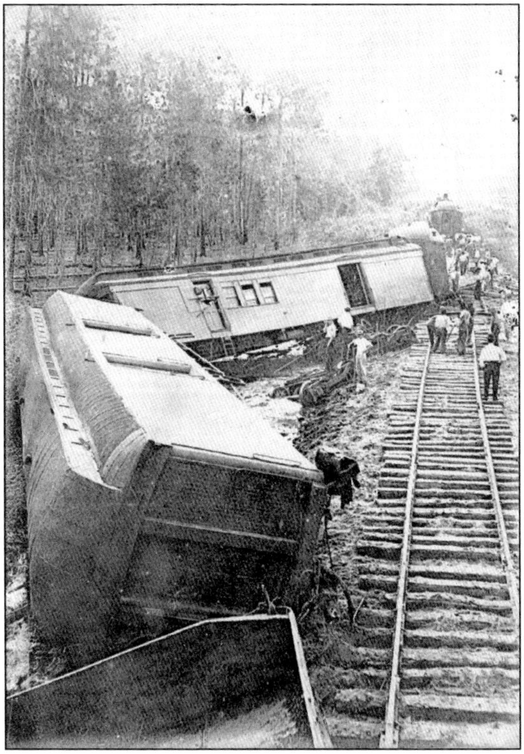

Vandals Loot the Goods from Overturned Railcars. Vandals were not shy in the removal of a rail section that had caused considerable damage to Seaboard tracks and cars near Knight's Station in 1911. Knight's Station crossing was near the intersection of Route 39 and Thonotosassa Road.

Is Visiting A Train Wreck Site a Social Occasion? A train wreck in downtown Plant City attracted plenty of spectators in 1904. Ladies came out with their parasols to have a look at the chaos created on the downtown train tracks. The manpower used to right the overturned train cars could take days and cause a delay in the mail and shipments of goods.

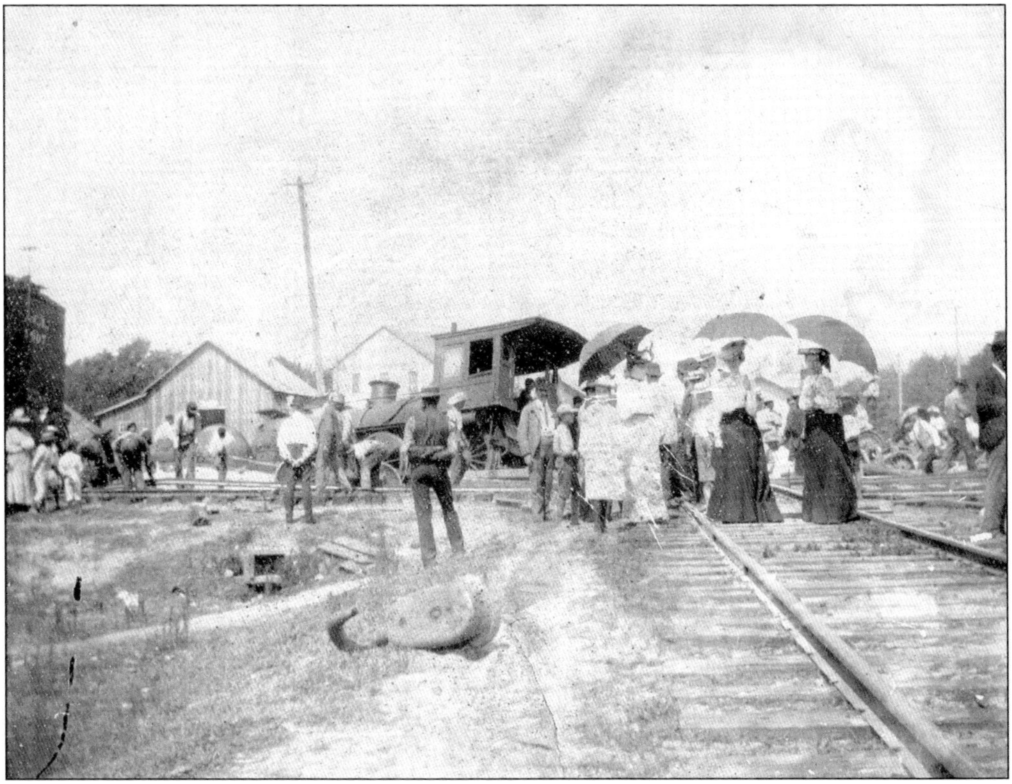

PLANT CITY LED BY OFFICIALS. The community was prospering under the leadership of local businessmen who had come to Plant City with a desire to develop the community into one that they could be proud of. They were pioneers and the descendants of pioneers who settled here prior to the incorporation of Plant City in 1885.

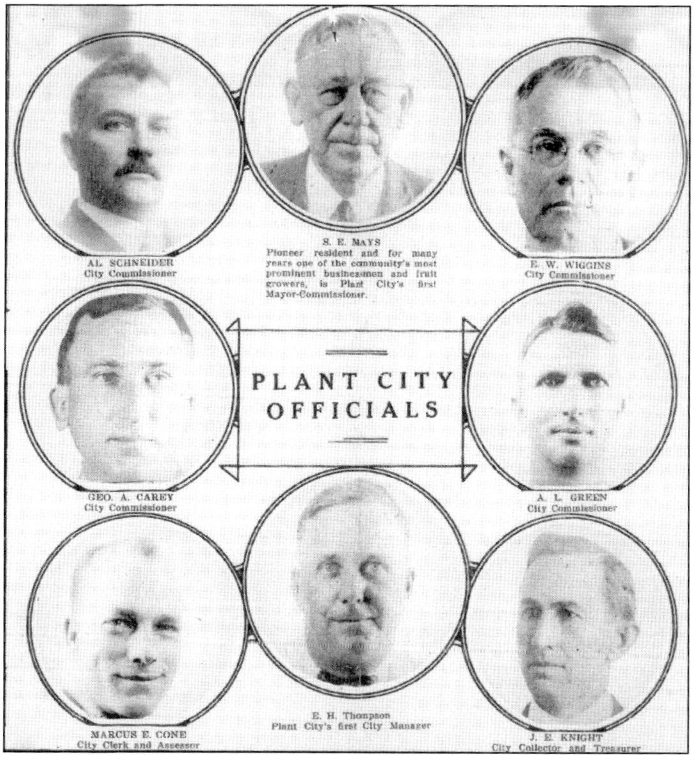

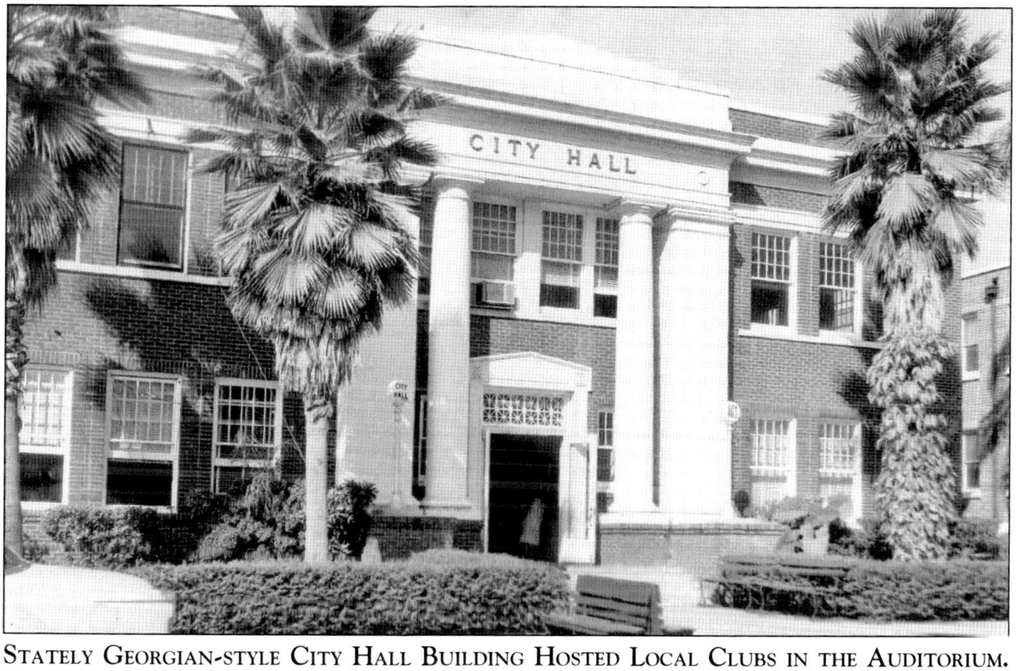

STATELY GEORGIAN-STYLE CITY HALL BUILDING HOSTED LOCAL CLUBS IN THE AUDITORIUM. The social clubs of the community used the auditorium in the city hall building for their regular club meetings prior to the opening of the Hotel Plant. The hotel offered meeting space, and guests and members could combine their business and pleasure. The city hall also housed the fire department.

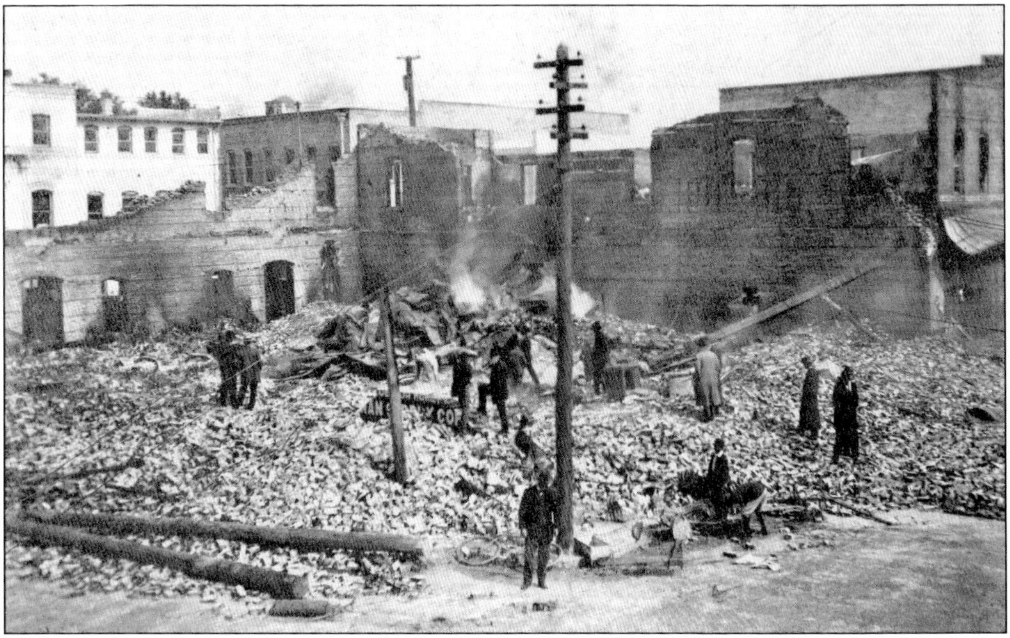

Downtown Fire Destroys Businesses, Nothing Left But Ashes. The 1915 fire, believed to have been caused by an arsonist, destroyed the Opera House, which was located on the third floor of the Mays Building at North Drane and Evers Streets. Plant City High School commencement exercises had been held at the Opera House. Under new ownership, the Mays Building became known as the Wells & Sons Company.

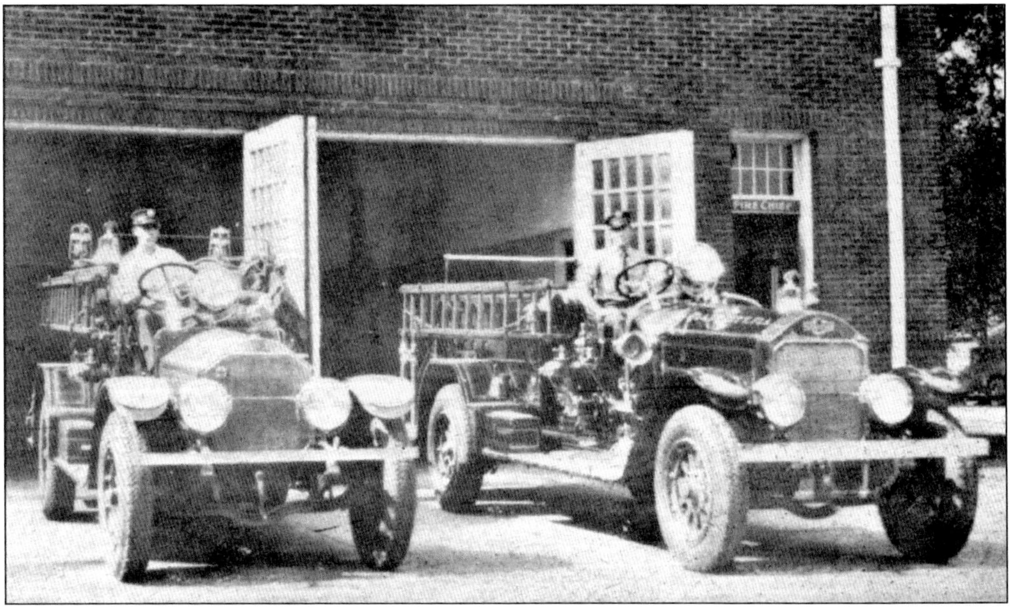

Plant City Fire Department to the Rescue. City hall housed all the city offices, including the fire department. The first-floor location featured large bay doors to accommodate the fire trucks. The fire chief and his crew were ably assisted by local volunteers, who were students from the nearby Plant City High School. A local fire emergency alarm called the volunteers to duty.

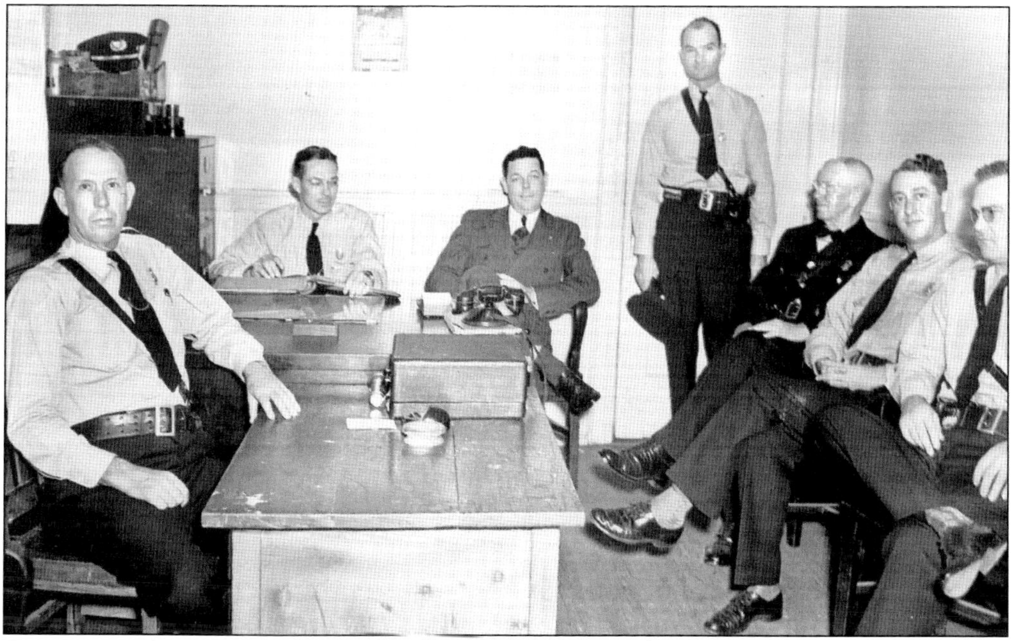

COMMUNITY OUTGROWS CITY HALL. It seems to be a crowded room as local officials wait for court to convene in Chief Harrell West's office in city hall in 1943. Pictured from left to right are Officer C.M. Stanley, Chief Harrell B. West, Judge James D. Bruton Jr., and Officers Bill Meredith, Lon House, Russell Holsberry, and Seymour Sparkman.

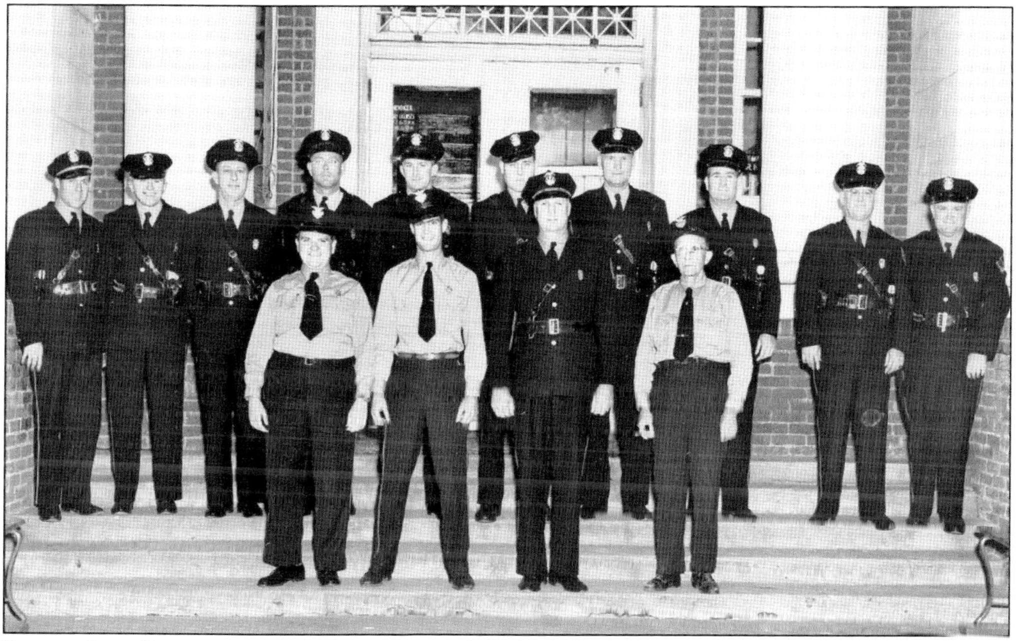

PLANT CITY POLICE DEPARTMENT, 1953. The Plant City Police Department proudly stands on the front steps of the city hall. Pictured from left to right are (front row) Gerald Thompson, Howard Surrency, Chief Bob Spooner, and H.E. Galyean; (back row) Hilton Horton, Joe Grubbs, Russell Holsberry, Jim Hart, Dick Driggers, Haywood Frazier, Joe Flint, Ron McCall, Seymore Sparkman, and Ray Simmons. (Courtesy of Mrs. T.J. McCall.)

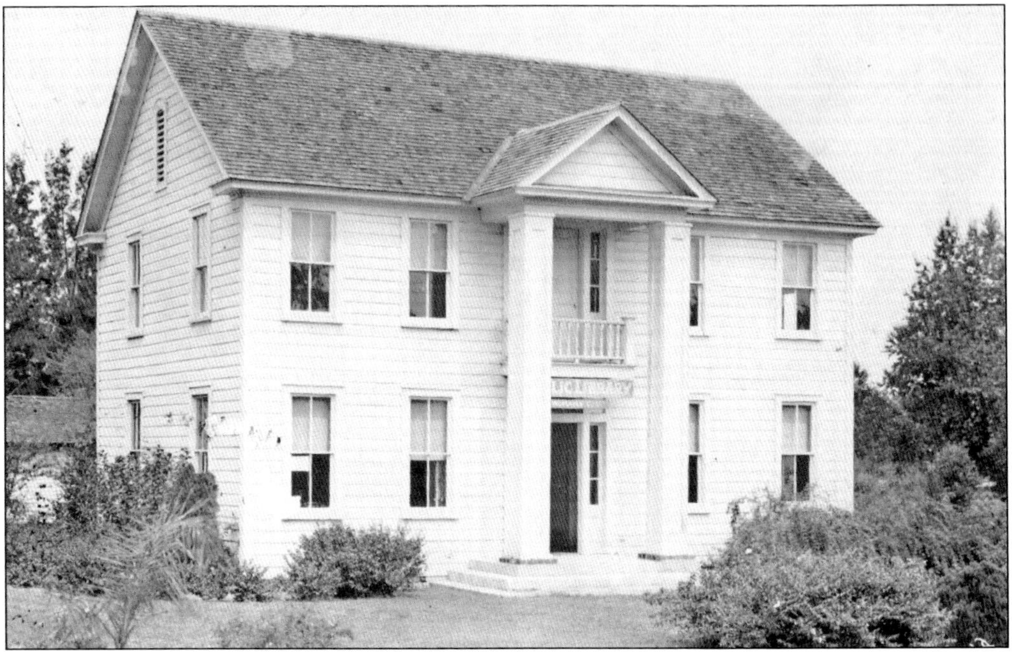

Plant City Public Library and Clubhouse of the Woman's Club of Plant City, 1933–1959. Located at the corner of Wheeler and McClendon Streets, this building was spared by the 1907 fire. The Miller (formerly Strickland) home, it was moved from Haines and Palmer Streets to the Wheeler/McClendon Street site. Materials from the building were salvaged when the building was demolished to make way for a new and modern library.

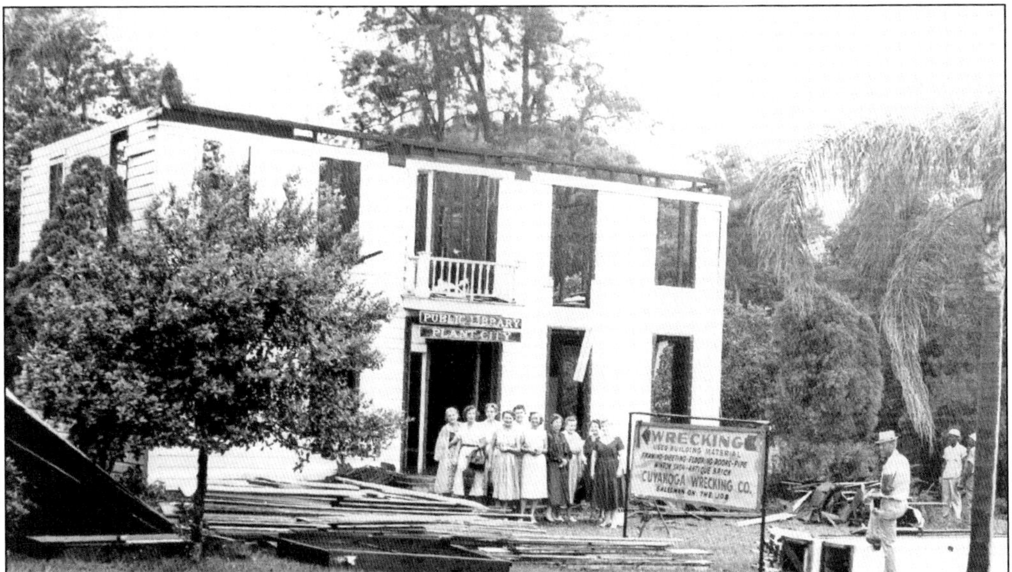

Wrecking Ball is Out With the Old, Making Room for the New. Members of the Woman's Club Division of Library Service pose in front of the old library building and clubhouse before it was demolished in June 1959 to make way for the new public library building on the same site. After having worked for years to fulfill their dreams of a new facility, employees raised funds by salvaging building materials from the two-story, wooden building.

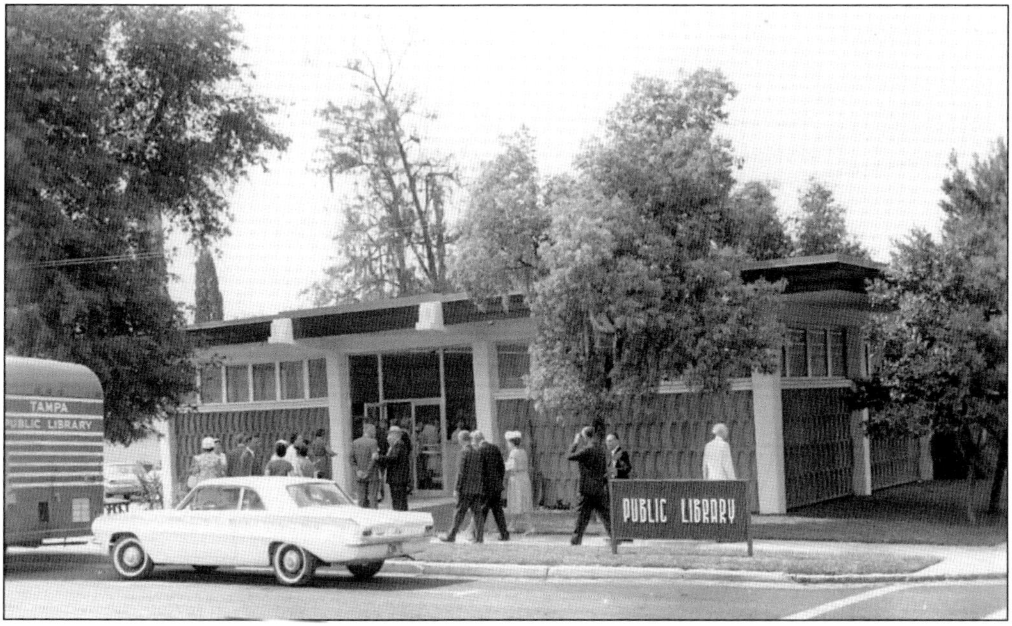

NEW PUBLIC LIBRARY OPEN IN PLANT CITY. Plant Citians and their guests came out for the opening of the new Plant City Public Library. Dedication ceremonies were held in December 1960. The award-winning library offered an expanded collection and new services to its patrons. (Courtesy of Gladys Jeffcoat Photo Studio and Camera Shop.)

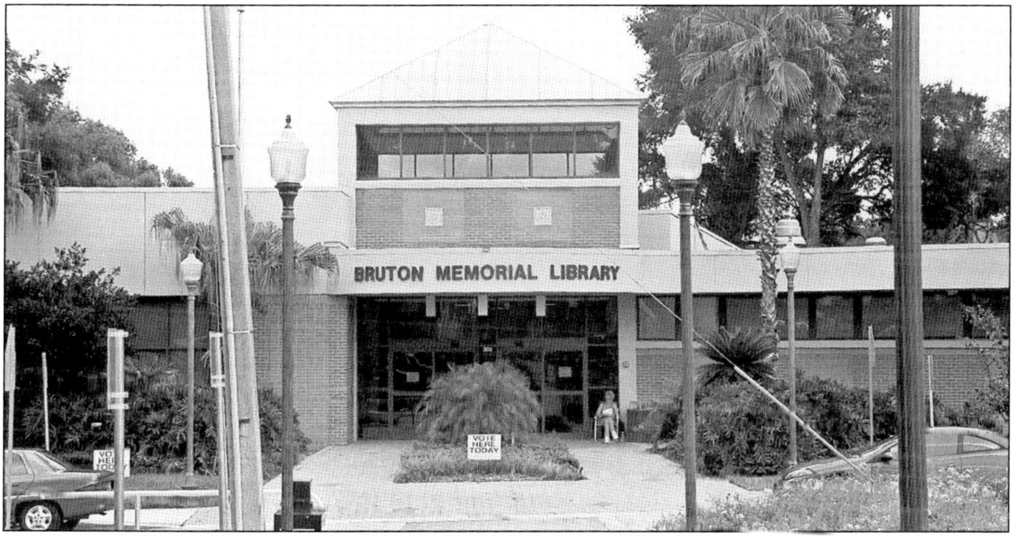

BRUTON MEMORIAL LIBRARY. Started by the Plant City Woman's Club in 1927, the library continued as their volunteer project until 1959, when the residents of the city voted to tax themselves to have public library service. A small library was built by the city, a staff was hired, and the library became a department of the city government. The library was enlarged and remodeled in 1994 and is now named in honor and memory of Quintilla Geer Bruton and Judge James D. Bruton Jr. The library is a beautiful and spacious 20,000-square-foot facility that houses three study and/or conference rooms, study and teaching space for 120, the Friends of the Library Tech Room with two computers connected to a scanner and a color printer, a screened reading porch, and the Mary Noel Moody Community. (Courtesy of John Briggs.)

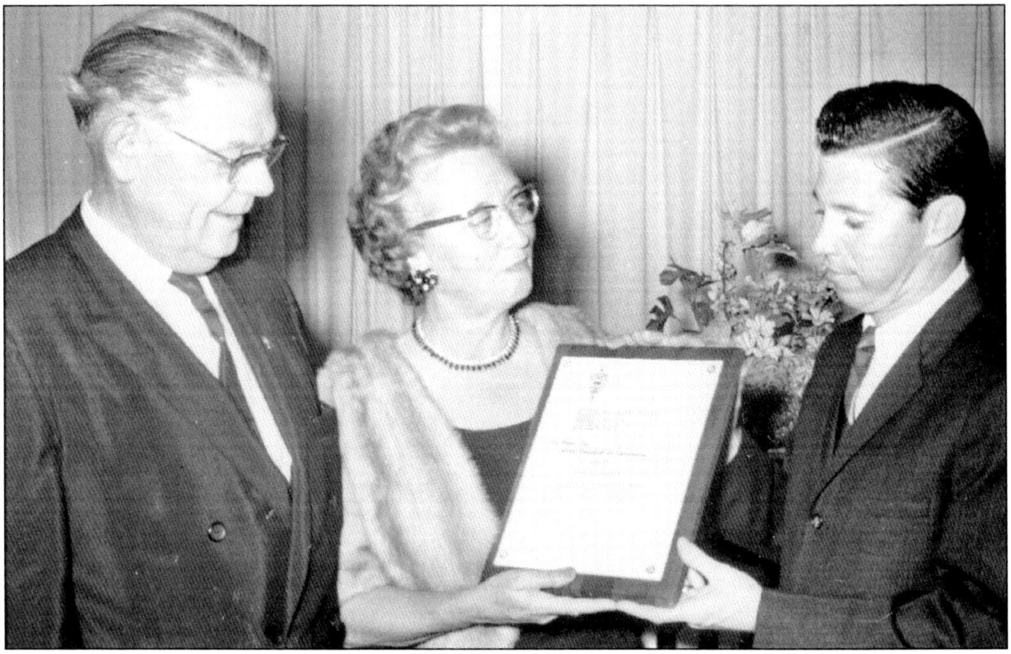

QUINTILLA GEER BRUTON PRESENTED DISTINGUISHED AWARD, 1963. The Plant City chapter of the Jaycees recognized a local outstanding citizen, Mrs. James D. Bruton Jr. (Quintilla Geer Bruton), for spearheading the successful campaign to build a new public library in Plant City. Pictured from left to right are Judge James D. Bruton Jr., Quintilla, and Dan Borchardt. (Courtesy of Bill Friend's Studio.)

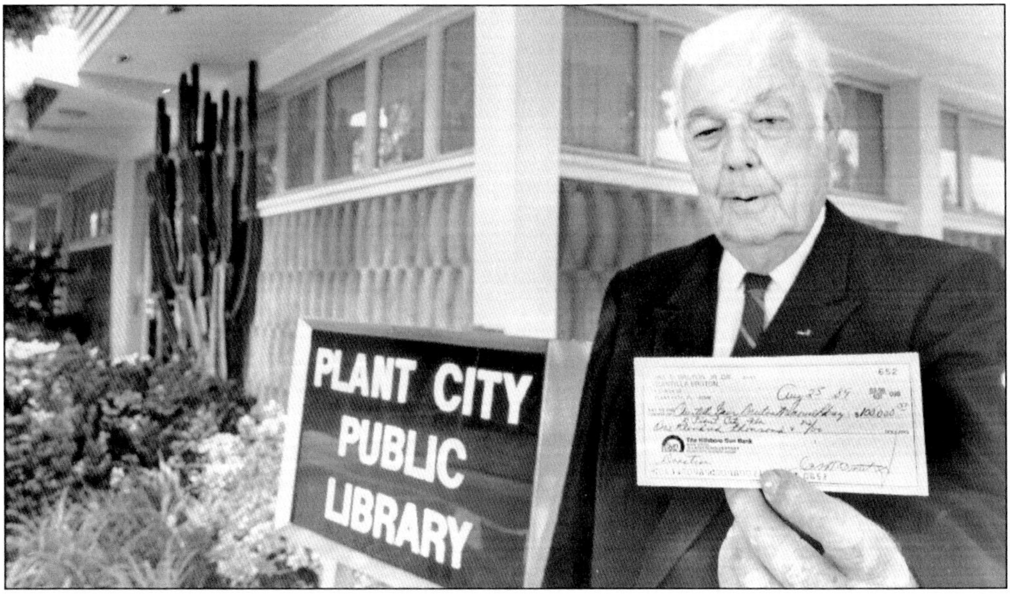

QUINTILLA GEER BRUTON MEMORIAL LIBRARY RECEIVES $100,000 GIFT. Retired Circuit Judge James D. Bruton Jr. was very generous with his gift of $100,000 to the Quintilla Geer Bruton Memorial Library. The library was named after his late wife, a longtime supporter of the library. The August 1989 gift was a great addition to the funding by the City of Plant City's library expansion project.

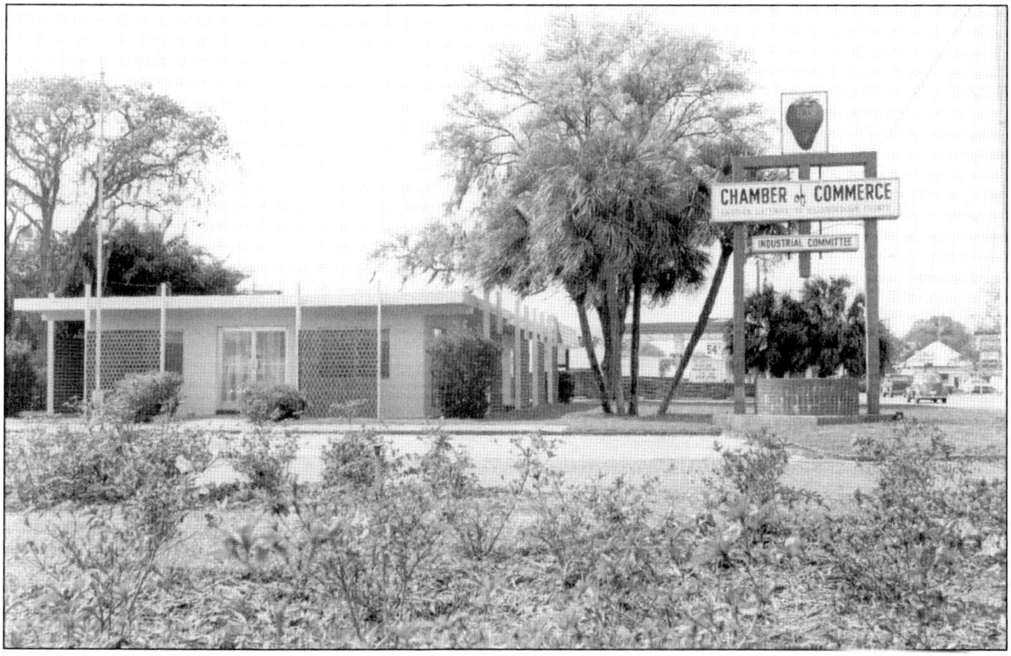

BUSINESS COMMUNITY SERVED BY THE GREATER PLANT CITY CHAMBER OF COMMERCE. The Chamber of Commerce of Plant City was located at the eastern gateway to the downtown area. Local agriculture and industry attracted new interest to town. Plant City had expanded its city limits to encourage new growth and development.

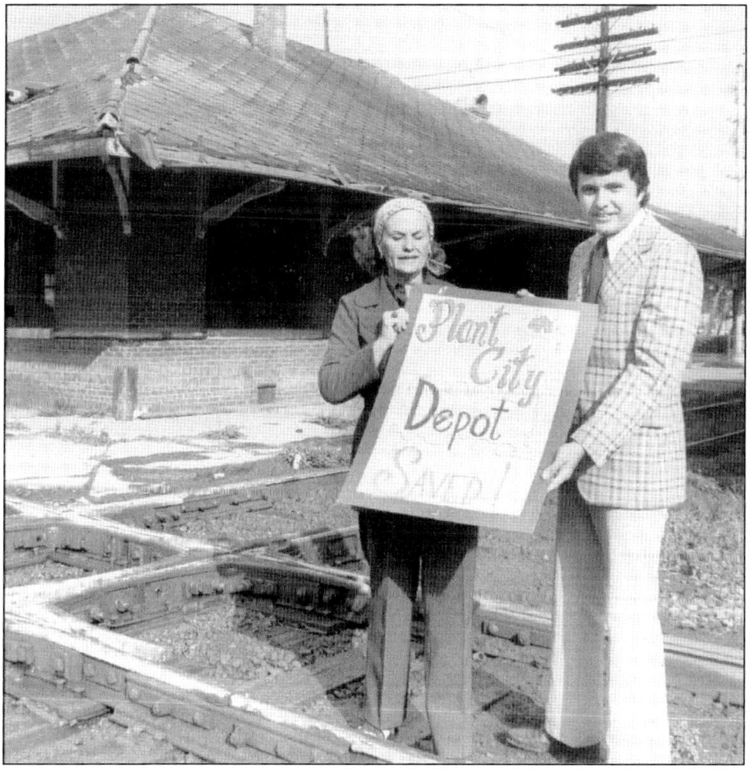

PLANT CITY DEPOT SAVED. Plant City's historic Union Station Depot was in a state of disrepair after being boarded up for years. The local arts council stepped up to the "palette" and focused their energy on saving the historic property. Listed on the National Register of Historic Sites, the depot has been restored and serves as a local visitor center and museum. Pictured here are arts council member Catherine Clark (left) and city commissioner Jerry Thomas.

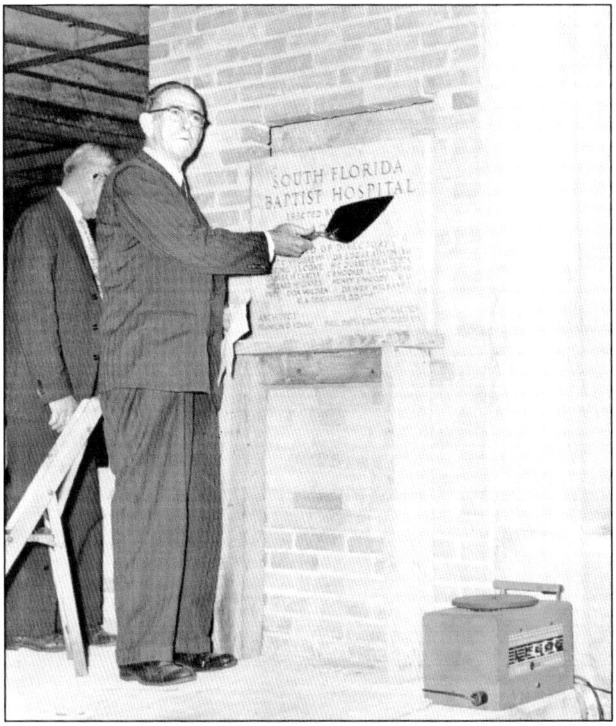

Cornerstone Laid for Plant City's South Florida Baptist Hospital. The new hospital was opened on December 29, 1953. Pictured is Dr. T.C. Maguire. Other board members were Dr. Edgar Austin, A. Boring, J.L. Cone, H.C. Durrett, L.H. Duyck, Grover H. Carter, C.R. Hooker, L.T. Langford, Willard McGinnes, Henry S. Moody, R.G. Pate, Dewey Willbanks, and C.A. Leichliter. The project architect was Franklin O. Adams, and the contractor was Paul Smith Construction Company.

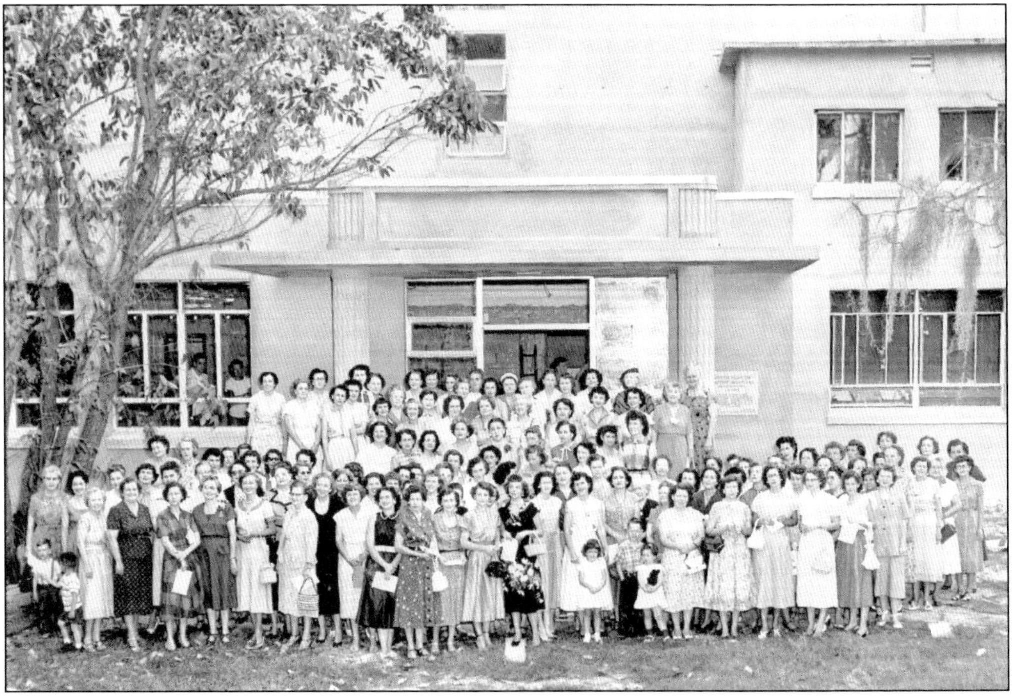

New Hospital's Wealth of Fund-raising is Supported by Local Woman's Club. South Florida Baptist Hospital was nearly complete when the Woman's Club paused in their fund-raising activities to pose on the front steps of the new medical facility. Women's organizations in the community have continued to support the financial needs of the hospital.

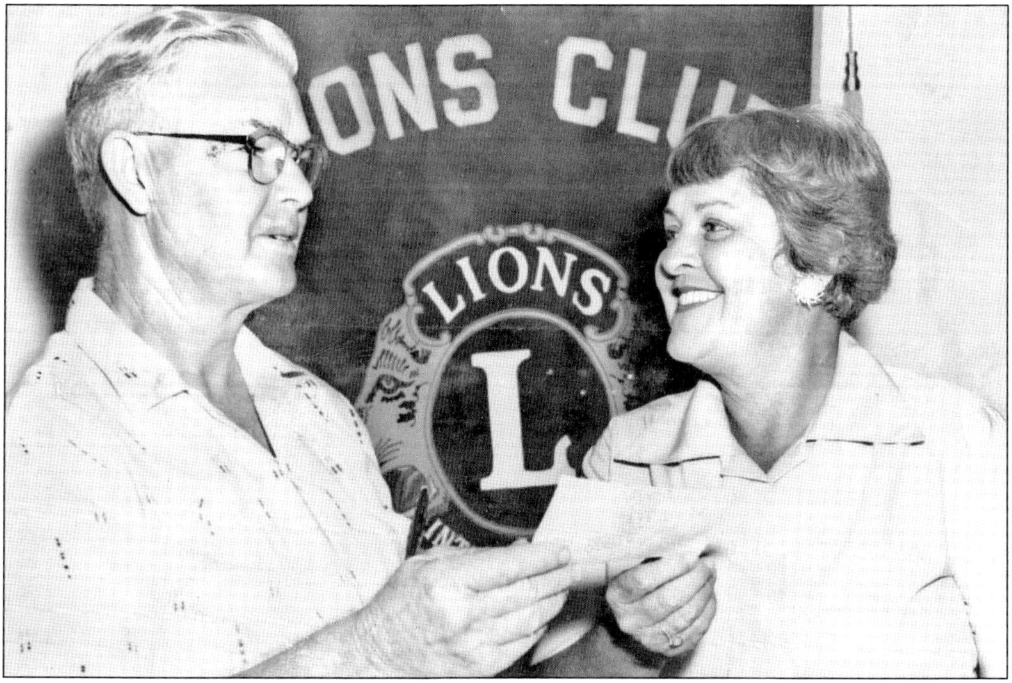

Plant City Lions Club Supports Local Girl Scouts. Mr. Glen Knox of the Plant City Lions Club makes a presentation to Mrs. Topsie Merriwether representing the local girl scouts in 1960. (Courtesy of Bill Friend's Studio.)

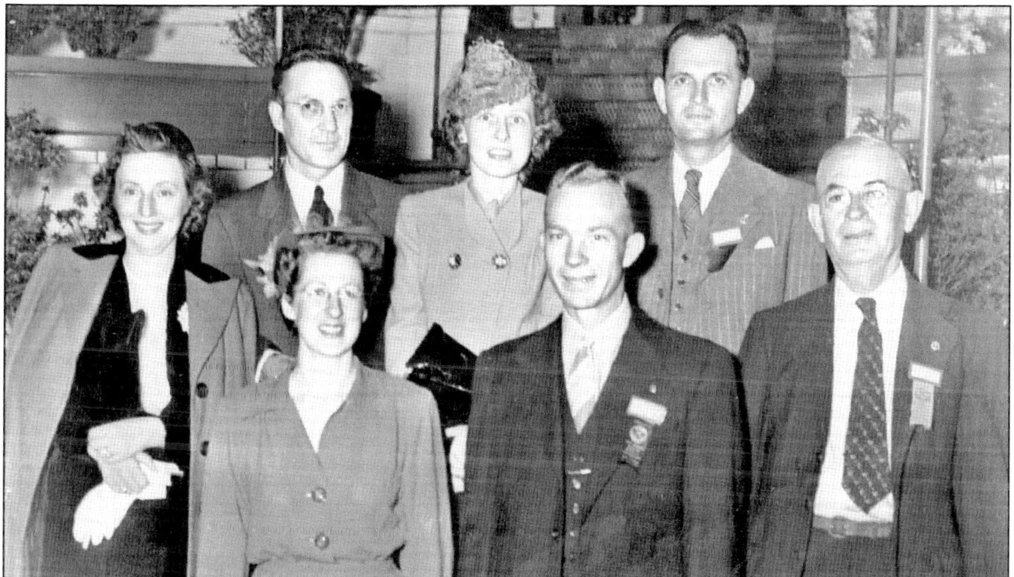

Plant City Kiwanis Club Members Attend State Convention. Plant City was proudly represented at the 1940 Kiwanis State Convention in Jacksonville. Pictured from left to right are (front row) Sara and Dr. Luman Black; and Henry H. Huff, club secretary; (back row) Vaviel and Lew J. Prosser; and Evelyn and Chester McDonald, Kiwanis president. Organized in 1921, the Kiwanis Club was Plant City's first men's civic club. Membership included the town's prominent business and professional men.

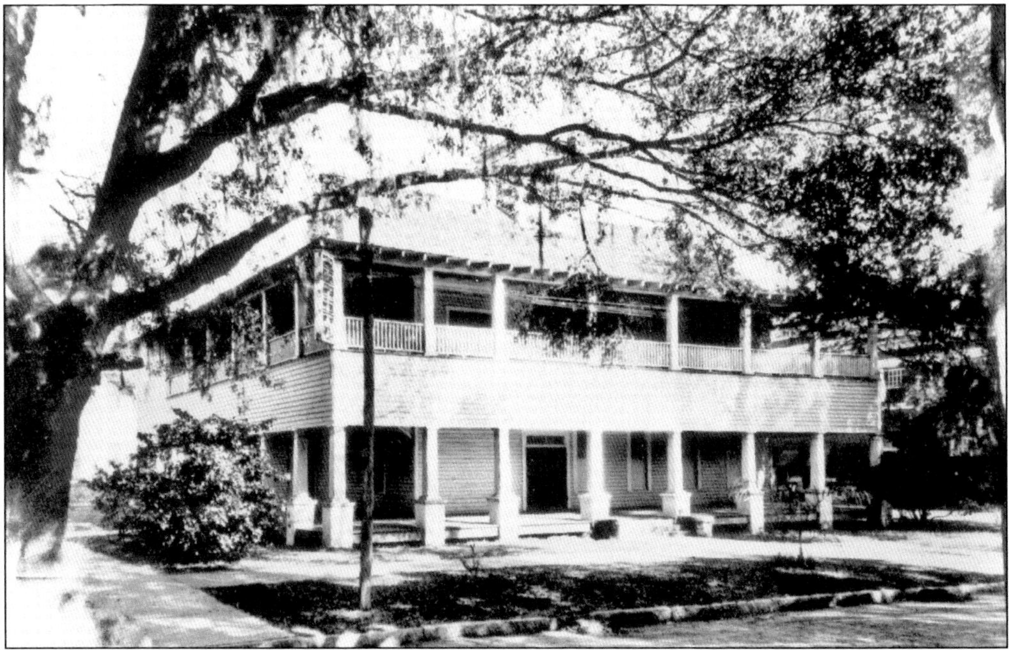

Masonic Lodge, July 1985. One of Plant City's oldest wooden structures of residential orientation was used by the Masons as their lodge. In 1914, the property, located at the corner of Mahoney and Evers Streets, had a value of $10,000. Included was a lodge room, meeting room, council room, banquet hall, and kitchen. The property was purchased by the City of Plant City, who in turn sold it to the First Baptist Church for expansion.

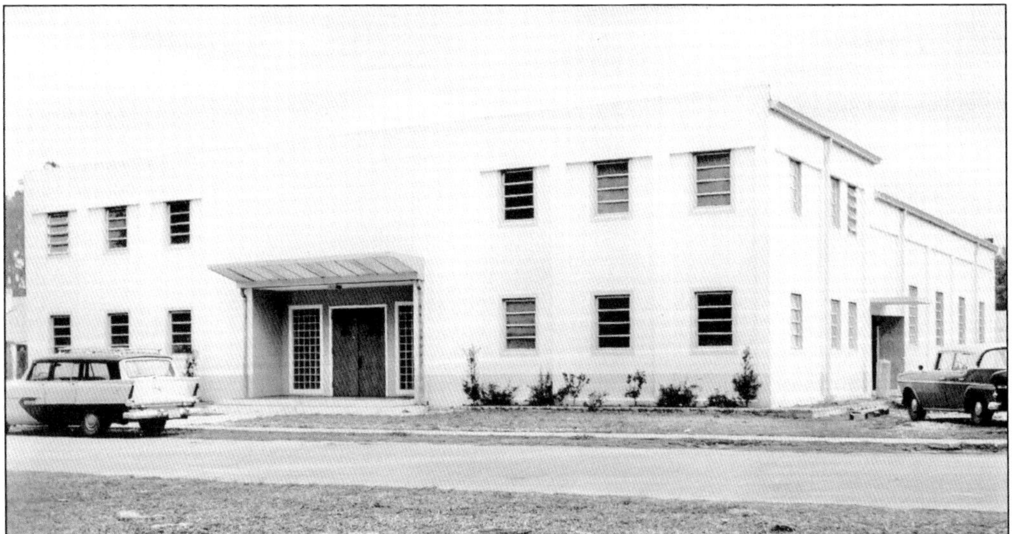

New Masonic Lodge Building. The new location of the Plant City Lodge No. 79 was at the apex of West Reynolds Street and Thonotosassa Road. Chartered January 13, 1876, as Ebeneezer Lodge, the lodge changed its name and moved from Shiloh to Plant City in 1885. In 1914, the officers were Thomas C. Calmes, high priest; Eben B. Trask, treasurer; and Olin Seymour Wright, secretary; there were 90 members. Regular convocations were held the second Friday in each month.

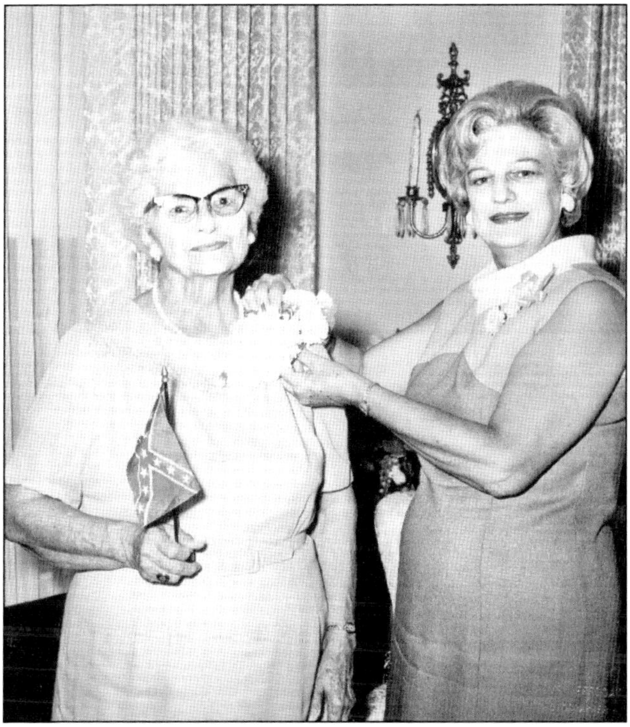

UNITED DAUGHTERS OF THE CONFEDERACY CELEBRATES MEMORIES OF THE CONFEDERACY. The Plant City chapter of the United Daughters of the Confederacy (UDC) was organized in 1927. Pictured here is Mrs. T. Pearce (left), a real daughter of the Confederacy, as she is being honored at a ceremony in October 1965. Making the presentation is Mrs. William Dee (Lilah) Chisolm, local chapter president of the United Daughters of the Confederacy. Plant City's last two surviving Confederate veterans were Charles Isom and Col. E.T. Roux.

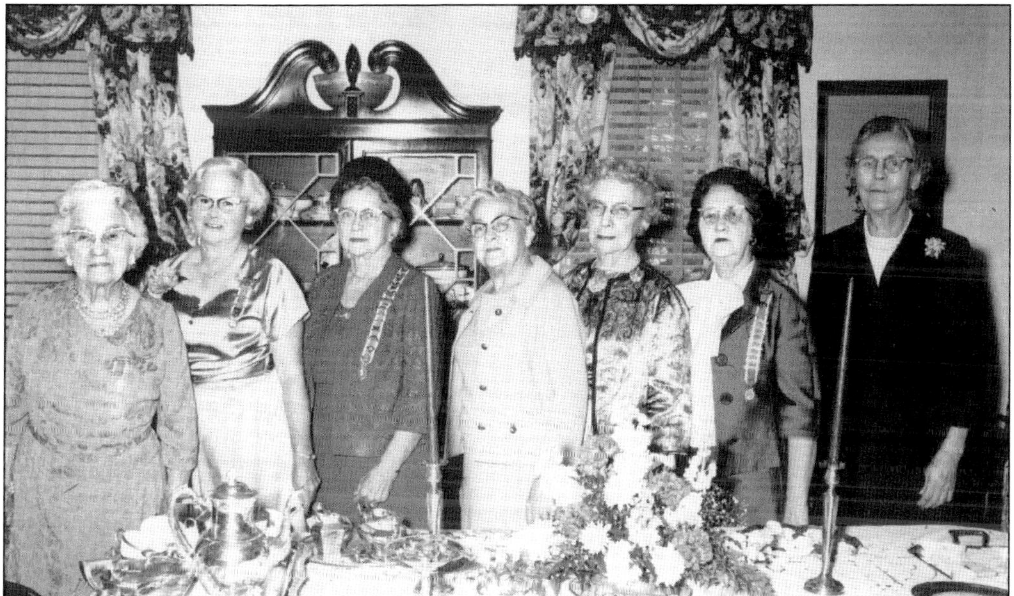

DAUGHTERS OF THE AMERICAN REVOLUTION CHAPTER TEA AT THE HOME OF MRS. ALBERT SCHNEIDER. The Daughters of the American Revolution, Echebucasassa Chapter, was organized in 1929. Members gathered for tea at the home of Mrs. Annie Schneider. Pictured from left to right are Mrs. Schneider, Mrs. Euridice Simmons, Mrs. Olga Davis, Mrs. Annie Eberhardt, Mrs. Alice E. Warner, Mrs. Bessie Lamar Calvert, and Miss Wilmoth Herron.

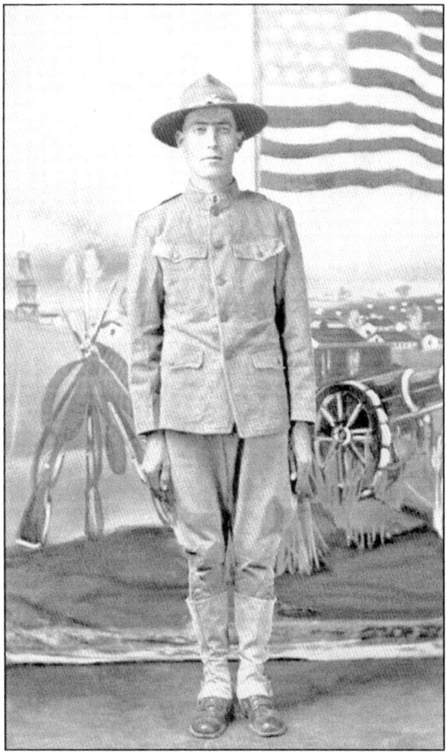

Local Man Ready for Service to His Country. Bartow Jesse Smith (1887–1936) stands at attention at Camp Jackson, South Carolina, on October 25, 1918. Bartow Jesse was born on November 27, 1887, in Zephyrhills, Pasco County, Florida, to James Porter Smith and Elizabeth Kersey Smith. According to military records, he had blue eyes and brown hair, and he was tall and of medium stature. Smith worked for Boyett and Sparkman as a butcher in Plant City and enjoyed entertaining friends and family with his harmonica playing. He died September 13, 1936, in Plant City and was buried in Geiger Cemetery, Zephyrhills. (Courtesy of Brenda Smith Inlow.)

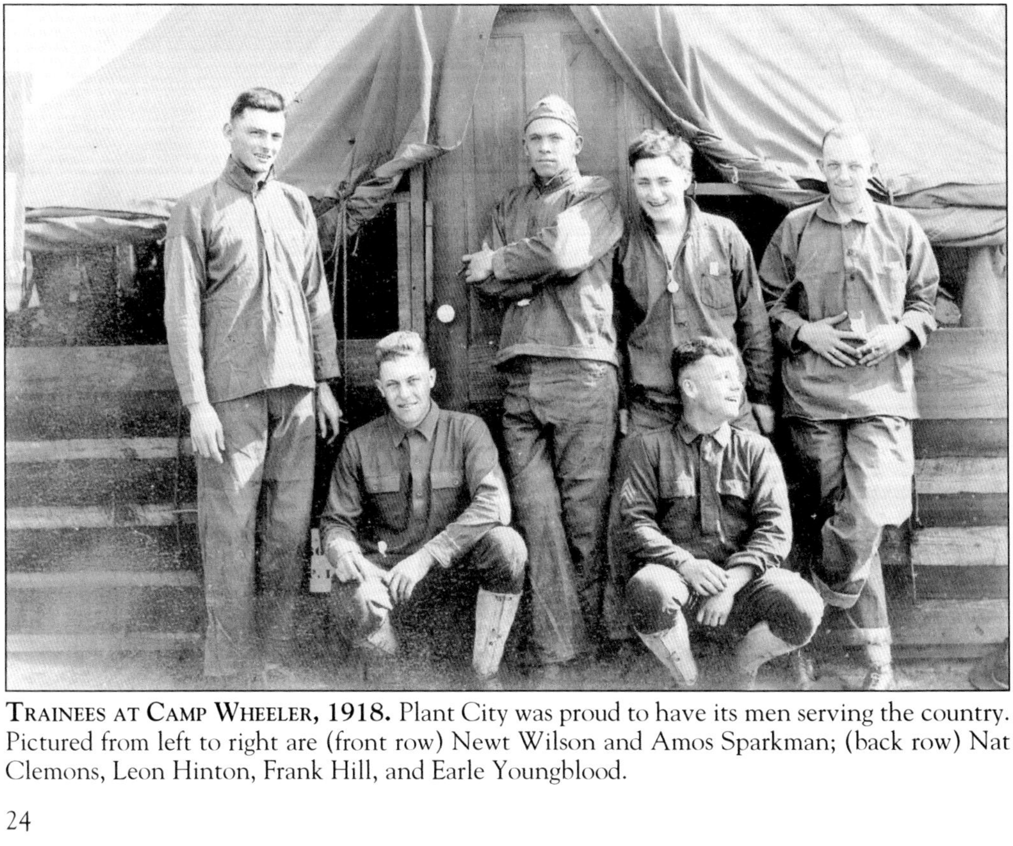

Trainees at Camp Wheeler, 1918. Plant City was proud to have its men serving the country. Pictured from left to right are (front row) Newt Wilson and Amos Sparkman; (back row) Nat Clemons, Leon Hinton, Frank Hill, and Earle Youngblood.

A.P. COOKE, EDITOR AND PUBLISHER OF *THE COURIER*. Mr. and Mrs. A.P. Cooke bought the local newspaper, *The Courier*, shortly after they moved to Plant City in 1944. Mr. Cooke had lived in the area prior to this time, having worked for the Peninsular Telephone Company and as state editor for the *Tampa Tribune*. Mr. Cooke edited and published *The Courier* until his death in 1952. He was a native of Cooperstown, New York. His weekly column "Just Roaming" was the platform for raising $3,000 to purchase a parcel of land used by the Plant City High School for physical education. The community honored him by naming the site A.P. Cooke–Courier Field.

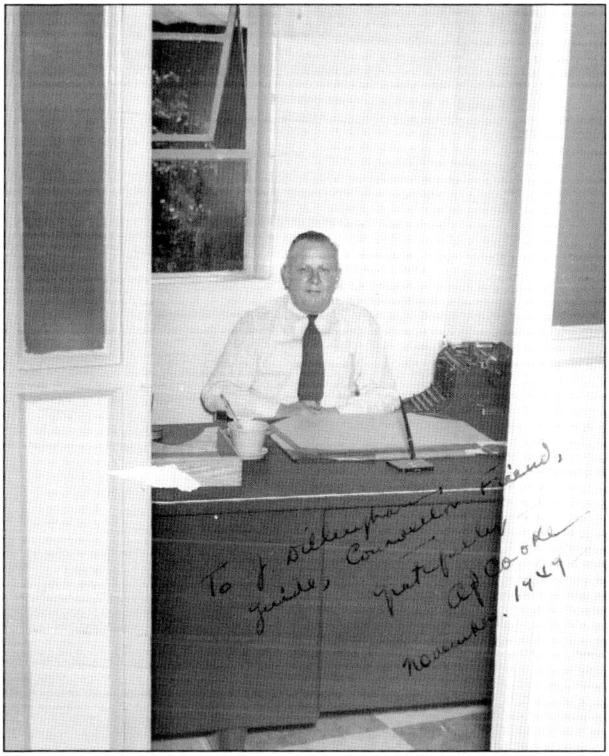

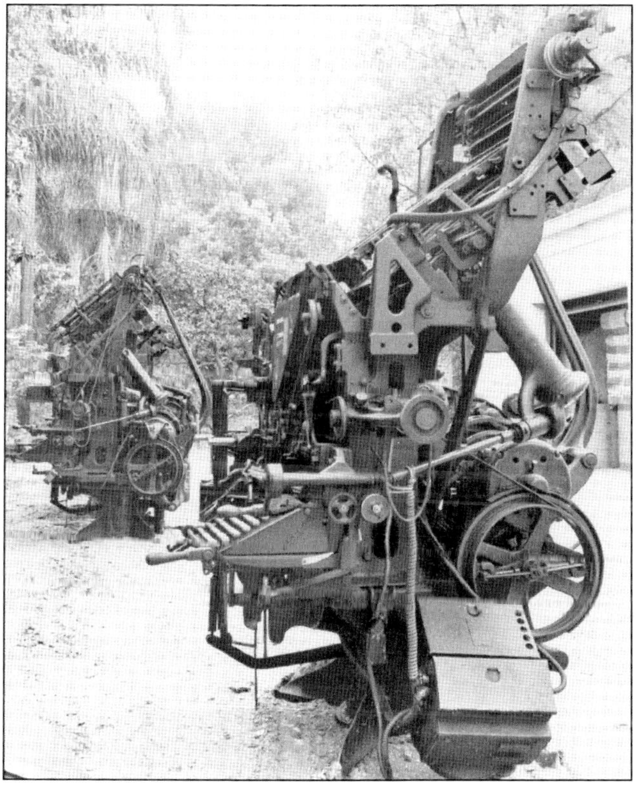

USE OF LINOTYPE MACHINE WAS DISCONTINUED IN 1976. The 1976 removal of old *Courier* linotypes machines marks the end of an era. As the name implies, the linotype is a machine that produces a solid "line of type." Introduced about 1886, it was used for generations by newspapers and general printers. It is a one-man machine: the operator sits in front with the copy to be set at the top of the keyboard, and he commences setting.

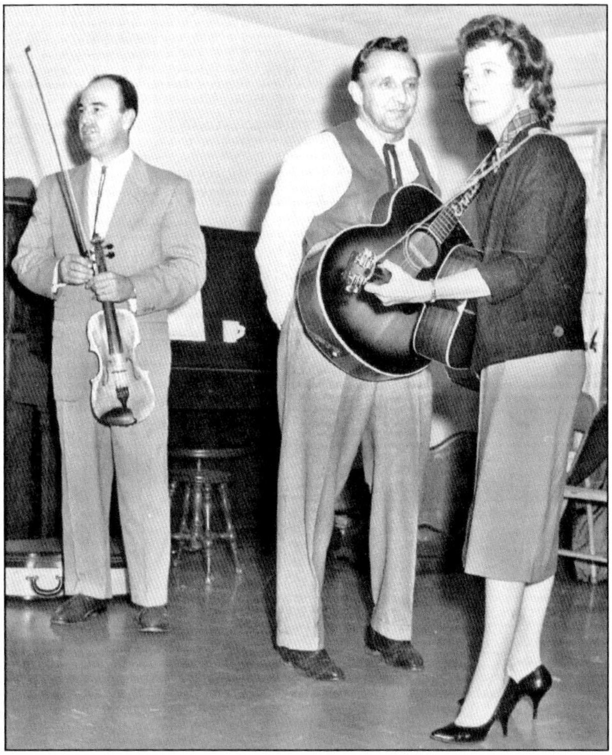

Winter Visitors Given a Warm Welcome. First Federal Savings and Loan Association (later Sunshine State) sponsored the "welcome back Winter Visitor" program each year after 1954. Pictured is WTVT television personality Ernie Lee (center) and his trio providing entertainment at the Welcome Back Dinner, December 1959.

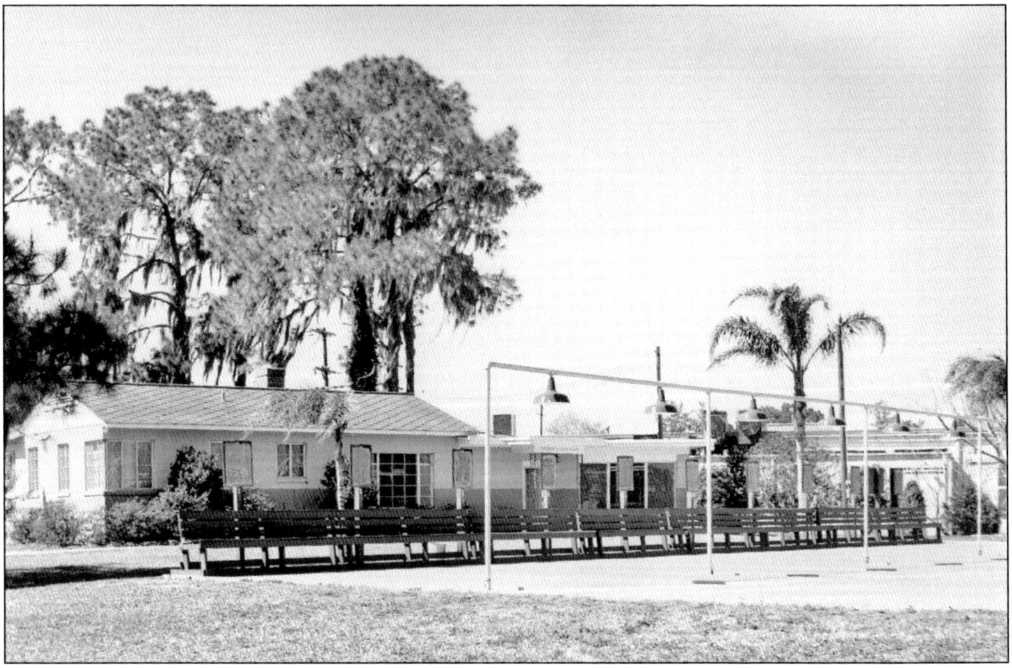

Welcome to the Sunshine State. Winter visitors to the Plant City area were always ready to enjoy a day of sunshine at the Winter Visitor's Center shuffleboard courts. While the men enjoyed the outdoors, the women could be found inside playing a game of bridge or planning for a social gathering.

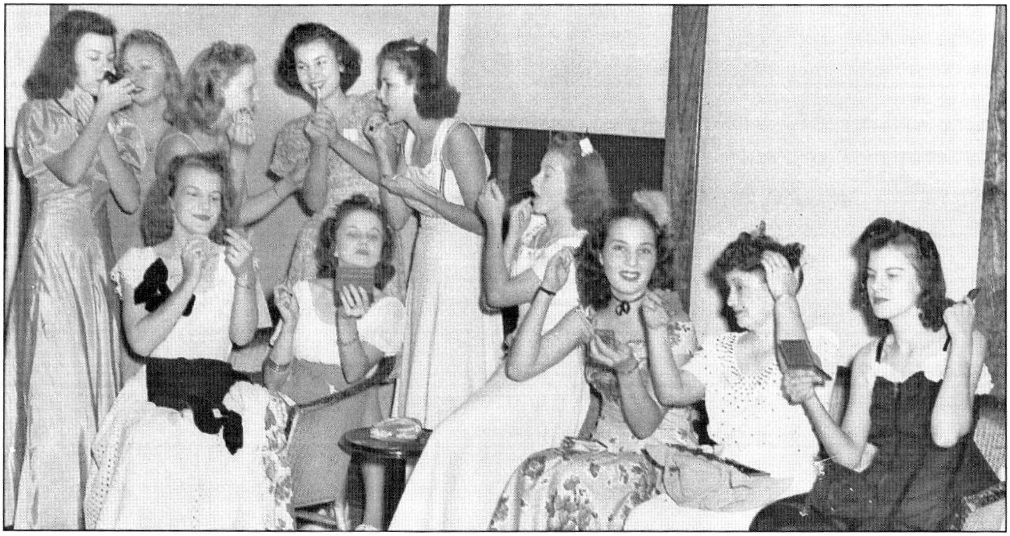

AND THE SHOW MUST GO ON. Shown here is a 1942 U.S.O. dance at the Fort Milton E. Hull Armory Building in Plant City, Florida. Pictured from left to right are (front row) Evalie Riles; Miriam Vannerson; Cecelia McColpin;Virginia Jordan; "Jeff"(Arthur) Coleman, the Plant City U.S.O. director; and Lillian Ergle; (back row) Annie Ruth Anderson; Edith McCall; Dot Willaford; unidentified; and Ernestine Martin. (Courtesy of Virginia Jordan Hull.)

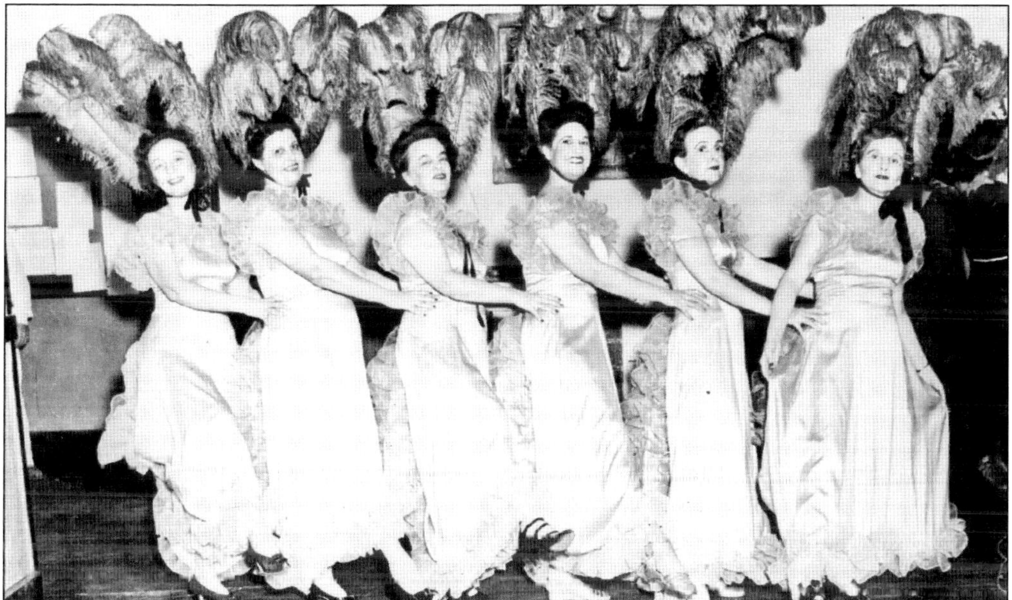

THE CAN-CAN GIRLS. Plant City's finest ladies kick up their heels with a little of the can-can. The fabulous home-talent production *Follies of '49* was presented by the Woman's Club's Welfare Department. The two-night show on January 28 and 29 played to a full house at the high school auditorium on Evers Street. Pictured from left to right are Vaviel Prosser, Lucile Langford, Lewie Belle Moore, Frances Hull, Geneva Ramsdell, and Mary Coleman. The souvenir program included a note from Bing Crosby: "Felicitations and best wishes to the Welfare Department on your Hospital Project. Hope the 'Follies of '49' will be a big success. Sincerely, Bing Crosby."

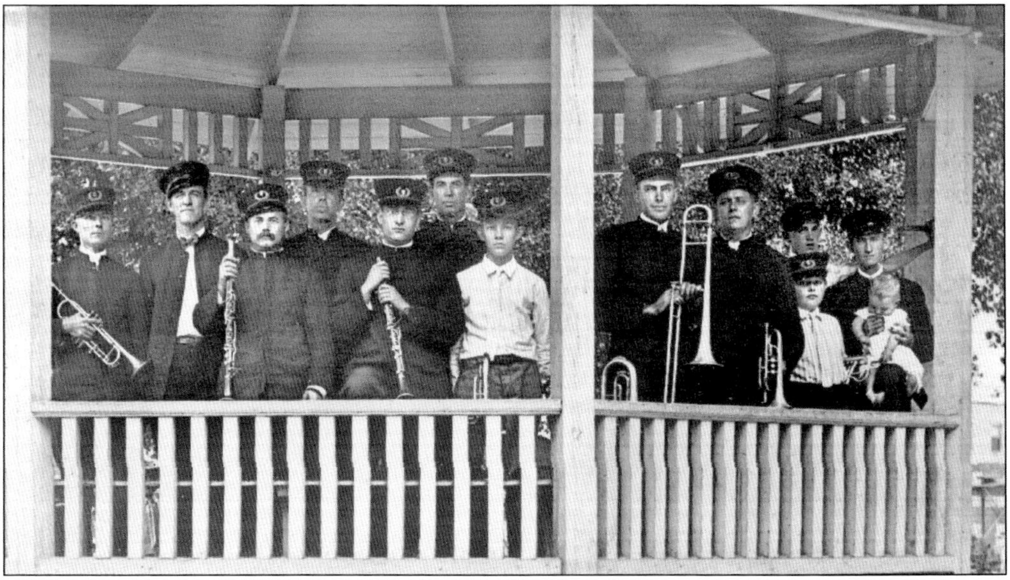

Plant City Band. Plant City's downtown bandstand, located at the northeast corner of Reynolds and Evers Streets, was always alive with music from the Plant City Band. Wooden gazebo structures were a popular spot for politicians to take the platform and announce their candidacy for office.

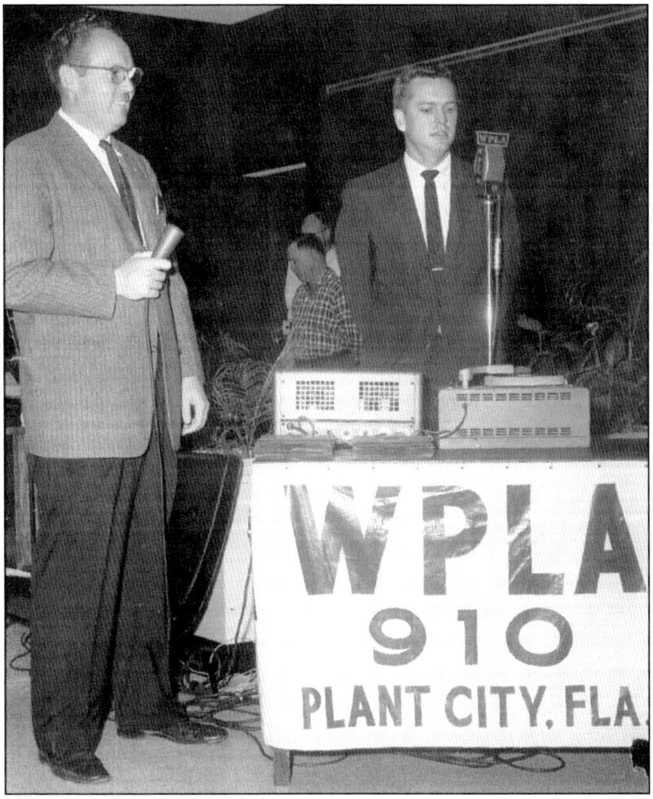

WPLA 910 Plant City, Fla. Local radio personalities were often on hand for a grand opening celebration. Remember the days of 45 records played on a turntable? Pictured from left to right are George Friend and Al Berry. Another local favorite radio show was *This and That*, a morning call-in show hosted by Al Berry and Ercelle Smith. A local favorite guest on the talk show was Aunt Maggie of Springhead. She usually had a few words of wisdom to share with the listeners.

Two

AGRICULTURE AND STRAWBERRIES

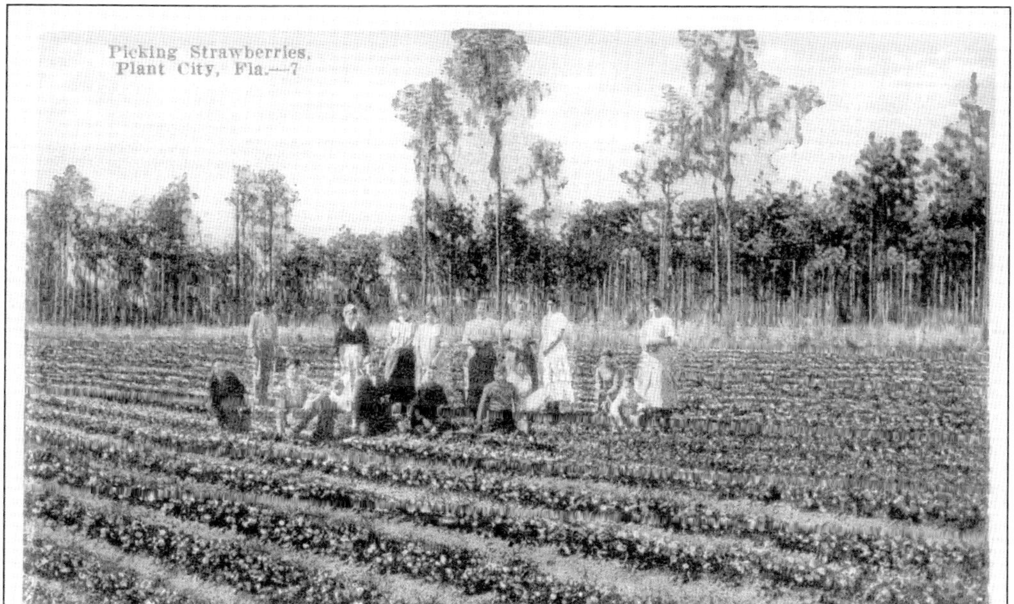

BERRY PICKING. Picking strawberries on the farm was a family affair. Schoolchildren attended Strawberry School so they could assist with the farm chores when picking time rolled around.

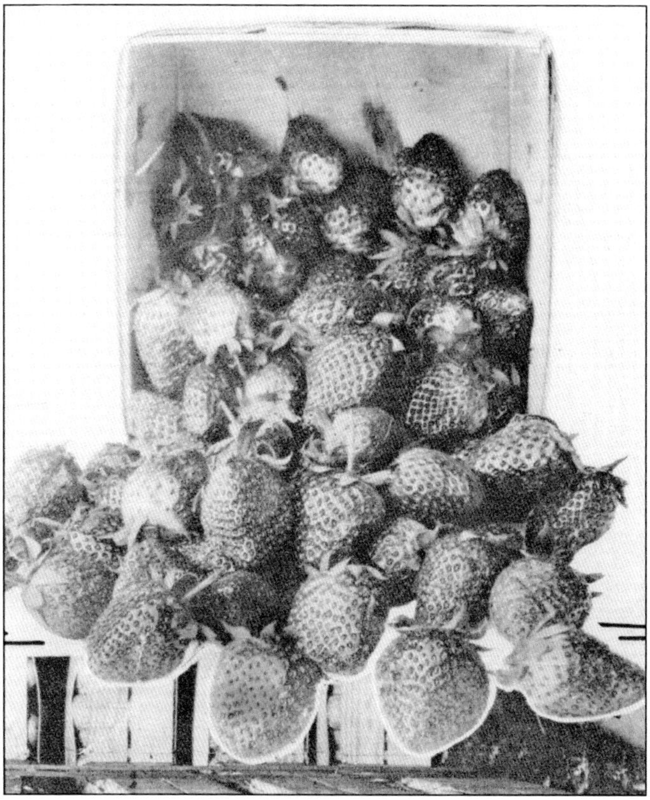

Short Cake Makin's. A bowl of Plant City strawberries, king of the local market from Thanksgiving to Easter, is first on the list of ingredients for delicious strawberry shortcake. In 1926, approximately four million quarts of strawberries were shipped by local growers. Strawberries continue to be a major source of agricultural income for the Plant City area.

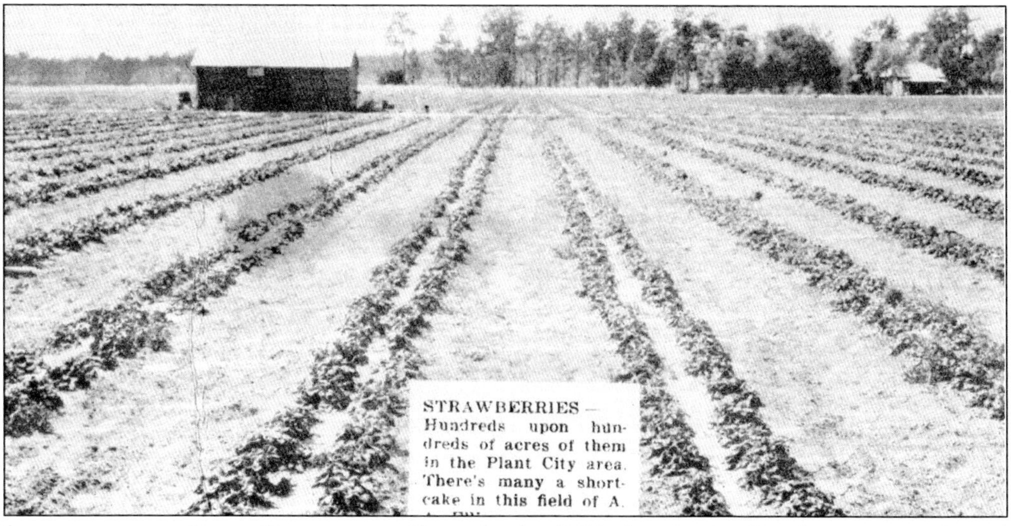

Strawberries in Fields Forever and Ever. In the 1920s, hundreds of local acres were planted in strawberries. Pictured in this field of local farmer A.A. Ellis are enough strawberries to make a very big shortcake. Homemade strawberry jam was favored as a topping for hot biscuits, fresh from the oven.

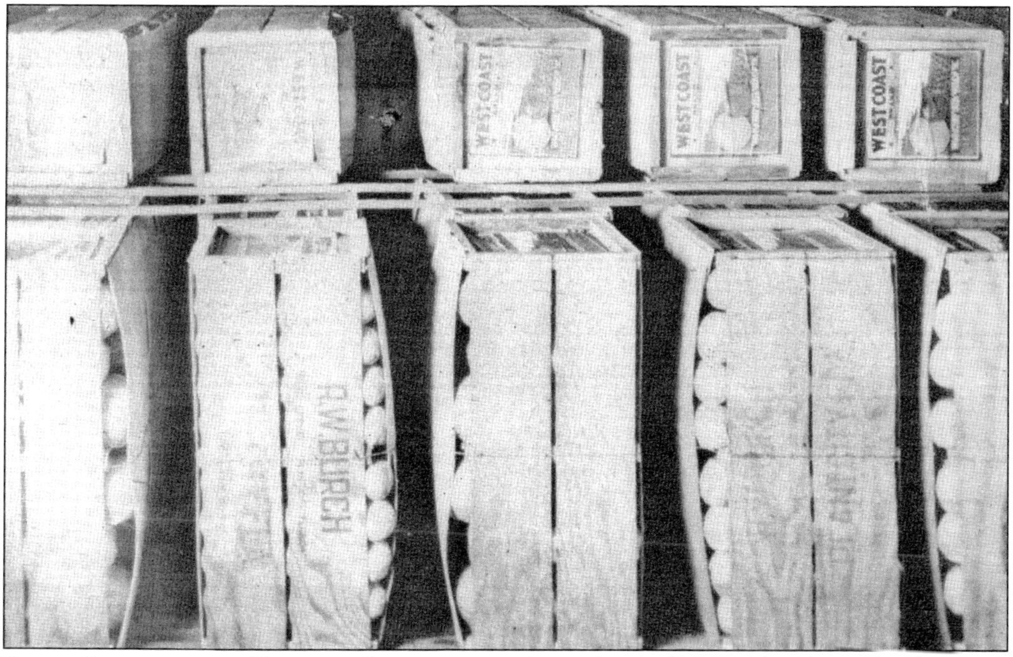

FRESH ORANGES FROM FLORIDA. Oranges were shipped on refrigerated rail cars by the R.W. Burch organization.

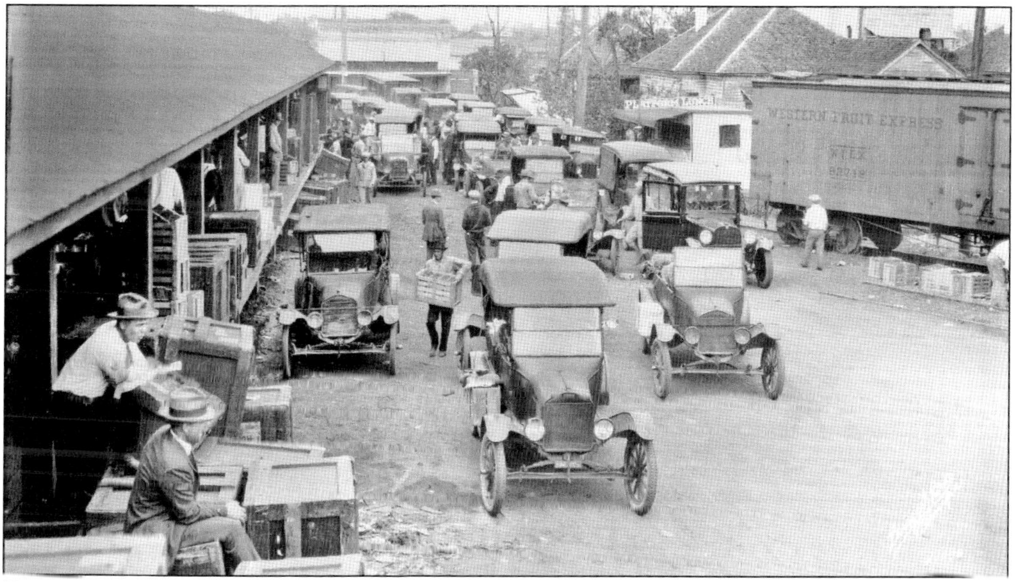

BIDDING FOR BERRIES IN 1926. Strawberry buyers inspect berries brought to market by local strawberry growers and make their bids right at the cars. Accepting the bid, strawberry grower Ben Faulkner carries a crate of fruit to the platform. This was called the Berry Yard because berries were sold in ponies (wooden boxes about three feet square). The berries were transported to the northern markets on the Western Fruit Express rail line. After bargaining with buyers, you could have a hot plate lunch at the Platform Lunch stand located next to the market. (Courtesy of Burgert Brothers No. V1096.)

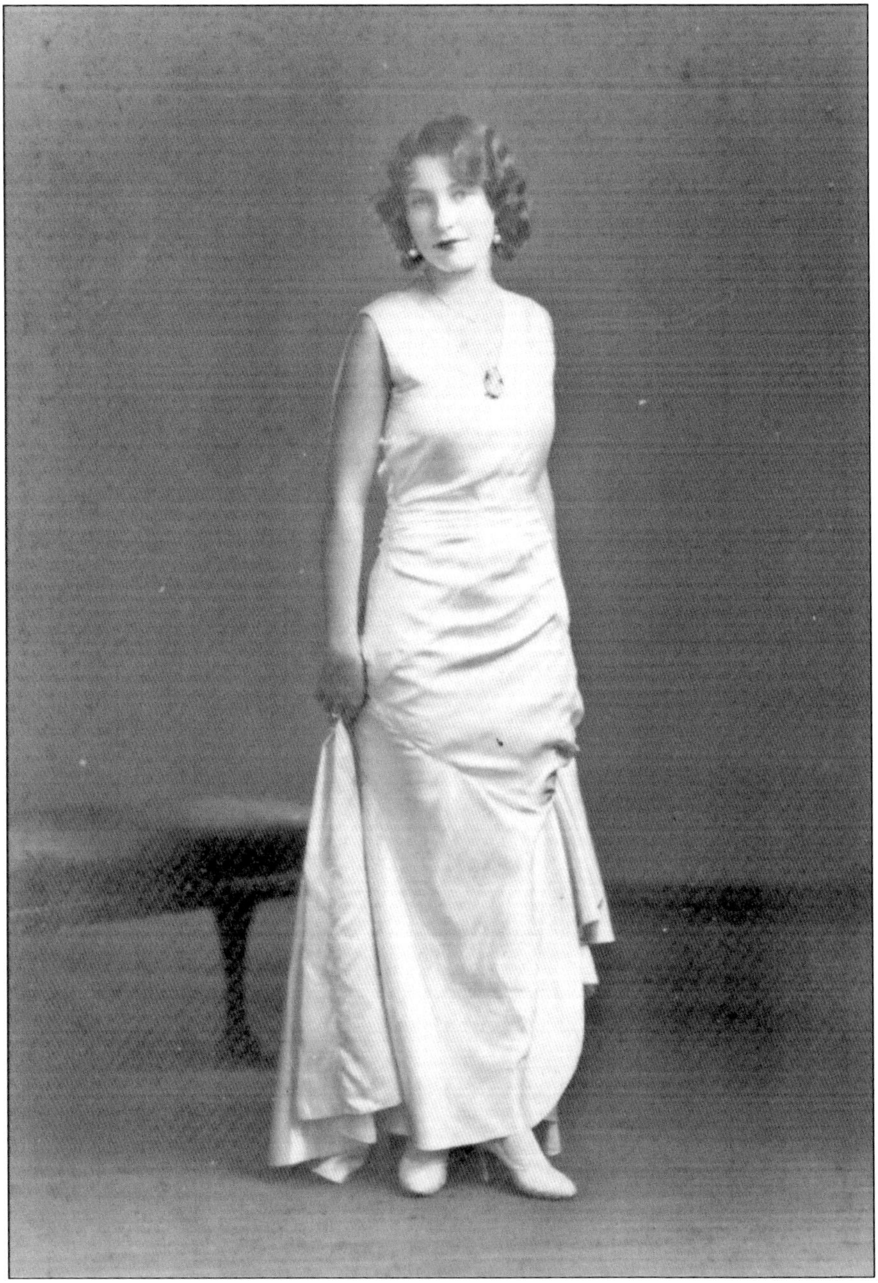

QUEEN CHARLOTTE ROSENBERG, FIRST QUEEN OF FLORIDA STRAWBERRY FESTIVAL. Miss Charlotte Rosenberg of Plant City was crowned queen of East Hillsborough's first annual strawberry festival at the opening ceremonies on Wednesday, March 12, 1930. The daughter of Mr. and Mrs. Sam Rosenberg of Plant City, she was a member of the senior class at Plant City High School. Her attendants were Miss Irvine Wilder, Miss Nettie Simmons, Miss Alice Sly, Miss Kathryn Dudley, and Miss Alice Maxey. The heralds were Elizabeth Carey, Marion Herring, Eugenia Sanchez, and Elizabeth Hull. The little pages were Helen Spear, Catherine Fletcher, Katherine Andrews, and Virginia Dennison. Elizabeth Carey was crowned queen in 1932, and Catherine Fletcher was crowned queen in 1940.

FLORIDA STRAWBERRY FESTIVAL PLANT CITY, FLA., MARCH 12-13-14-15, 1930. In the heart of the world's largest winter strawberry producing area were held four fun-filled days with all the strawberries you could eat. Opening day was designated Children's Day at the festival by Mayor G.A. Carey. The day was proclaimed a holiday and all business houses were expected to respect the City's proclamation by closing their doors to business for the afternoon and to do honor to this occasion by joining in the festivity of the day. The 1:00 p.m. parade had 10 units, including local officials, Queen Charlotte and court members, Plant City Band, Hillsborough High School Band of Tampa, a UDC float, and decorated cars.

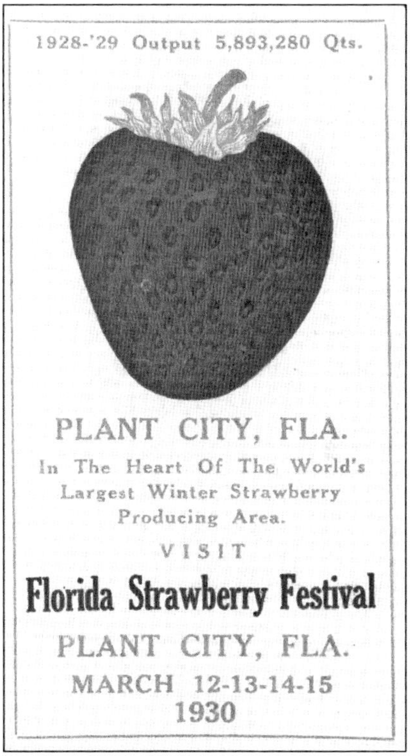

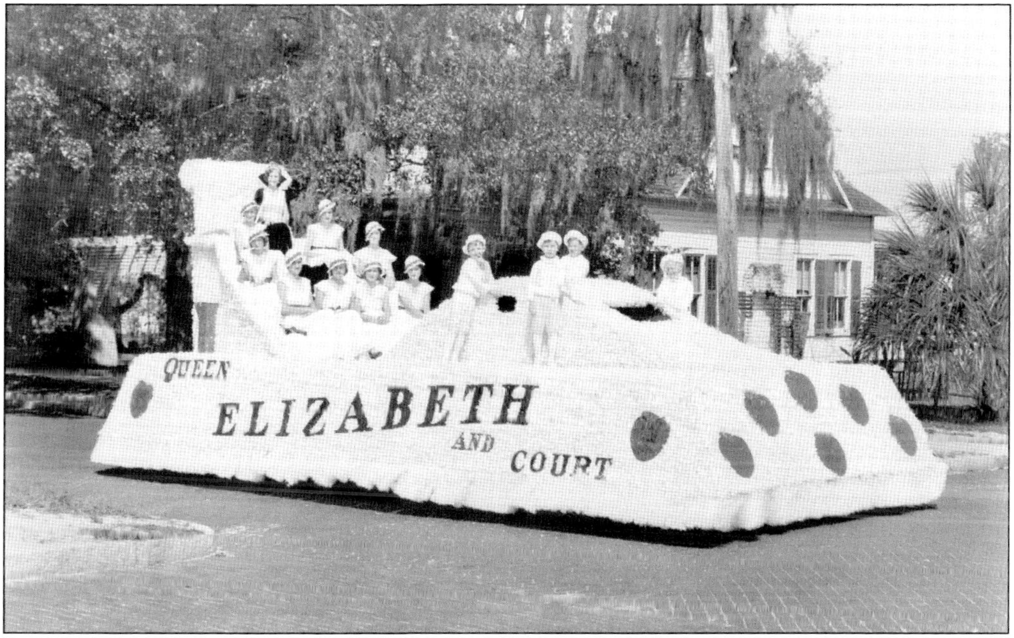

STRAWBERRY FESTIVAL QUEEN AND COURT ALONG PARADE ROUTE, 1932. The reigning queen, Elizabeth Carey (Turner) Stalnaker, and her court members Dot Gentry, Marian Herring, Winfred Yates, Elisie Coronet, Verna Jones, Ethel Randall, Ruby Pratt, and Loraine Paroline, participate in the 1932 parade. The pages were Ned Haven, William Reese Smith Jr., Jack Fewell, and unidentified.

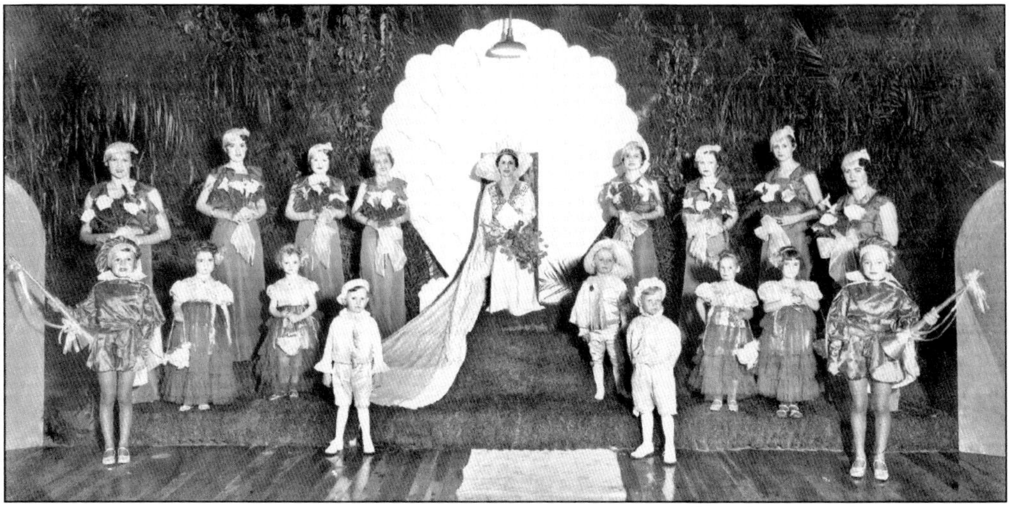

STRAWBERRY FESTIVAL QUEEN WITH COURT AND PAGES AT CORONATION, 1934. Queen Dorothy Adelson was the fifth queen of the Strawberry Festival. Pictured in the back row from left to right are court members Goldie Rice, Doyle Colding, Clara Nell Register, Lila Florence Craig, Dorothy Adelson (queen), Ermeldene Peeples, Edith Gentry, Elizabeth Buckalew, and Helen Read. The pages pictured from left to right in the front row are Margaret Whitney, Geraldine Bates, Joy Marley, Jimmie Barker, Arden Mays Merkle, Marcus E. Cone Jr., Barbara Alley, Betty Boring, and Katherine Coleman. Mrs. William Reece Smith Sr. (not pictured) served as chairman of the Coronation Committee. (Courtesy of William Reece Smith Jr.; a Hockett photo.)

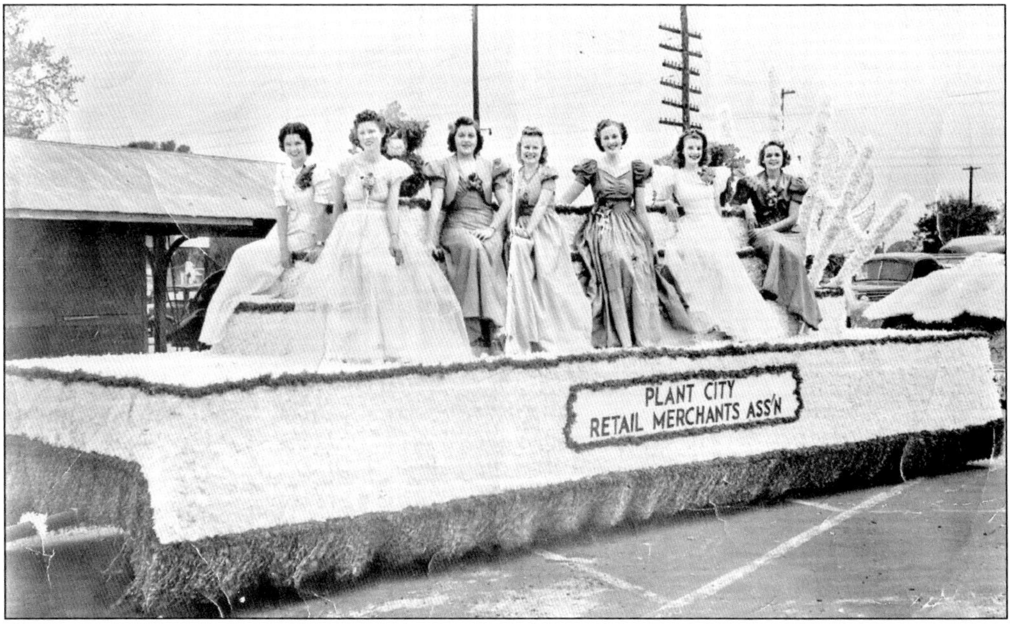

FLORIDA STRAWBERRY FESTIVAL PARADE FLOAT OF PLANT CITY RETAIL MERCHANTS ASSOCIATION, 1938. Pretty young ladies were all smiles as they waved to the well-wishers along the parade route. Pictured from left to right are Mary Frances McQuinn Schroeder, Edra Carpenter Baker, Virginia Moberly, Vonelle Smith Miles Robinson, Roynelle Wolfe, Evalie Riles, and Katherine Fisher Draughon.

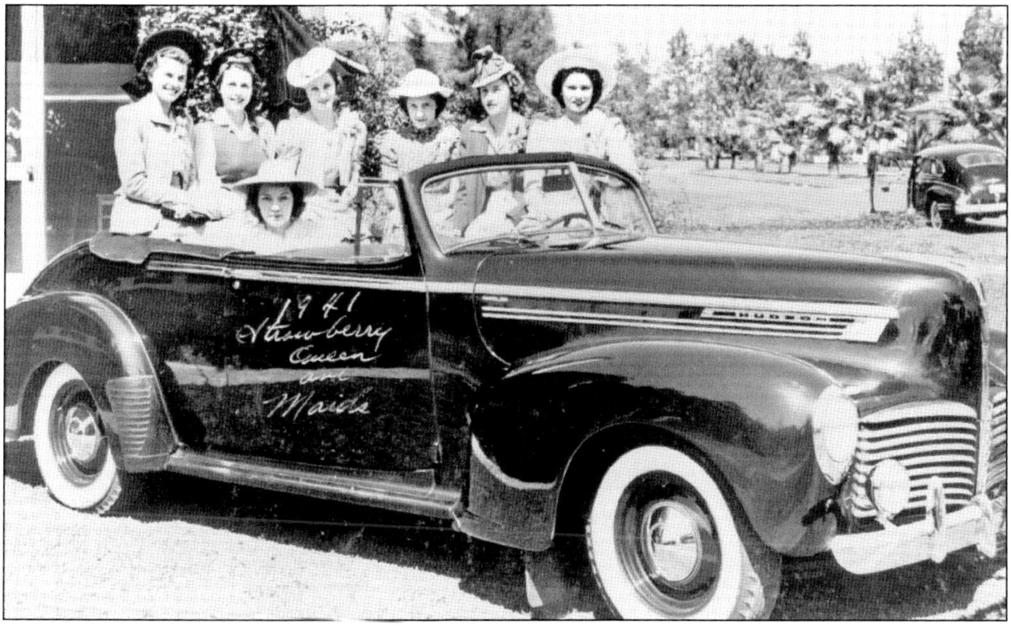

What a Beauty! The 1941 Florida Strawberry Festival Queen and her court are off to a social event in a white side-walled Hudson convertible. Pictured from left to right are Lillian Ergle, Jane Langford (queen), Louise Gardner, Virginia Jordan, Florance Anderson, Marjorie Rogers, and Agatha Jean Sampson.

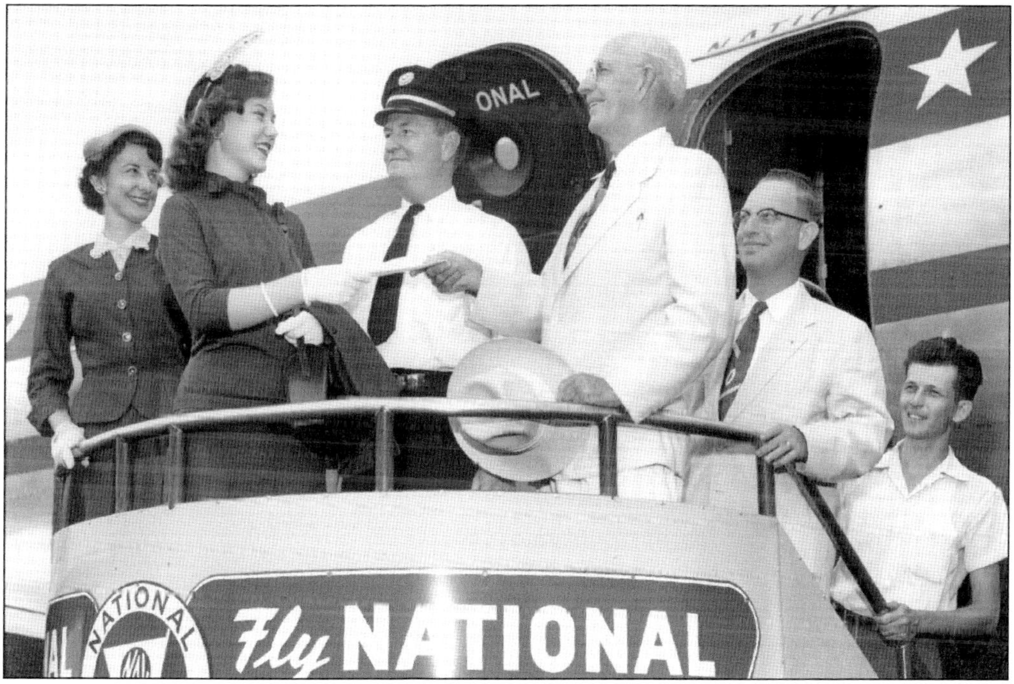

Strawberry Festival Queen Travels First Class; Fly National Airline of the Stars. Pictured from left to right are Doris Andrews, 1955 Florida Strawberry Festival queen Betty Clements, National Airlines captain Glasgow, Ben E. Rawlins, Paul S. Buchman, and Bill Gunn.

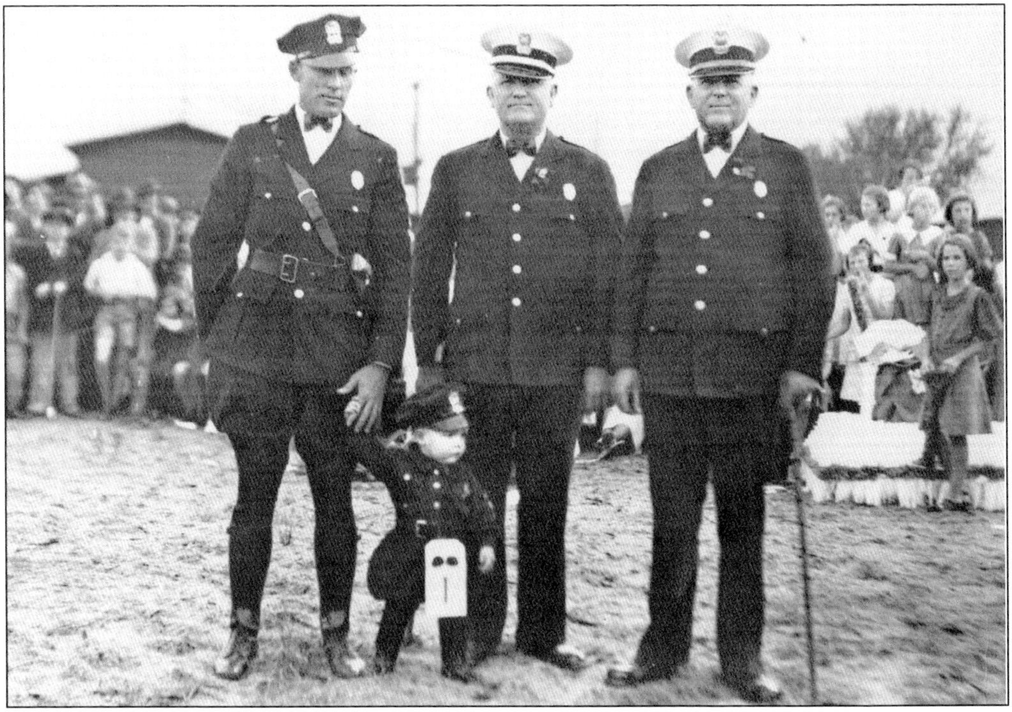

YOUNG MAN IN UNIFORM IS NO. 1 ENTRY. The men in uniform took a moment to pause with the No. 1 officer at the 1936 Florida Strawberry Festival baby parade. Pictured from left to right are T.J. McCall and son James C. McCall, Officer ? Kirkland, and police chief J.A. Abbott. T.J. McCall was named city manager in 1941.

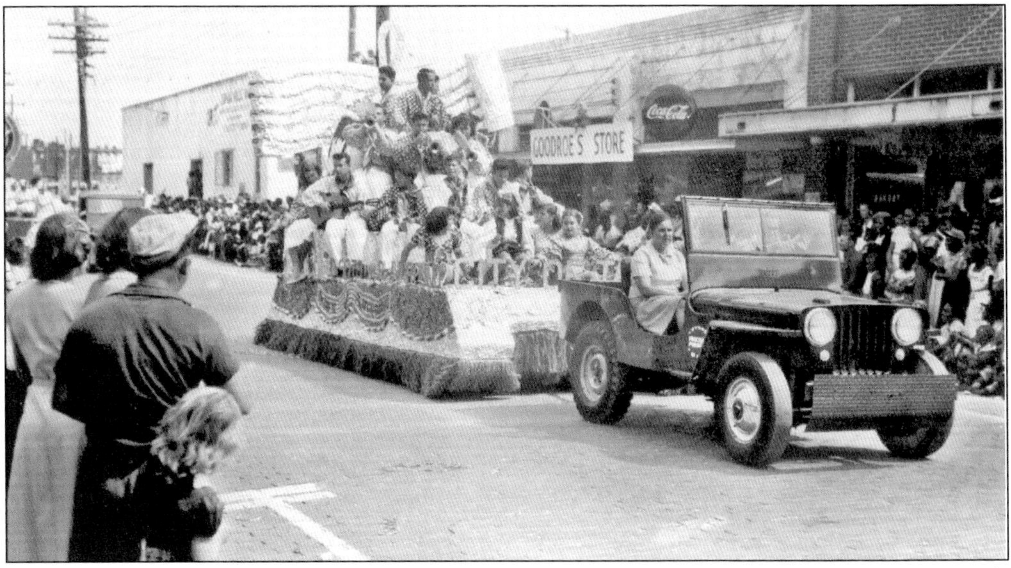

BIG CROWD ALONG THE PARADE ROUTE. Spectators lined up along Haines Street to watch the annual Florida Strawberry Festival Parade. Floats were pulled by jeeps, trucks, and cars representing businesses, civic organizations, and officials. Haines Street was named for Col. Henry S. Haines, the rail chief for Gen. Robert E. Lee during the War between the States. The name was changed to Dr. M.L. King Jr. Boulevard to honor the late Dr. King.

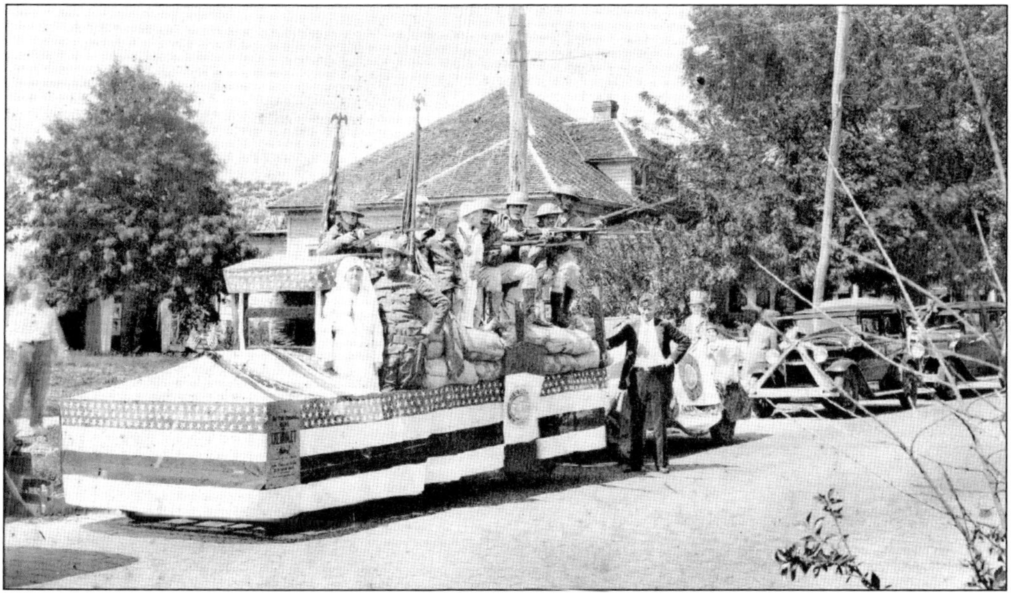

PARADE ENTRY WITH A PATRIOTIC FLAIR. Patriotism has long been a theme for parade entries across America. This float, an advertisement for Chevrolet, showed the local spirit of America. Pictured with his hand on his hip is Clyde Noble Simmons, who moved to Plant City in 1921 from Bridgeport, Pennsylvania. (Courtesy of Anna Ellen "Nancy" S. Duffield, by Leavitt Photo Co.)

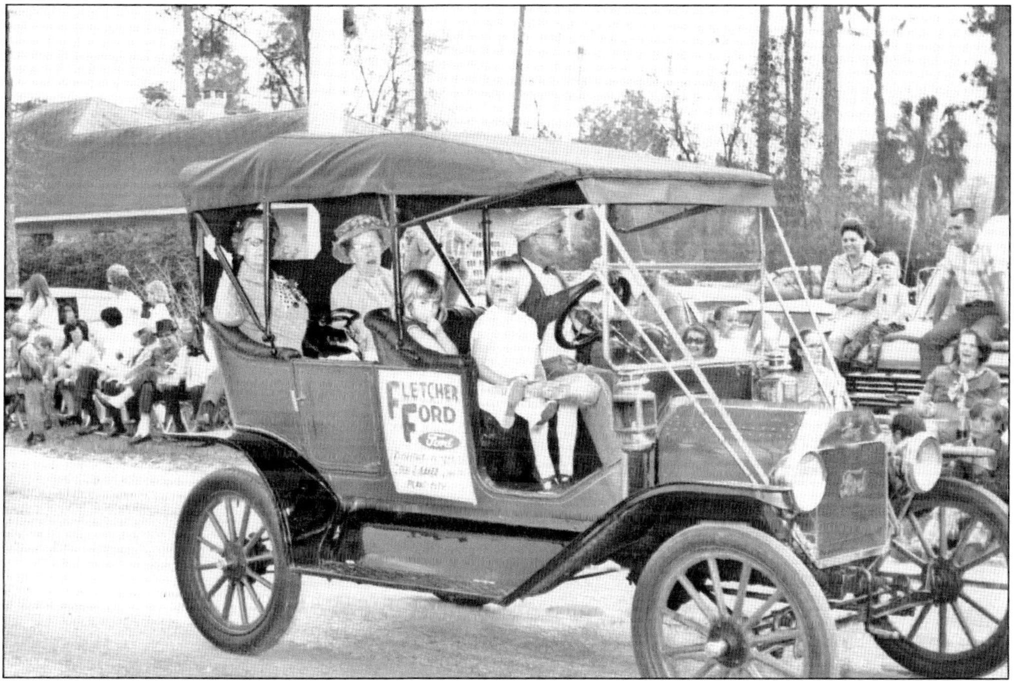

LONGTIME FRIENDS ENJOYING THE PARADE. The early-model Ford car was a standing entry in the annual Florida Strawberry Festival Parade. Enjoying the festivities from the back seat are Mrs. Nita Fletcher (left) of Fletcher Ford and Mrs. Ula Miles (right) of Miles Motor Company, the local Plymouth and Willys dealership. (Courtesy of Gladys Jeffcoat Photographer.)

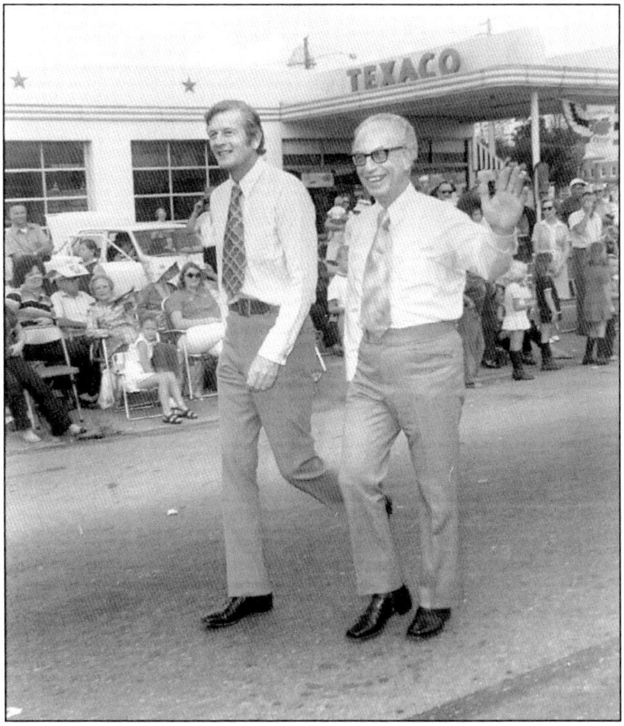

New York Mayor John Lindsay Waves to the Parade Watchers. New York City mayor John Lindsay writes in March 1972: "Dear Paul, Thank you again for your courage. I was proud to walk with you! Sincerely, John Lindsay 2 March 1972." (*New York Post*, Wednesday, March 1, 1972.) Mayor Lindsay does some shirt-sleeve campaigning as a participant in the Plant City Florida Strawberry Festival Parade. The Arthur Goldberg look-alike on his right is Paul S. Buchman, a Plant City official. (Courtesy of Beryle Soloman Buchman Wolff; Associated Press Wirephoto.)

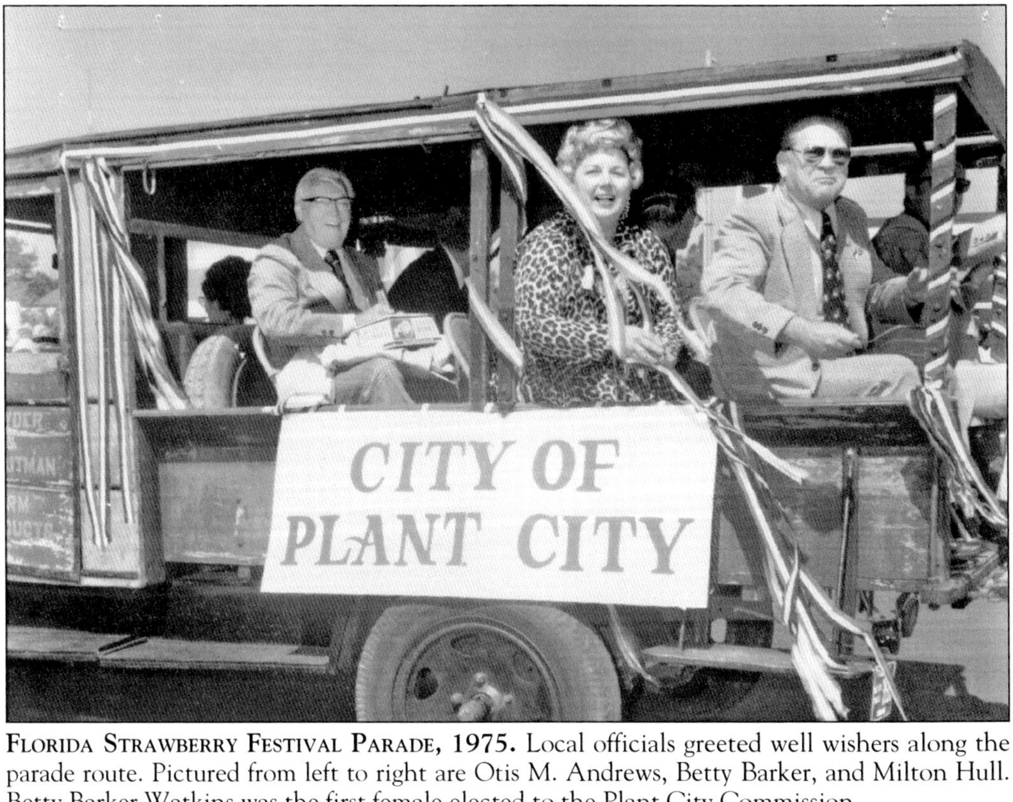

Florida Strawberry Festival Parade, 1975. Local officials greeted well wishers along the parade route. Pictured from left to right are Otis M. Andrews, Betty Barker, and Milton Hull. Betty Barker Watkins was the first female elected to the Plant City Commission.

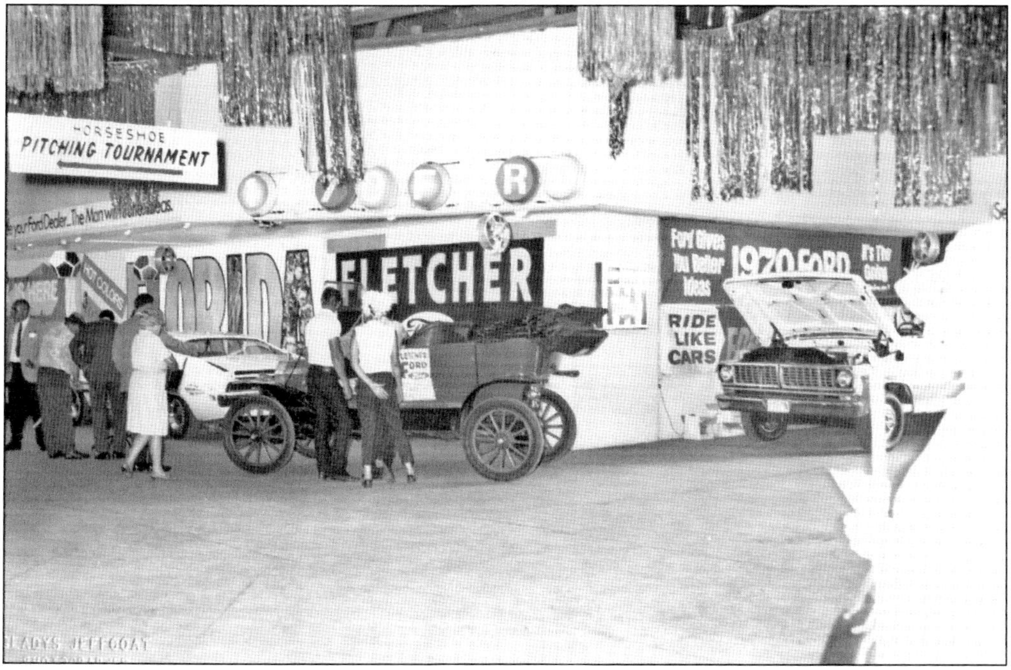

FORD GIVES YOU BETTER IDEAS. The year was 1970 and a local dealer, Fletcher Ford, had an exhibit in the Main Exhibit Hall at the Florida Strawberry Festival. Ford's new pick-up trucks were said to "ride like cars." New "hot" colors were available. (Courtesy of Gladys Jeffcoat.)

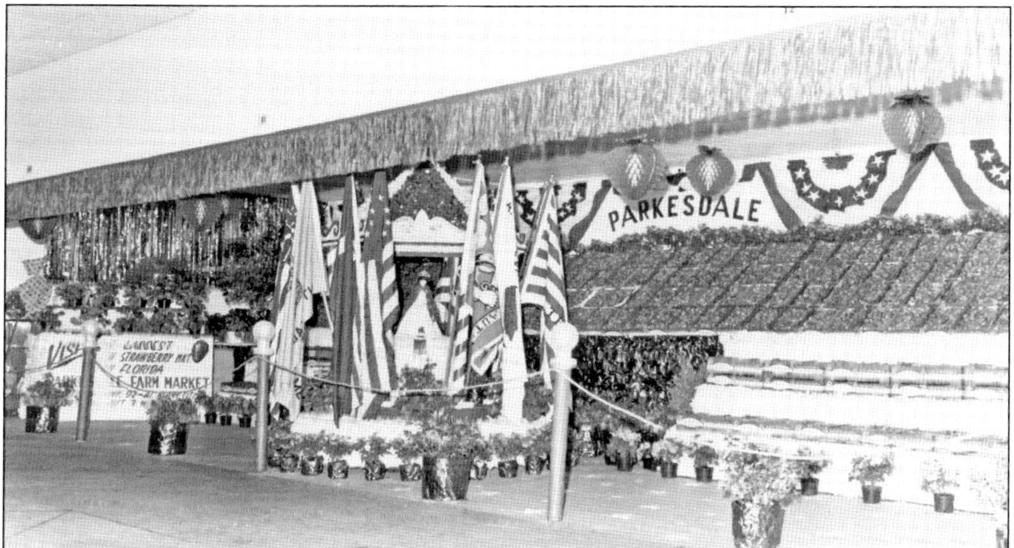

PARKESDALE—LARGEST STRAWBERRY MARKET IN FLORIDA. Parkesdale Farm's booth exhibit at the 1975 Florida Strawberry Festival received the "Berriest Bunch" Award. Owned by R.E. (Roy) Parke & Sons, Parkesdale Farm has had one of the largest exhibits of fresh berries at the festival for many years.

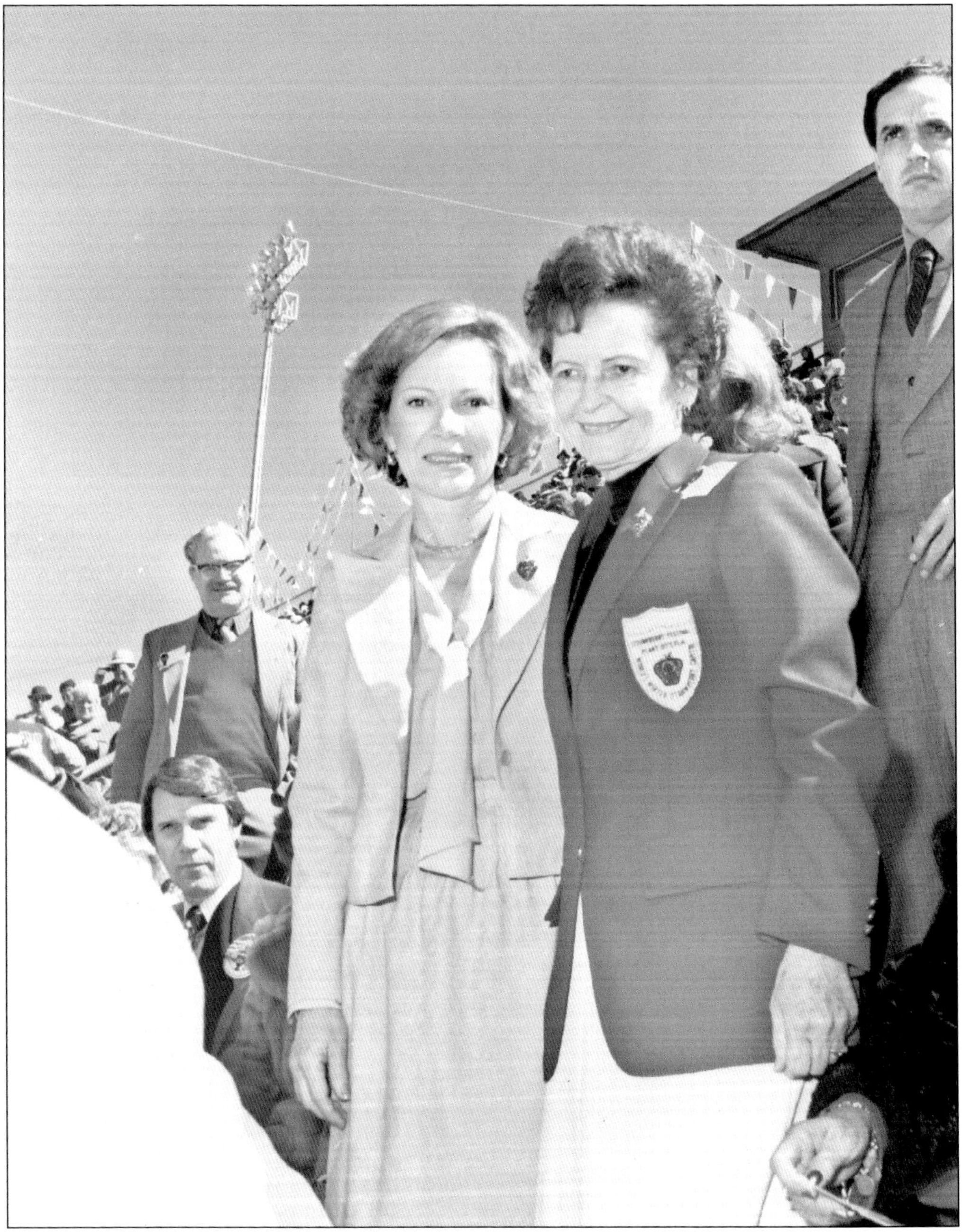

MARCH 3, 1980, SCHNEIDER STADIUM, PLANT CITY: 45TH ANNUAL FLORIDA STRAWBERRY FESTIVAL PARADE REVIEW. First Lady Rosalyn Carter, wife of President Jimmy Carter, and Nettie M. Draughon, city manager and associate director of the Florida Strawberry Festival, are enjoying the parade from the stadium at the fairgrounds. Also pictured from left to right are (standing) Richard M. Olson, city clerk and finance director; Harold Taylor, president of the First National Bank; and one of Mrs. Carter's Secret Service security guards.

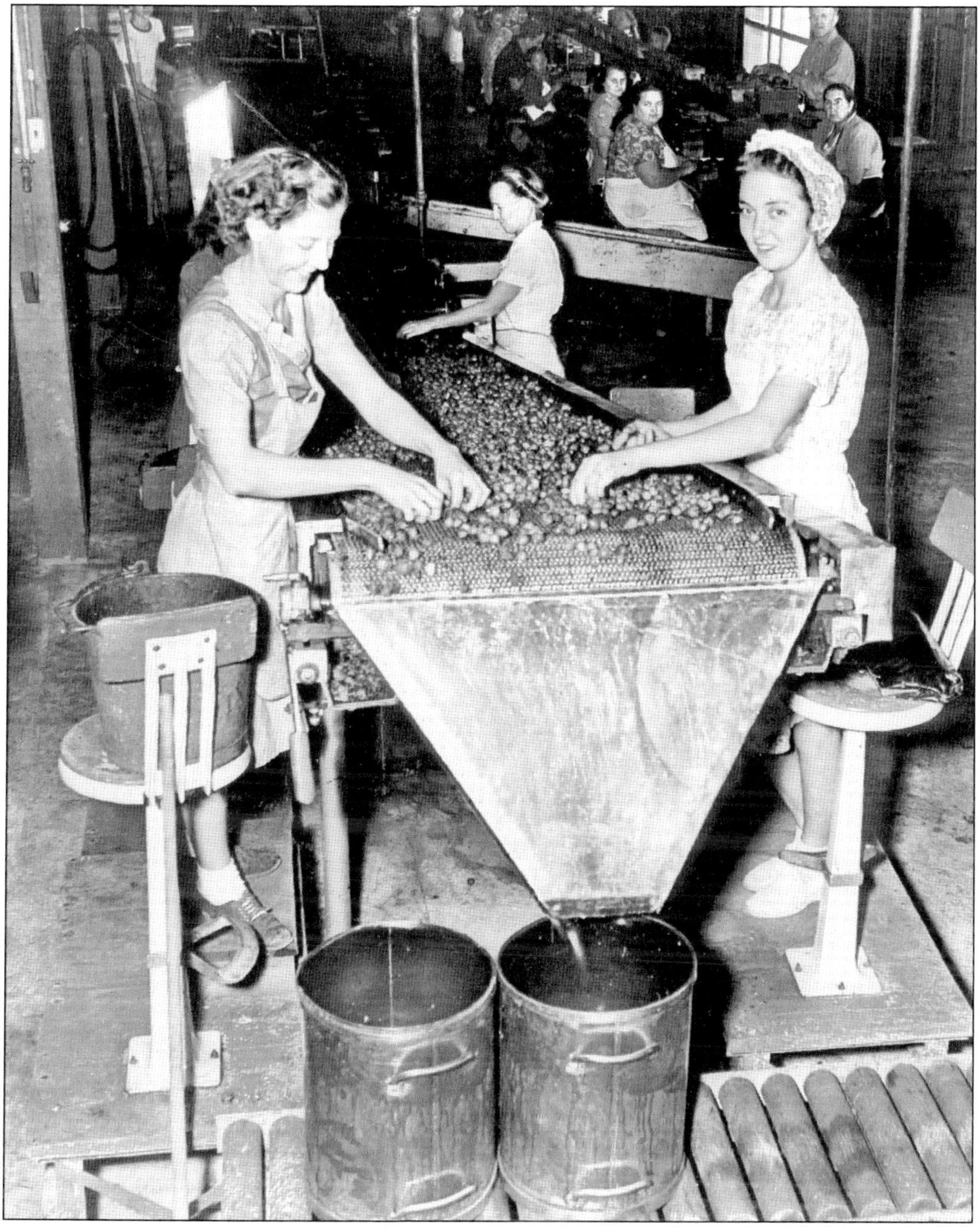

The Berriest Best of the Strawberries. Two workers carefully select berries at Processing Shed No. 4 at the Farmers' Market in Plant City. Strawberries brought to market were sorted and graded by hand. A sign on the production line read "NO TALKING." (Courtesy of Robertson & Fresh Photographers.)

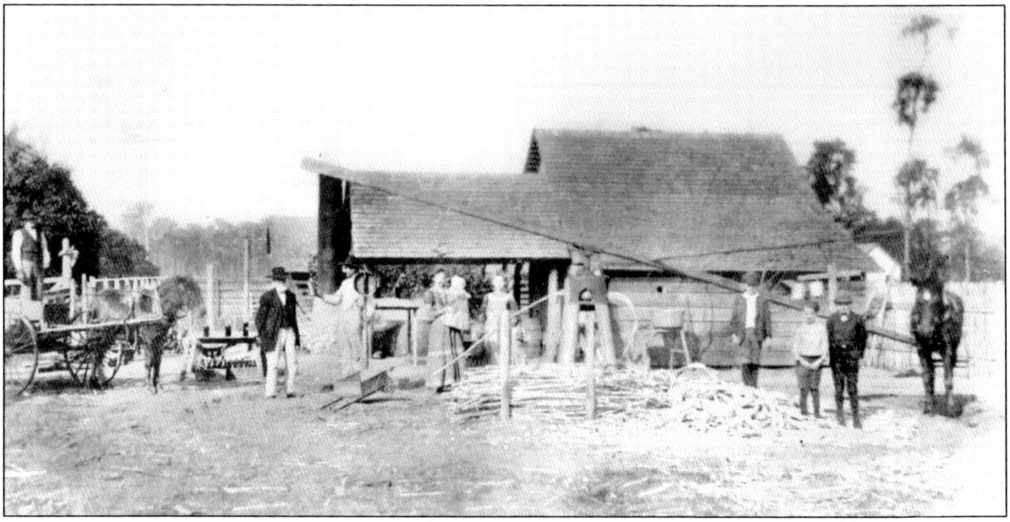

AN OLD-FASHIONED CANE GRINDING. Cane-grinding mills like this one were essential to early farm families. Modern cane mills extracted more juice from the cane, thus increasing the yield of syrup. Pictured from left to right are J.W. Browning (in the wagon), Berrian Platt, Bartlett Hamilton, May Howell Blanton (with a baby), Mrs. Hamilton, and Hamilton boys Wayne, Ray, and Ralph. (Courtesy of EHHS DeVane Collection.)

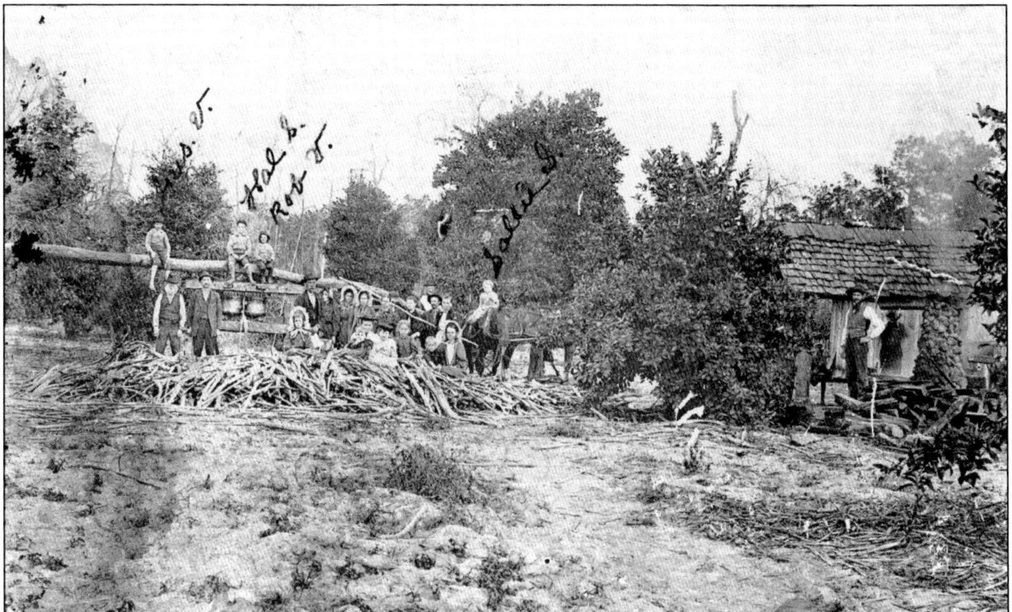

SUGAR-MAKING ON A COLD DAY IN JANUARY 1891. This picture is of sugar-making at the mill on Mr. Beaty's farm near Plant City. Cane grindings were popular in the early days. Identified in this photo from left to right are (standing at far left) "Old Man" Beaty and Bill Beaty; (seated on the cane grinding pole) Gus Venning, Hal Shannon, and Rob Venning; and (seated on the horse) Sallie Shannon. Others named in the photo but unidentified are Ella, Minnie, Fannie, and Allice Beaty (neé Platt); T.M. and Minnie Louise Venning; ? Garrison (Mary Platt Garrison's husband); Mrs. Mary Garrison; ? Lindley; Fannie Lindley (neé Beaty); Minnie Shannon; and Charlie Shannon.

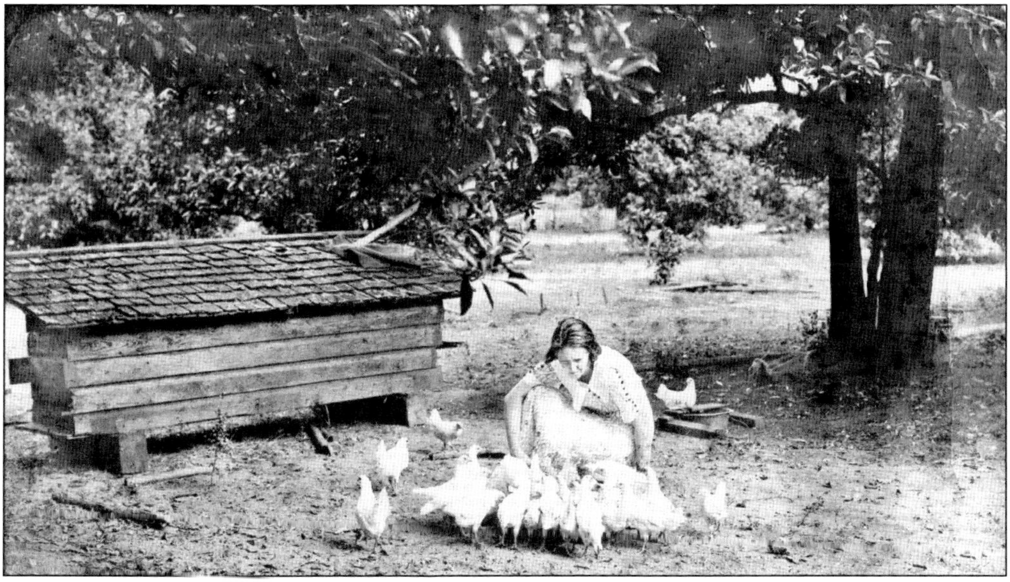

MOMMA'S PRIZE CHICKEN STOCK. Mrs. Denver Hawthorne (Myrtis Avant) raised chickens in the orange grove of Denver Hawthorne at Knights, Florida, around 1930. This method has proven very satisfactory to the oranges and the chickens also. (Courtesy of the Hawthorne Family Collection; by the Agricultural Extension Service, Gainesville, Florida.)

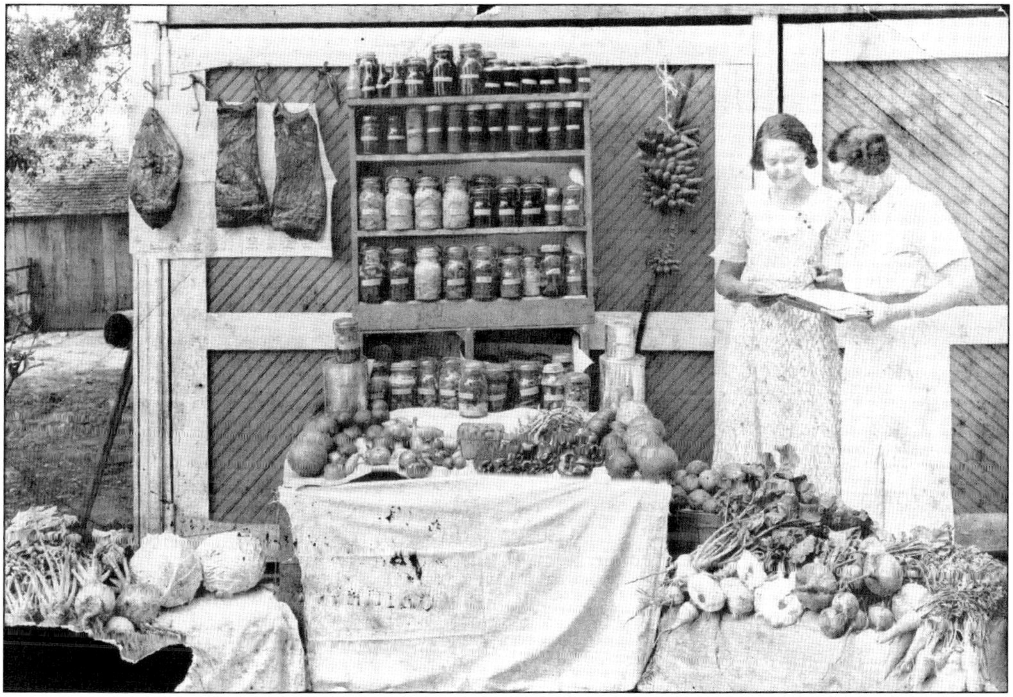

ON THE HAWTHORNE FAMILY FARM, KNIGHTS, FLORIDA. Pictured from left to right are Mrs. Denver Hawthorne (Myrtis Avant) and the Agricultural Extension Service agent, with a display of Live-at-Home products, outside the barn of the Hawthorne farm at Knights, Florida, around 1930. (Courtesy of the Hawthorne Family Collection; by the Agricultural Extension Service, Gainesville, Florida.)

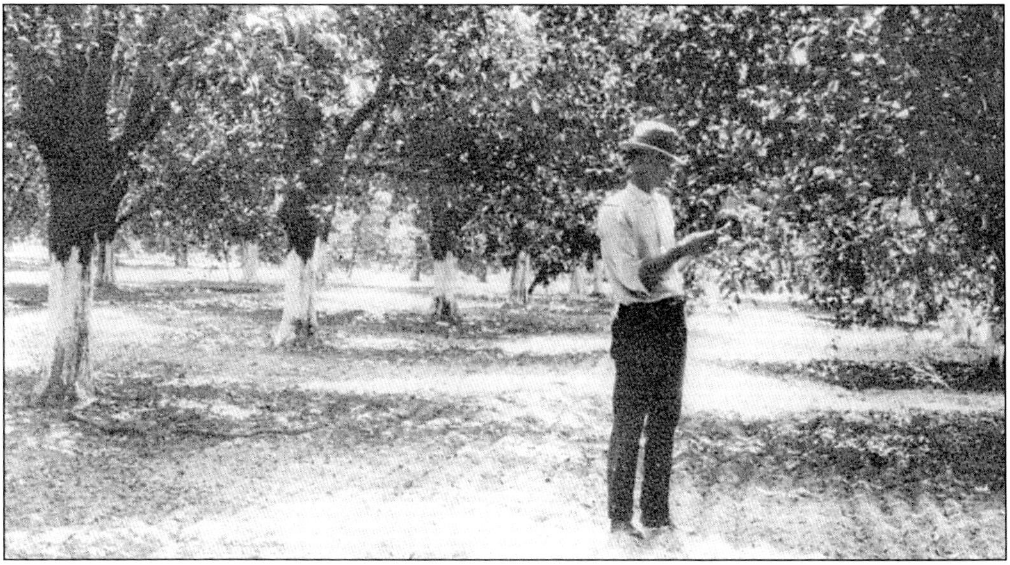

The S.E. Mays Orange Grove at Riverview, One of the Most Productive in All of Florida. Prof. Samuel E. Mays of Peru (Riverview) was among the first to plant orange trees in the county. His son S.E. Mays Jr. expanded his father's grove until at one time it covered nearly 300 acres. Plant City and its surrounding land offer some of the best soils for growing orange trees. A well-producing orange grove offered a nice income. In fact, this section of Florida offers the farmer its best soil to produce more revenue for the money than any other area.

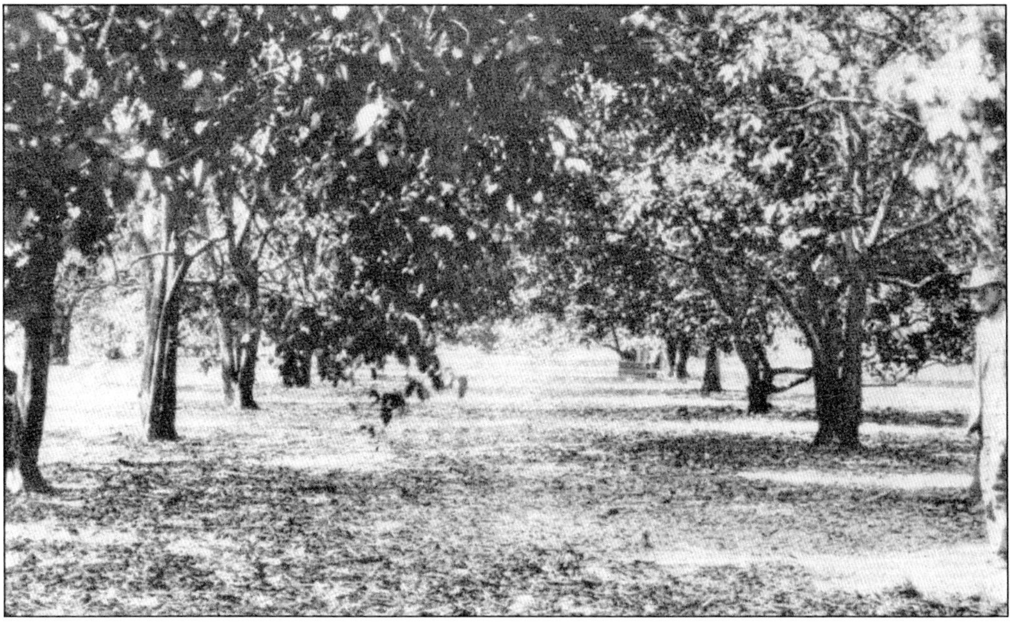

Grapefruit on the H.J. Moody Farm at Riverview, One of the County's Best Farming Sections. Citrus was an important crop grown in the East Hillsborough County area. The Florida Citrus Exchange was formed in 1909, with headquarters in Tampa. Processing plants in the area sectioned the grapefruits for canning. The sweet smell of the fruit filled the air when the processing plants were being run during their season.

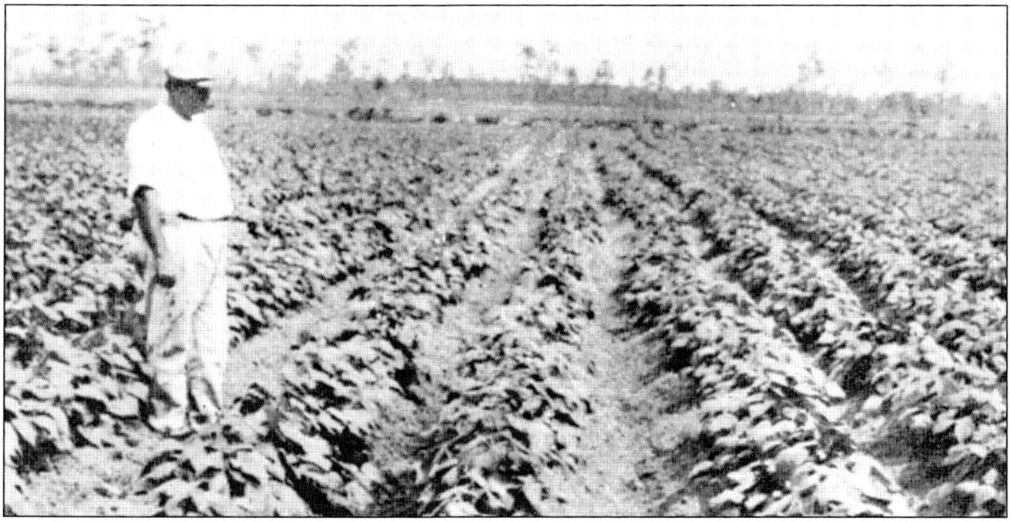

BEANS ON THE FARM OF D.M. DOWELL, IN THE RICH WIMAUMA SECTION. The soil and climate of the area strongly supported the growing of vegetables, including beans. Other crops grown were okra, squash, peas, and eggplant.

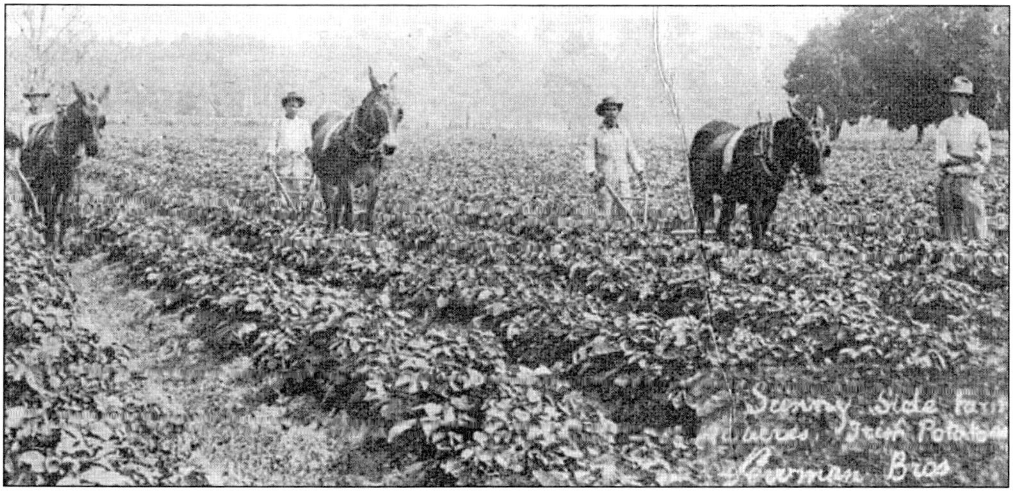

IRISH POTATOES AREN'T JUST GROWN IN IRELAND. Irish potatoes were just one of the many crops grown profitably by the Newman brothers on their well-known Plant City farm. An important food source, potatoes are the most widely cultivated vegetable in the world. Over one million Irish people left their country during the potato blight in the mid-1800s.

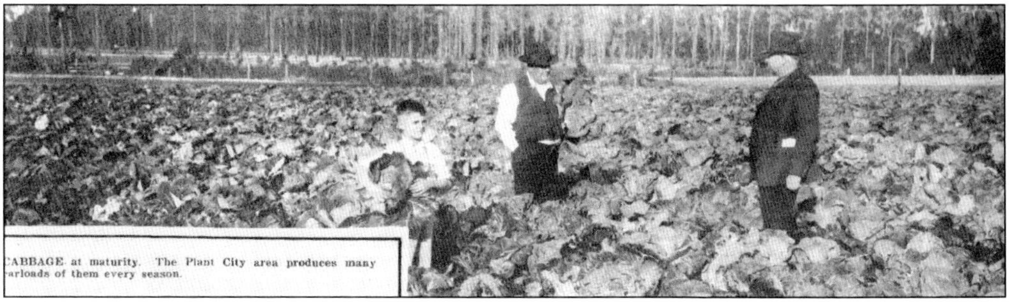

CABBAGE AT MATURITY. The Plant City area produces many carloads of them every season. Cabbage is a hardy vegetable that grows especially well in fertile soils. Cabbage is a good source of vitamins and has disease-preventive properties. Shaped in round, pointed, or flattened heads, varieties occur with green, red, or purple leaves.

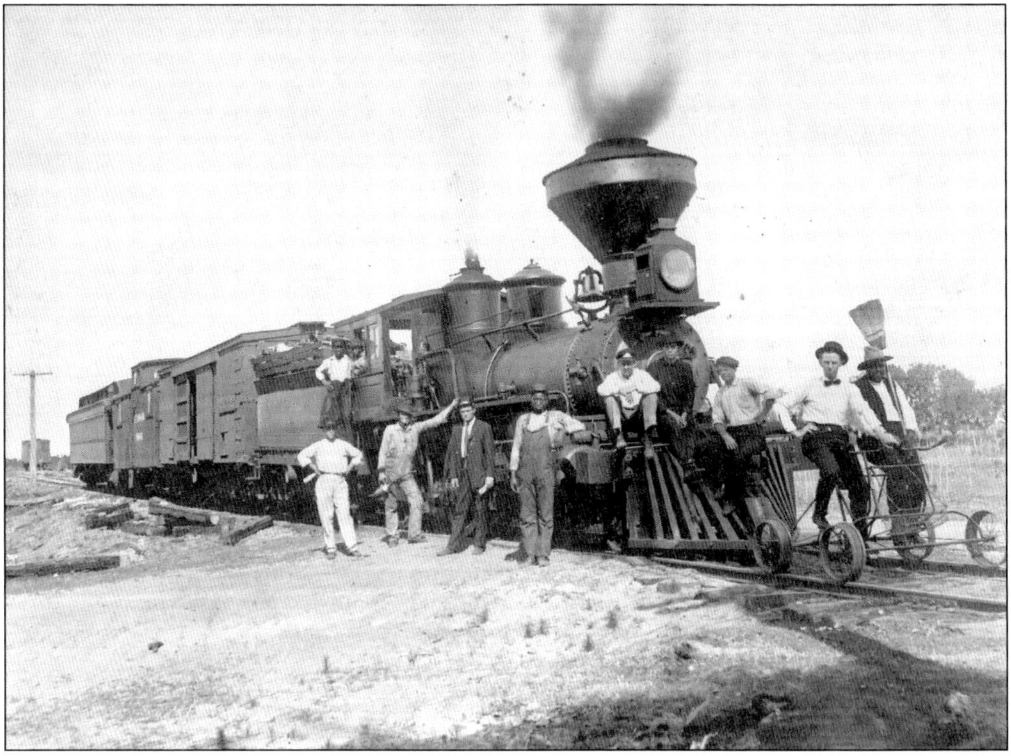

THE VEGGIE TRAIN. Taken in 1907, this photo shows the "Vegetable Train," which ran between Turkey Creek and Palmetto, Florida, and made pick-ups from farmers along the route. Freshly picked vegetables were packed in crates and placed along the track for pick-up. A train man rode ahead of the engine with a broom to sweep the track and keep it free of gravel.

Three

EDUCATION

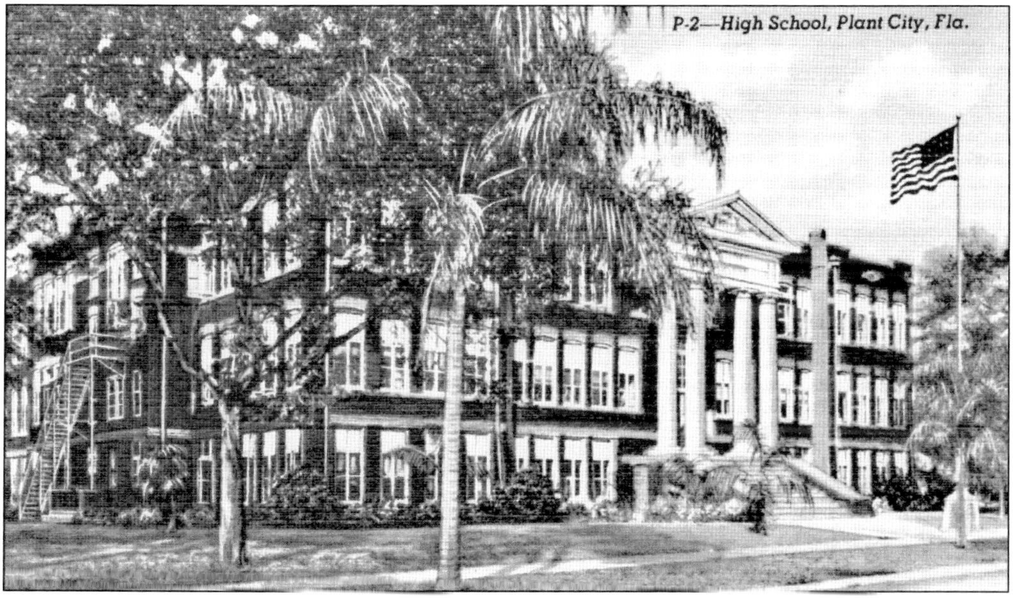

PLANT CITY HIGH SCHOOL. Construction started on May 19, 1914, with funding from a $10,000 bond issue. This modified Georgia-revival building is a three-story, red brick structure with decorative blond brick from Macon, Georgia, as accent trim. After much community discussion, it was decided that the original plan would be changed and the building made to face both Collins and Evers Streets. The facade elevations feature central, four-bay, fluted, pedimented Doric columns, with porticos on the second, or main, level. The building is located on an entire block in one of Plant City's oldest residential neighborhoods and stands as an impressive contrast to the predominant frame housing that lines the tree-shaded brick streets. Listed on the National Register of Historic Sites, the building is owned by the City of Plant City and managed by the East Hillsborough Historical Society. The society houses its offices, pioneer museums, and archives center here. Other displays of agricultural, classroom, photography, and railroad memorabilia are present. The auditorium is used for community musical and theater productions.

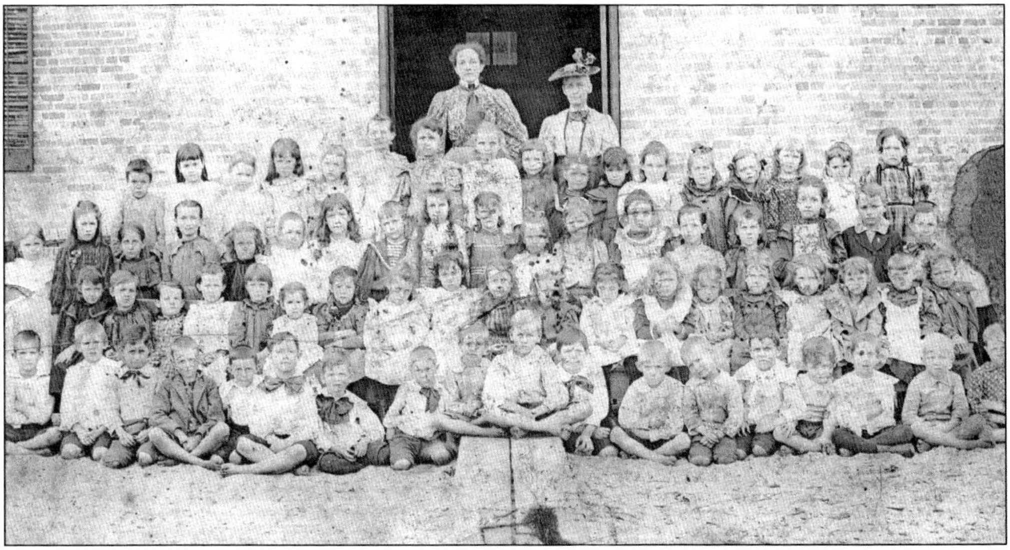

First and Second Grade, Plant City School, 1895–1896. The first- and second-grade students pose for their class picture in the entryway of the grammar-school building at the corner of Wheeler and Baker Streets. The teachers pictured are Miss Laura Keller (Mrs. P.A. Merrin), second-grade teacher, at left, and Mrs. Esther D. Burney, first-grade teacher, at right. (Courtesy of Mrs. Arthur Coleman.)

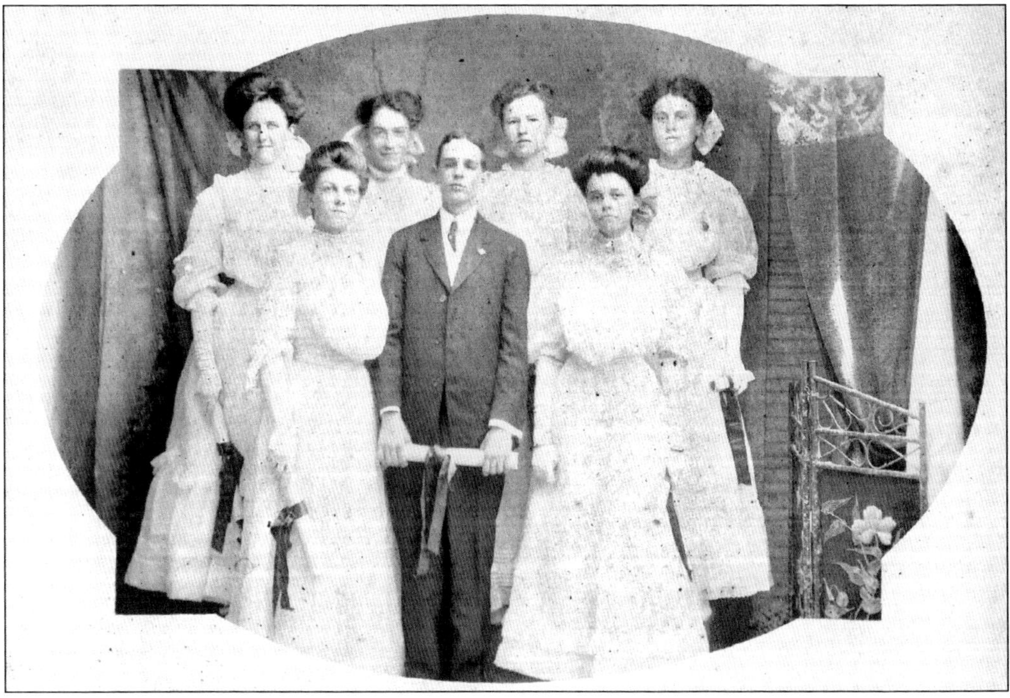

Class of 1907, Plant City High School. The graduates are proud of their accomplishments during the commencement exercises. With their diplomas in hand, pictured from left to right are (front row) Josephine Schneider Land, Walter Griffin, and Florence Smith Root; (back row) Mamie Roy Walker, Ellen Vining Swindall, Maud DeVane Hays, and Mae Collins Boone Sweat.

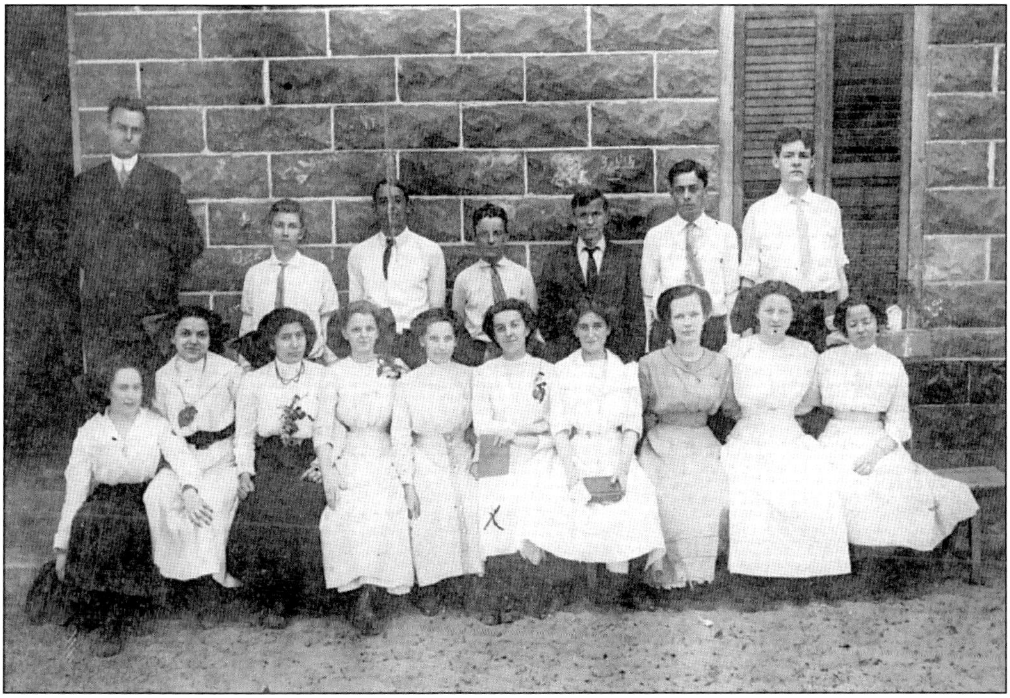

JUNIOR CLASS OF 1911, PLANT CITY HIGH SCHOOL. The Plant City High School was located at the corner of Wheeler and Mahoney Streets. Pictured from left to right are (front row) Herberta Hathcock, Victoria Coleman (Mrs. Paul D. Barns), Fannie Clair Franklin, Viva Griffin, Irene Merrin, Tallie Slone, Mattie Young, Hilda Causey, Connie DeVane, and Eugenia Barker; (back row) Clyde Beck (language teacher), Chester Branch, Fred Fischer, ? Causey, Richard Merrin, Gresham Causey, and Fred Durrance.

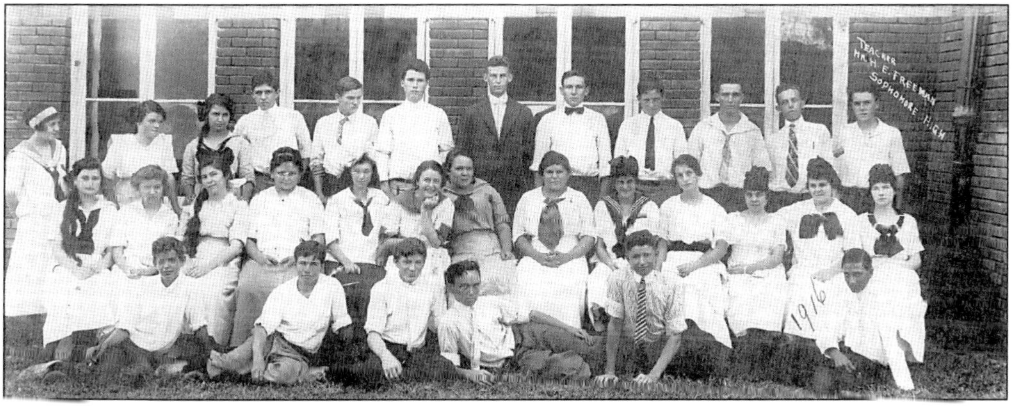

SOPHOMORE CLASS OF 1916, PLANT CITY HIGH SCHOOL. Pictured from left to right are (front row) Sterling Meldrim, Broward Green, Marshall Lair, Harley Smith, Sumter Barker, and Johnnie Wood; (middle row) Ina Nulter, unidentified, Celiee Strickland, Mae Register, Carmelita McEwen, Minnie Mae Hull, Bertha Thomas, Isabel Miller, Jewell DeVane, Eunice Stafford, Emma Holloway, Marie Parker, and Annie Smith; (back row) Edna Anderson, Viola Parramore, Foy Strong, Ernest Harpor, Carl Curry, Wade Branch, Prof. Henry Freeman, Rowe Taylor, unidentified, Lanier Rocker, Clarence Martin, and LaRue Collins.

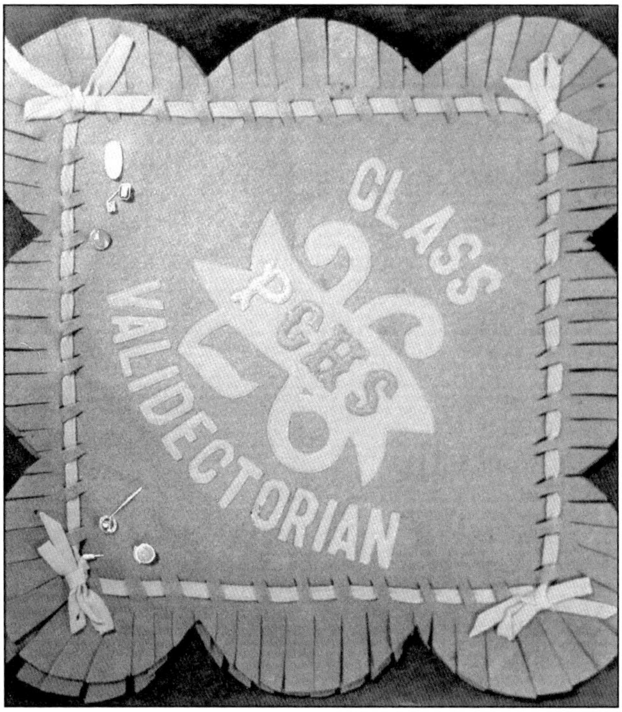

VALEDICTORIAN PLANT CITY HIGH SCHOOL, CLASS OF 1926. Quintilla Geer Bruton was born in Walton, Kentucky, on December 16, 1907. She came to Plant City on Thanksgiving Day in 1923 with her parents, Celia Exular Wooten and James Arthur Geer, and sister Odessa Geer. She was valedictorian for the Class of 1926 at Plant City High School. The two seniors vying for the position were Quintilla Geer and James D. Bruton Jr. After James completed law school at the University of Florida, they would become Mr. and Mrs. James D. Bruton Jr. in 1932. Quintilla attended Tampa Business College and Brewster Vocational School in Tampa. Plant City would always be their hometown. (Courtesy of John Briggs.)

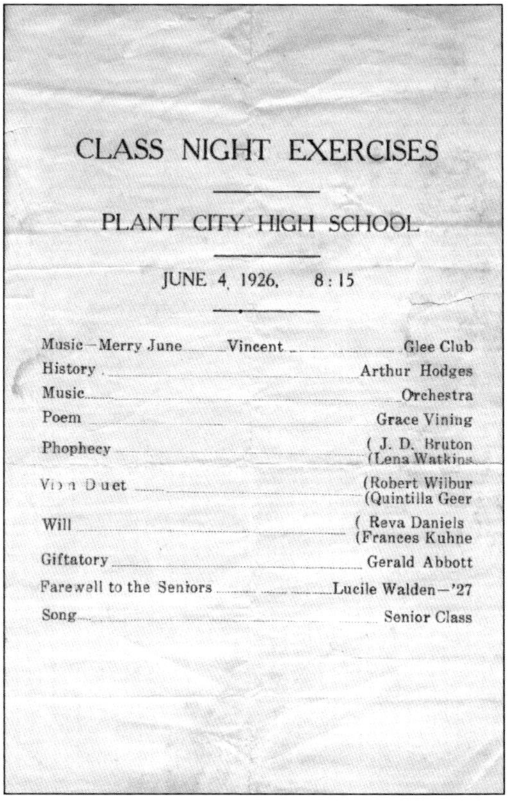

CLASS NIGHT EXERCISES

PLANT CITY HIGH SCHOOL

JUNE 4, 1926, 8:15

Music—Merry June .... Vincent	Glee Club
History	Arthur Hodges
Music	Orchestra
Poem	Grace Vining
Phophecy	(J. D. Bruton (Lena Watkins
Vi n Duet	(Robert Wilbur (Quintilla Geer
Will	(Reva Daniels (Frances Kuhne
Giftatory	Gerald Abbott
Farewell to the Seniors	Lucile Walden—'27
Song	Senior Class

CLASS NIGHT EXERCISES. Members listed on the senior class roster of Plant City High School in June 1926 were as follows: Ellis Hawkins, Helen Brown, Gerald Abbott, Reva Daniels, Maxine Purcell, Ila Poppell, Quintilla Geer, O.D. Pemberton, Lena Watkins, James D. Bruton Jr., Frances Kuhne, Arthur Hodges, Roselie Lacy, Roy Goheen, Beulah Maxey, Horace Miley, Evelyn Cassels, Calffrey Taylor, Bettye Draughon, Edmund Staff, Meribeth Henderson, Henry Robinson, Dorothy Merlino, Wilbur Purcell, Lessie Hull, Margaret Holloway, Earl Green, Josephine Mays, Ella Mae Faulkner, J.W. Register Jr., Macel Holsberry, Elbert Lowry, Louise McDonald, Robert Wilbur, Violet Witte, Park Hamilton, Juanita Ekis, Lester Knox, Georgia Davis, James Frierson, Wilbur Cahow, Dorothy Williams, Warren Wilson, Mildred Bowman, Tom Weber, Rubye McIntosh, William Aris, Grace Vining, Fletcher Lett, F.M. Carter Jr., Hazel Holsberry, and Clyde Futch.

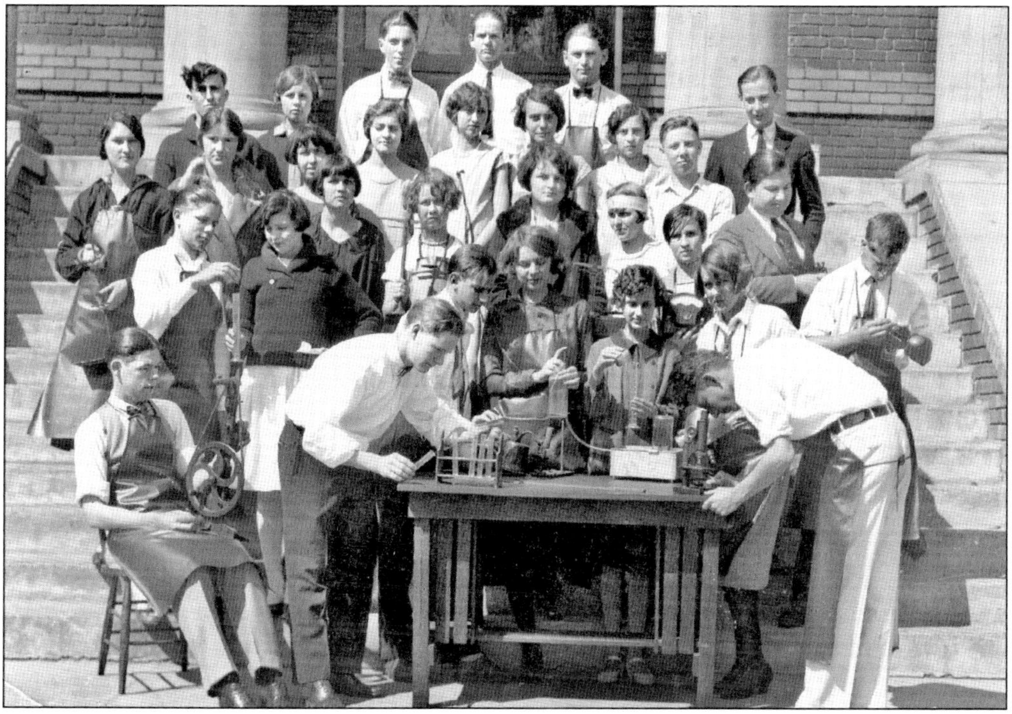

Science Class Is All Experimental. Several prominent Plant City retirees are pictured in this 1926 Plant City High School senior science class. Seated left is retired Circuit Judge James D. Bruton Jr.; standing to his right is artist Bill Miller; standing top right in the dark suit is Robert M. Wilbur, former manager of Borden, Inc.; and the third girl from his left is Quintilla Geer Bruton.The motto for this senior class was "Build For Character Not For Fame." Such was not the case, as members of this graduating class went on in life to become prominent and successful in their professional and personal lives.

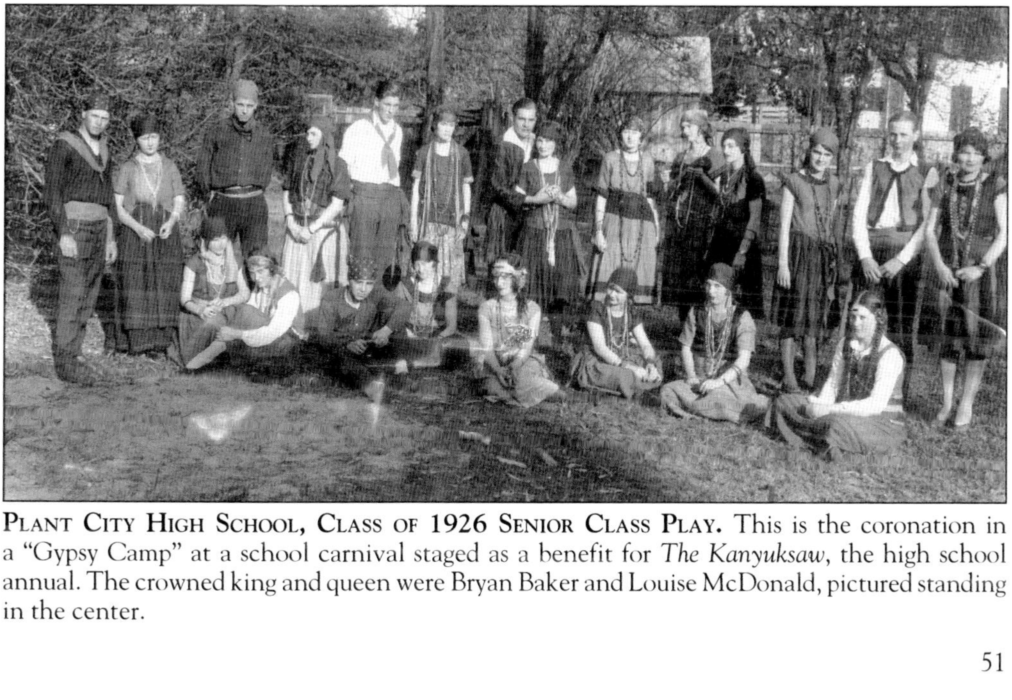

Plant City High School, Class of 1926 Senior Class Play. This is the coronation in a "Gypsy Camp" at a school carnival staged as a benefit for *The Kanyuksaw*, the high school annual. The crowned king and queen were Bryan Baker and Louise McDonald, pictured standing in the center.

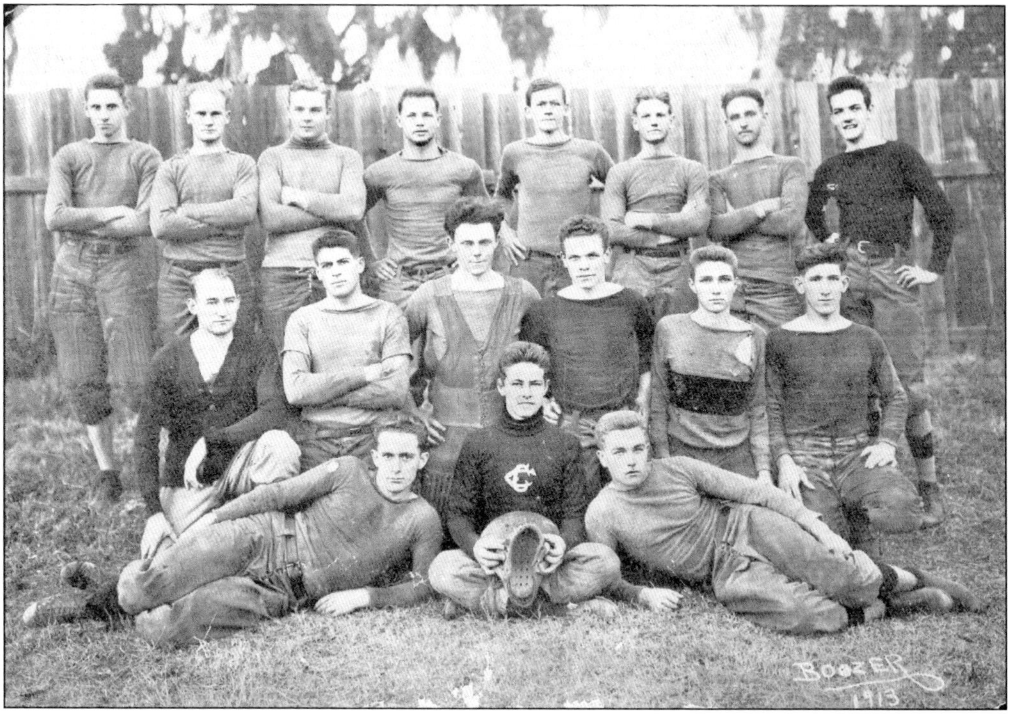

BOOZER 1913. Shown here is the Plant City High School 1913 football team. Before the days of shoulder pads, leg padding, mouth guards, and helmets, the rough and tough boys of Plant City High School's football team take time for a photo shoot.

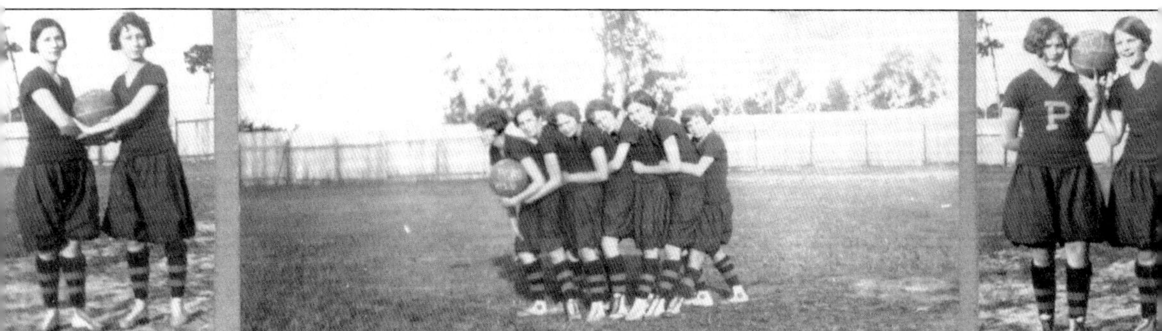

PLANT CITY HIGH SCHOOL GIRLS' BASKETBALL TEAM. Sugar and spice and everything nice, the members of the girls' basketball team were always ready for the camera. This photo was taken for *The Kanyuksaw*, the yearbook for Plant City High School.

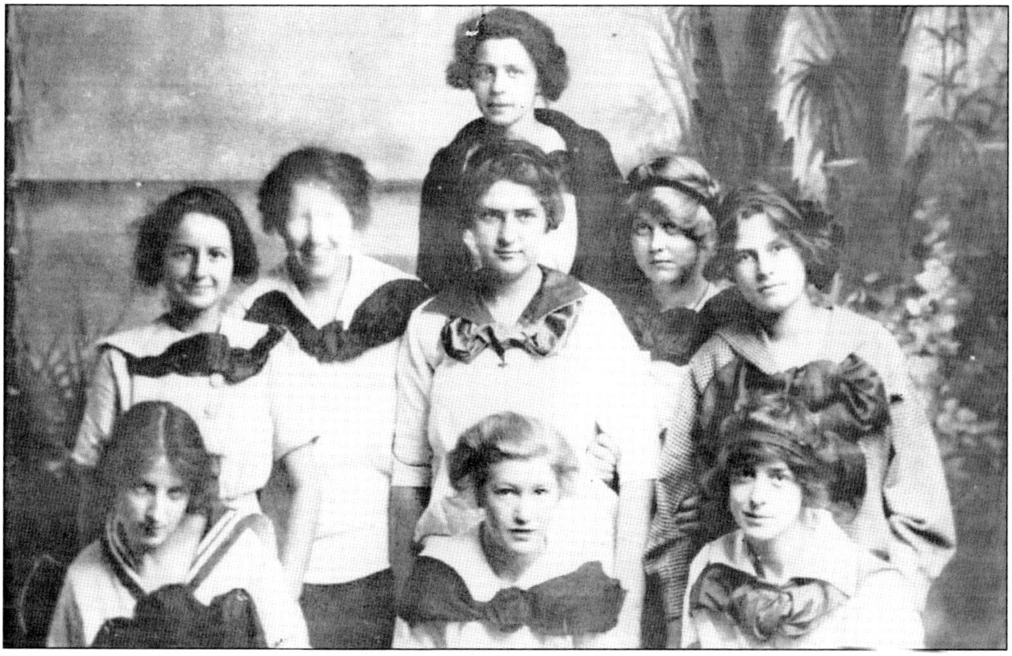

Plant City High School Girls' Basketball Team, 1914. Pictured from left to right are (front row) Addie (Boyette) Spangler, Almerine (Maney) Merrin, and Pallas (Wright) Crum; (middle row) Gertrude (Methvin) May, Ula (Lightsey) Miles, Gladys (Hamilton) Vann, Lila (Ferris) Walden, and Evelyn (Crum) Tipton; (back row) Coach Juno (Wright) Coleman. (Courtesy of Evelyn Tipton.)

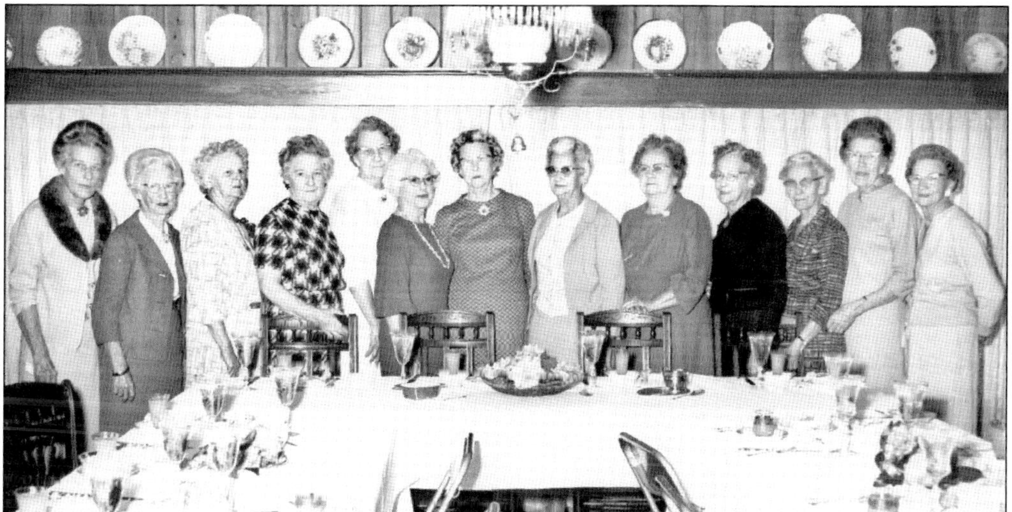

Fifty-Year Reunion of the 1914 Plant City High School Girls' Basketball Team. Team members and their guests gathered for an evening of dinner and fellowship at the home of Mrs J.A. Miles Sr. Pictured from left to right are Evelyn Crum Tipton, guests Audrey May McColpin and Viva Griffin Alexander, Addie Boyette Spangler, Maude Griffin Carlton, Gertrude Methvin May, Lela Farris Walden, guests Sarah Sparkman McKinney and Mary Blackburn, Pallas Wright Crum, guest Irene Merrin, Ula Lightsey Miles, and Estelle Venning Ross. (Courtesy of Evelyn Tipton.)

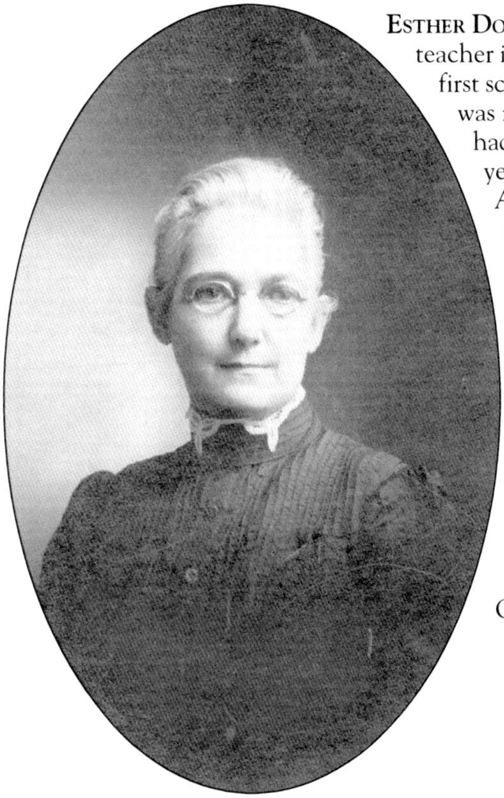

Esther Dorothy Burney. For 45 years, Mrs. Burney was a teacher in this city. She and her husband established the first school here in 1885, and the first grammar school was named for her. Mrs. Burney died at age 82. She had been a teacher for 62 years, having taught 17 years in Mississippi before coming to Plant City. A memorial service was held in the auditorium of Plant City High School. Grammar school let out at noon that day, and the high school dismissed following the memorial service. Funeral services were held October 5, 1931, at the Presbyterian church at 4:00 p.m. Dr. A.R. Larrick conducted the services, and interment was made in Oaklawn Cemetery under direction of Wells & Company. Mrs. Burney was survived by a sister, Mrs. R.N. Wommack, of Houston, Texas; two nephews, Edward and Lawrence Garland of Plant City; and two stepsons, J.A and W.M. Burney, of Plant City. (Courtesy of Tri-Color Engraving Co., Tampa, Florida.)

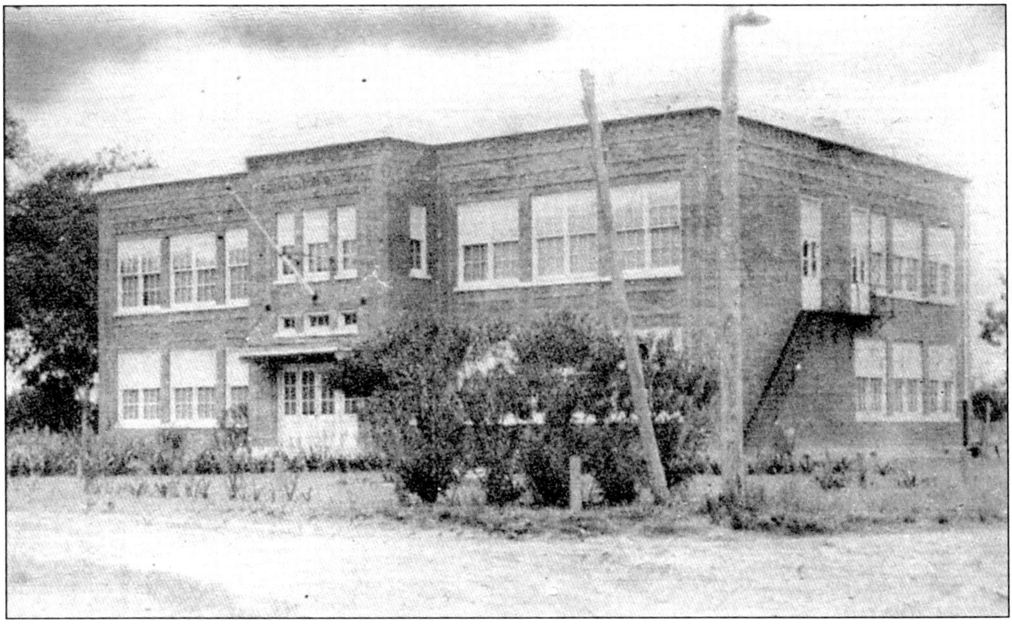

Esther D. Burney School. The need for a new elementary school was met with the construction of a new school on South Evers Street in 1923. Named for one of Plant City's earliest teachers, Esther D. Burney School was Plant City's first stand-alone grammar school.

STONEWALL JACKSON GRAMMAR SCHOOL. Claude Green received his certificate of completion on April 10, 1931, from Stonewall Jackson Grammar School. Jackson School was on the east side of Plant City. Most students who attended Jackson School walked to school and either brought their lunch from home or walked to one of the nearby lunchrooms. Having successfully completed the grammar-school course, Green was ready to enter junior high school. Edna Loving was the principal at Stonewall Jackson; W.H. Cassels was the supervising principal.

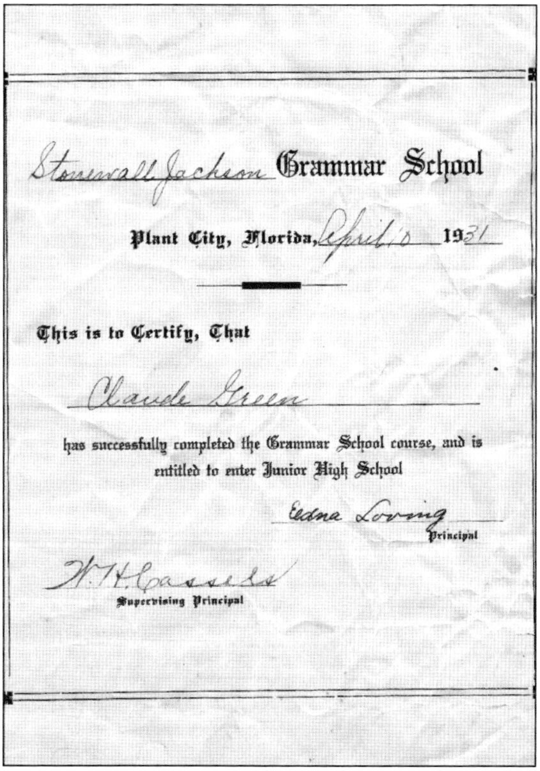

Stonewall Jackson Grammar School

Plant City, Florida, April 10 1931

This is to Certify, That

Claude Green

has successfully completed the Grammar School course, and is entitled to enter Junior High School

Edna Loving
Principal

W.H. Cassels
Supervising Principal

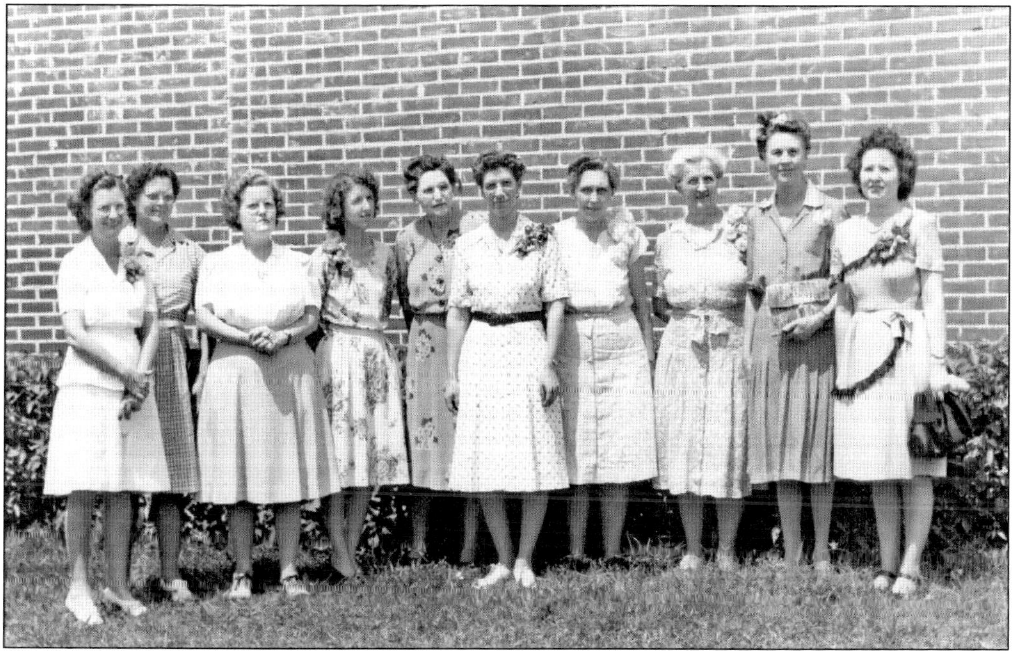

JACKSON ELEMENTARY SCHOOL FACULTY, JUNE 1946. Pictured from left to right are Aldine Griffin, Mary Sue DeVane, Bessie McGlammory, Margaret McKey, Lucile Robinson, Hazel Carlton, Mildred Johnson, Lillie Robinson, Wilmoth Herron, and Edna Sparkman. (Courtesy of McAllister's Photo Studio, Plant City, Florida.)

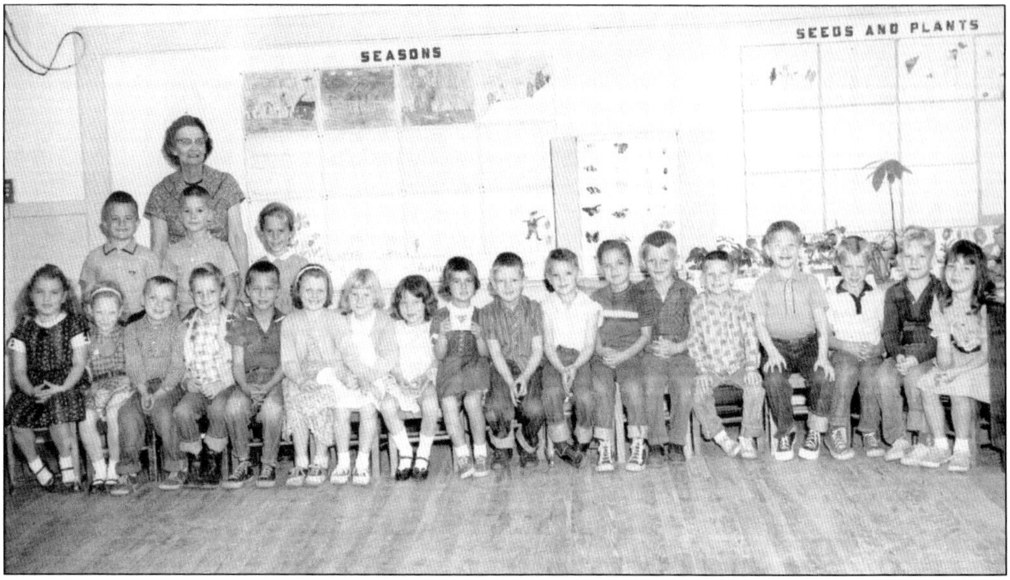

First Grade Class of 1961, Wilson Elementary School, Plant City. Miss Grace Platt taught at Wilson School, on the north side of Plant City. Identified in the photo are, from left to right, (front row) Susan Langland, at far left; (back row) two unidentified, Mary Lou Sinnett, and Miss Platt. Class photos were always taken shortly after the school year had begun. Letters were sent home to the parents telling them that school and classroom pictures would be taken. (Courtesy of Gladys Jeffcoat.)

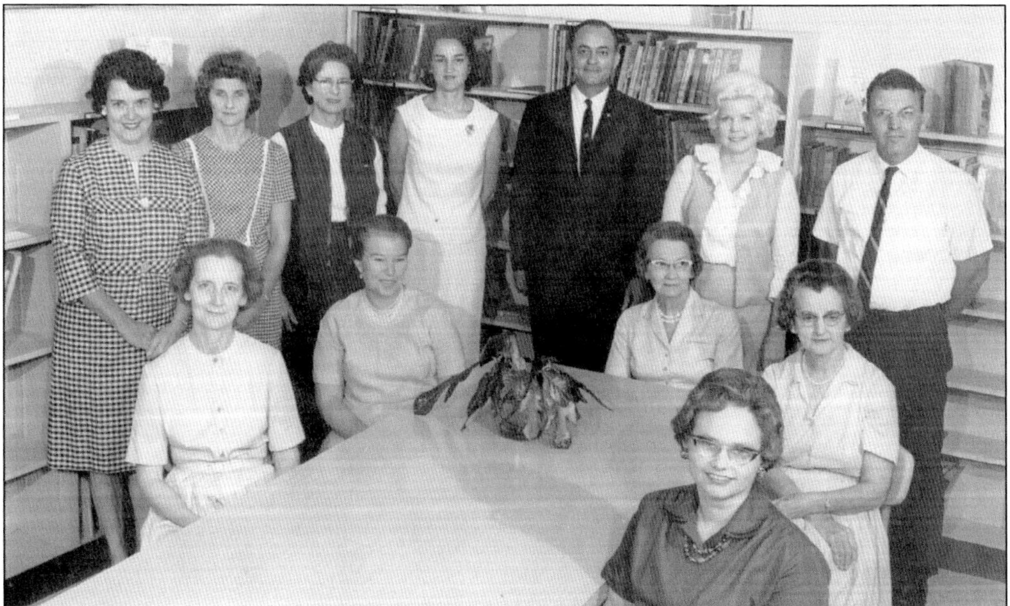

Wilson Elementary School, 1966–1967, Plant City, Florida. The teachers and staff would have their group photo taken for display in the offices of the principal. Pictured from left to right are (seated) Ida Bender, Evalina Vann, Grace Platt, Josephine Sparkman, and Margie Evans; (standing) secretary Jimmie Smith, Mary Martin, Bonnie Carter, Ann Martin, Principal Robert L. Cooper, Gloria Reid, and George Holbrook.

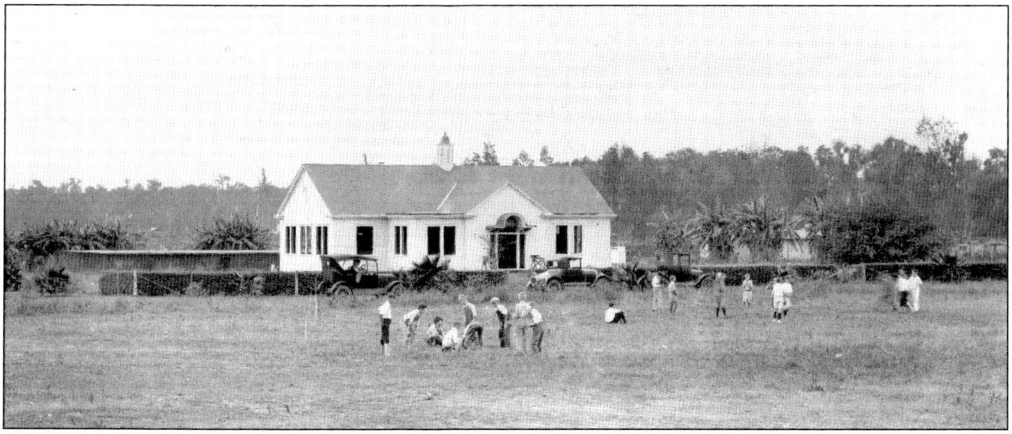

Courier Field in 1925. Courier Field, a large green space, was the location used for physical education classes for the 1914 Plant City High School. Boys are being coached in football. The agriculture school building is under construction, as the windows and interior are yet to be finished. The banana grove partially covers the livestock barn. A cannery was built as a service center for the agricultural agency to instruct homemakers in the processing of fruits, meats, and vegetables. The building has been renamed in honor of Dwight M. "Bud" Nifong, who served as an area supervisor of Hillsborough County Schools. (Courtesy of Burgert Brothers no. 15970.)

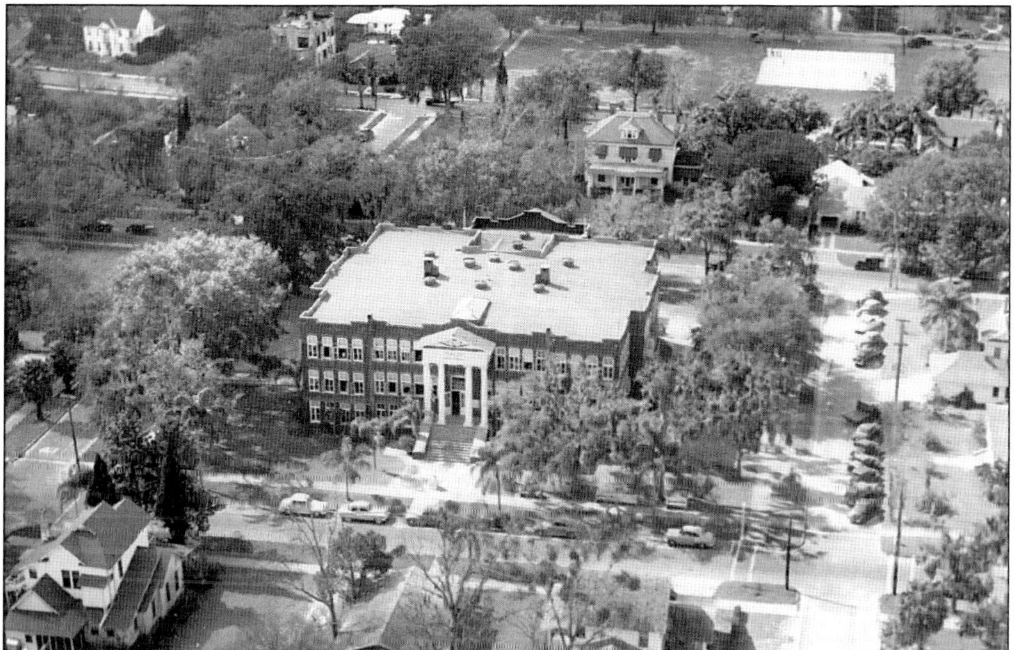

A Bird's-eye View of the 1914 Plant City High School Neighborhood. Pictured from left to right are (foreground) the E.S. Tyner home and Glenn Armstrong home; (center) 1914 Plant City High School, the home of Dr. J.W. Alsobrook, Courier Field (west portion), the Manee home, and the agricultural building; (background) the Woman's Club and public library building and the Dr. B.H. Sanchez home. The residential area, with its brick streets and granite curbs was heavy in lush vegetation, including massive oaks. Southern magnolia trees were seen in almost every yard. (Courtesy of Bill Friend's Studio.)

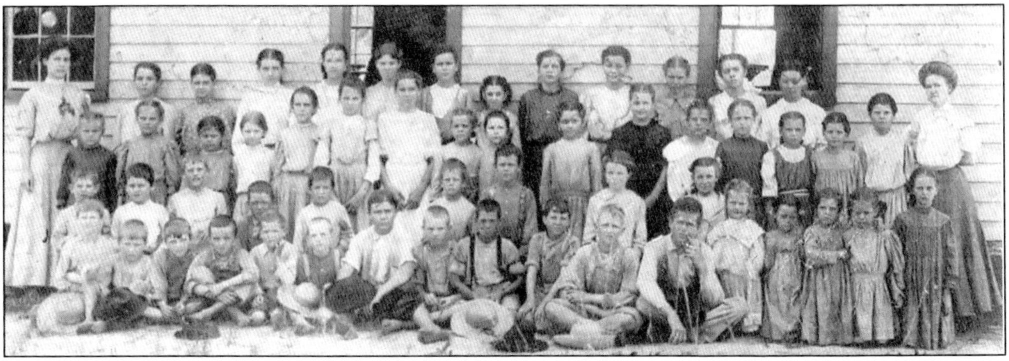

Springhead School, 1908. Pictured from left to right are (first row) Caswell Pollard, Olin English, Edgar ?, Gordon Clemons, Hugh Davis, Dewey Howell, Graville Hall, Willie Howell, Earl Davis, Claude ?, Albert ?, Morris Nesmith, Mable Pollard, Rosa Mae Yates, Donna ?, Bertha ?, and Rowena English; (second row) Norman Webb, ? Chalker, Leslie Webb, Russell Smith, Roy Hamilton, Wayne Ham, Ralph Ham, Irene English, Clara Howell, and Pearl Davis; (third row) Rosa Nesmith, Loca Carruthers, Myrtle Smith, Carrie English, ? Wetherington, Edna Clemons, Grace Howell, Janice Ham, Nita Hall, Maude Pollard, Maggie ?, Agnes Nesmith, Pauline Davis, and Jessie ?; (fourth row) teacher Lillian Lindley, Rose Howell, Maggie English, Laura English, Daisy Pollard, Texas Howell, Lura Doke, Josie Morgan, Mae ?, Myrtle Howell, Virginia Blanton, Charlie Hall, Ammer Davis, and teacher Ida Blanton. (Courtesy of EHHS DeVane Collection.)

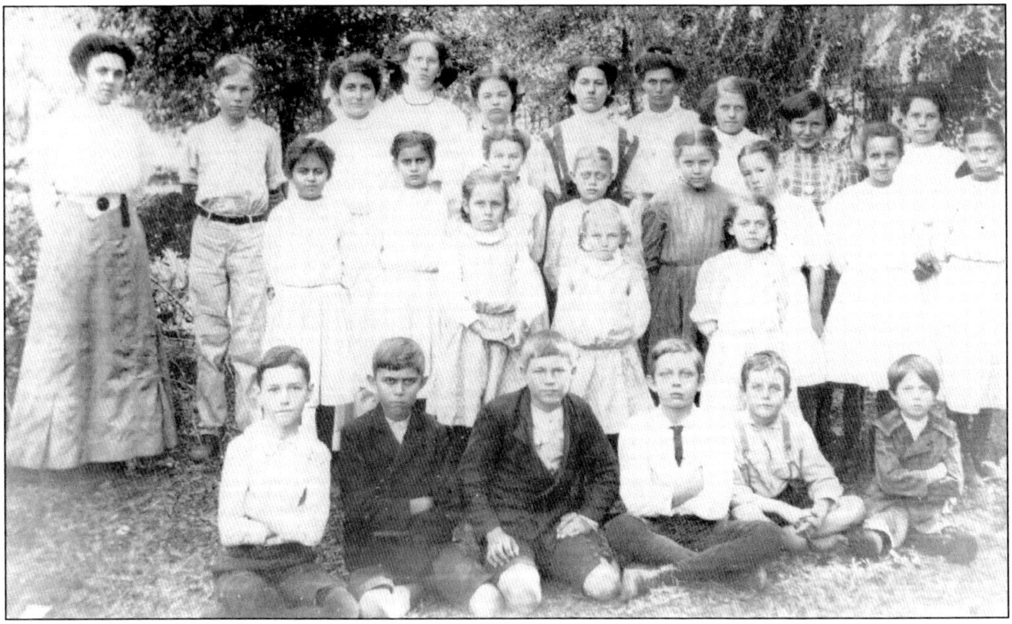

Alafia School, 1909. One of the oldest settlements in the interior of Hillsborough County is Alafia. Pioneer settlers came to the area in the early 1840s, homesteading land. Pictured from left to right are (first row) Fred Evers, Jasper Bacon, Robert Tatum, Clarence Martin, Ross Evers, and Hiram Evers; (second row) Lillie Butler, Addie Butler, Mary Lou Tatum, Eva Bacon, Baily Farnsworth, Ruth Evers, Lillian Evers, and Rosa Bacon; (third row) Annie Hagin, Grace Hagin, and Cora Bacon; (fourth row) teacher Florence Franklin, Victor Farnsworth, Pinkie Hagin, Lucile Farnsworth, Met Tatum, Bessie Hagin, Lottie Bacon, Ruth Martin, Bessie Frierson, and ? O'Riley.

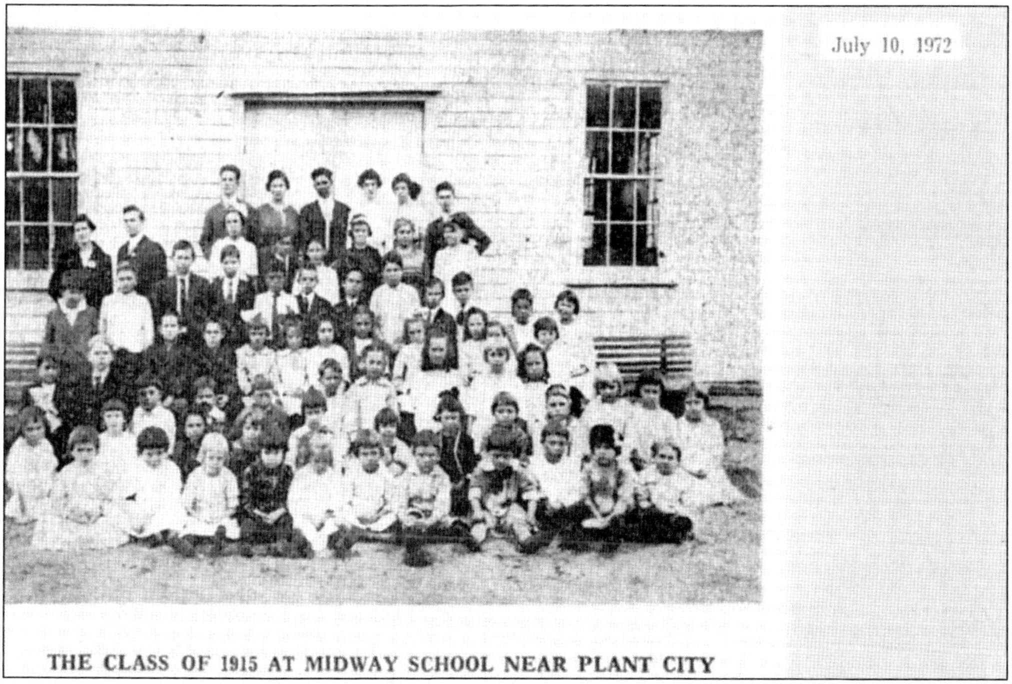

PEOPLE ARE WHAT MAKE A SCHOOL. Shown is a picture of John Cone with classmates at Midway School near Plant City. The Midway School, a frame building with only one room built in 1891, was torn down many years ago. (By the time it was dismantled a second room had been added by parent labor.) The school used to stand on Midway Road, northeast of Plant City, near the Midway Baptist Church. Mrs. Rebecca Branch was one of three teachers assigned to Midway, which housed grades six through nine at the time. John Cone, who traced the history of Midway School, said that he remembers one teacher who walked four miles to school each day and farmed on the side to make ends meet. His teacher taught grades one through eight until 4:00 p.m. each day. The school board paid her a monthly salary of $40.

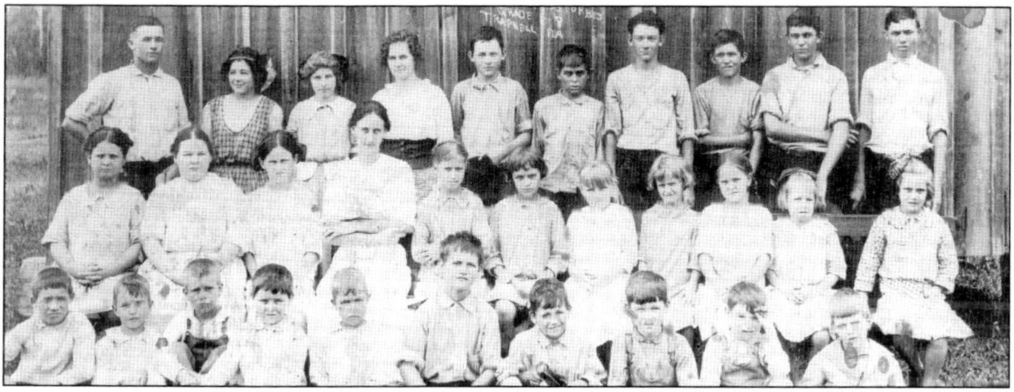

EIGHTH GRADE CLASS, TRAPNELL SCHOOL 1916. Pictured from left to right are (front row) Ellis Hawkins, Fletcher Lightsey, unidentified, Seymour Sparkman, three unidentified students, Emory B. Sparkman, unidentified; (middle row) Lois Hawkins, Mable McDonald, Bessie Lett, teacher Miss Mae Forbes, ? Johnson, Helen Johnson, two unidentified students, Mary Dale Trapnell, unidentified, Mary Sparkman; (back row) Alma McDonald, D. Trapnell, Hilda Trapnell, Ola Trapnell, unidentified, Sheldon Howard, W. McDonald, Floyd McDonald, H. McDonald, and ? Johnson.

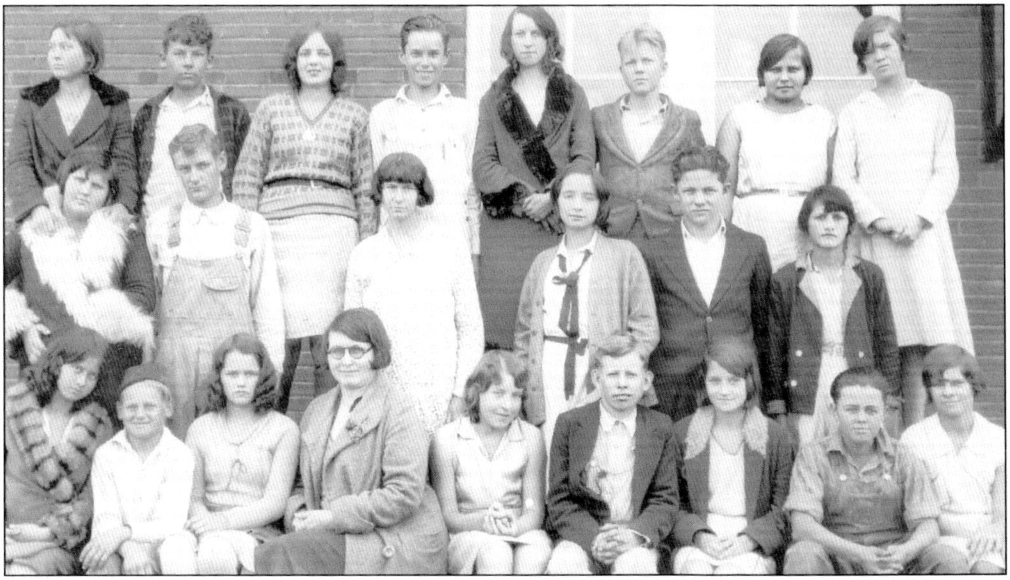

Turkey Creek School Grade Eight, December 1930. Turkey Creek School was one of the county school system's strawberry schools. Turkey Creek School was designed by architect Frank Winn in 1926. The contract for the school was awarded to Dudley and Nulter in September of the same year with a bid of $19,800.

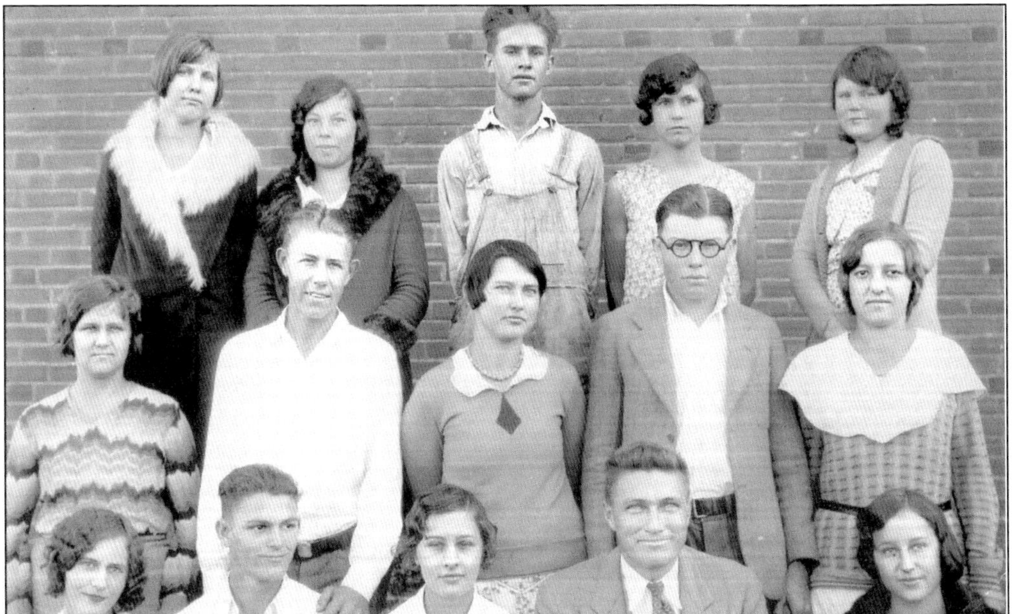

Turkey Creek Florida School Grade 11, December 1930. Typical of other rural schools, Turkey Creek School operated as a strawberry school. The "strawberry school" schedule allowed children to attend school in the summer so they would be free to harvest crops during the winter. This was essential to the local economy, providing the necessary labor for small farms, which depended on family labor and sharecroppers. Alumni of the Turkey Creek School have actively played a role in its restoration and recognition as a Hillsborough County Historic Landmark and listing as a National Register of Historic Places Site.

PINECREST SCHOOL. The faculty of Pinecrest School is pictured with Principal Garland Branch. This nine-member teacher team was all women. The Pinecrest school building also served as a site for many community social functions. When one of the local churches burned, services and weddings were held at the school. The wooden structure was torn down after being abandoned when local high schools were consolidated and students were bused to nearby Plant City High School.

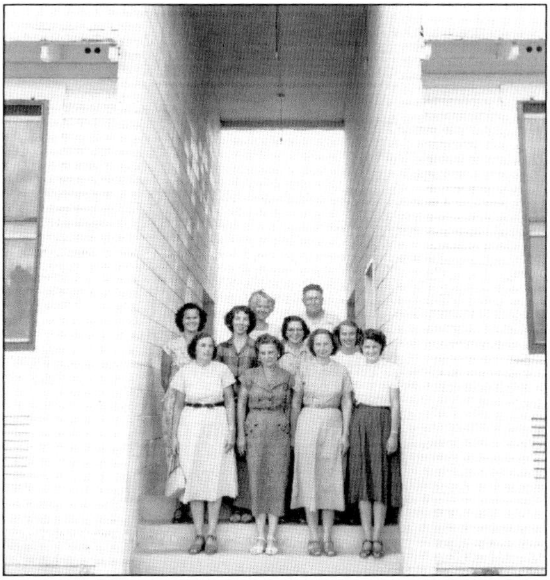

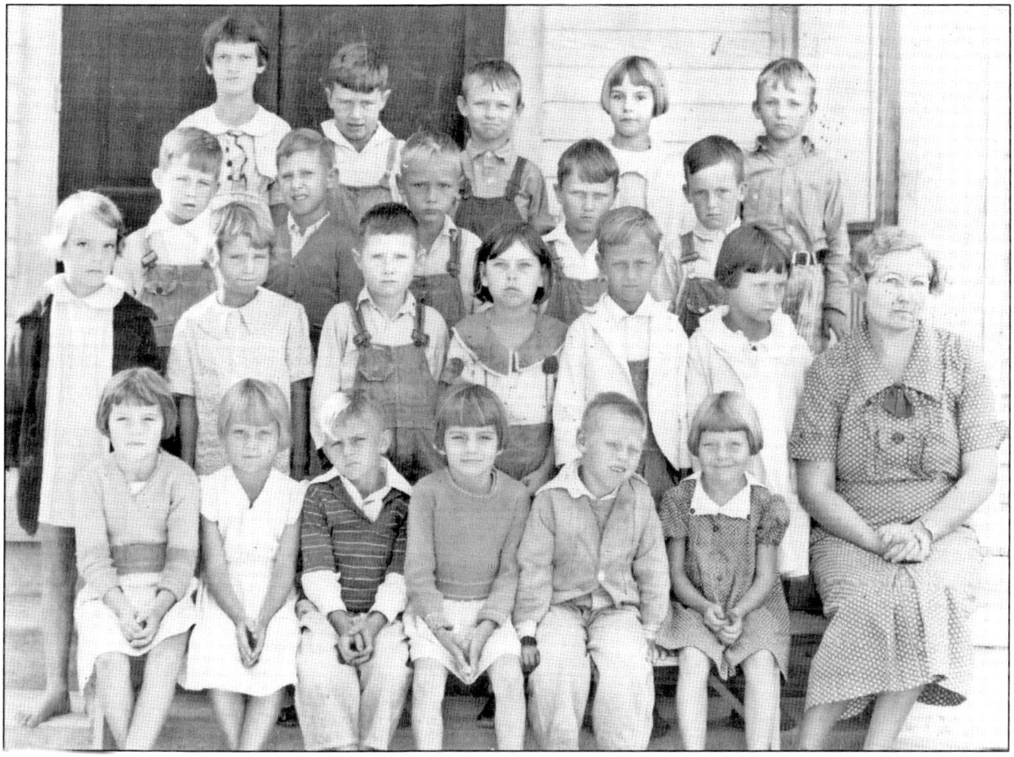

FIRST GRADE, HOPEWELL SCHOOL, 1936. Pictured are teacher Mrs. Ammer Davis Tomberlin and students Blanch Croft, Rodney Calvert, Louis Mattair, Josie Ann Musselwhite, T.S. Mattair, Lewis Croft, Lamar Jameson, Wallace Harvill, Howard Johnson, Buford Simmons, Josephine Dennison, Ruby Surrency, Geraldine Woodle, C.J. Powell, Maxine Gibb, Christine Culpepper, Jean Mangum, Alex Clark, and Hazel Brinson. Although the names are known, the order in which they appear is not. (Courtesy of Doris Tomberlin Howell and Joyce Tomberlin Wetherington.)

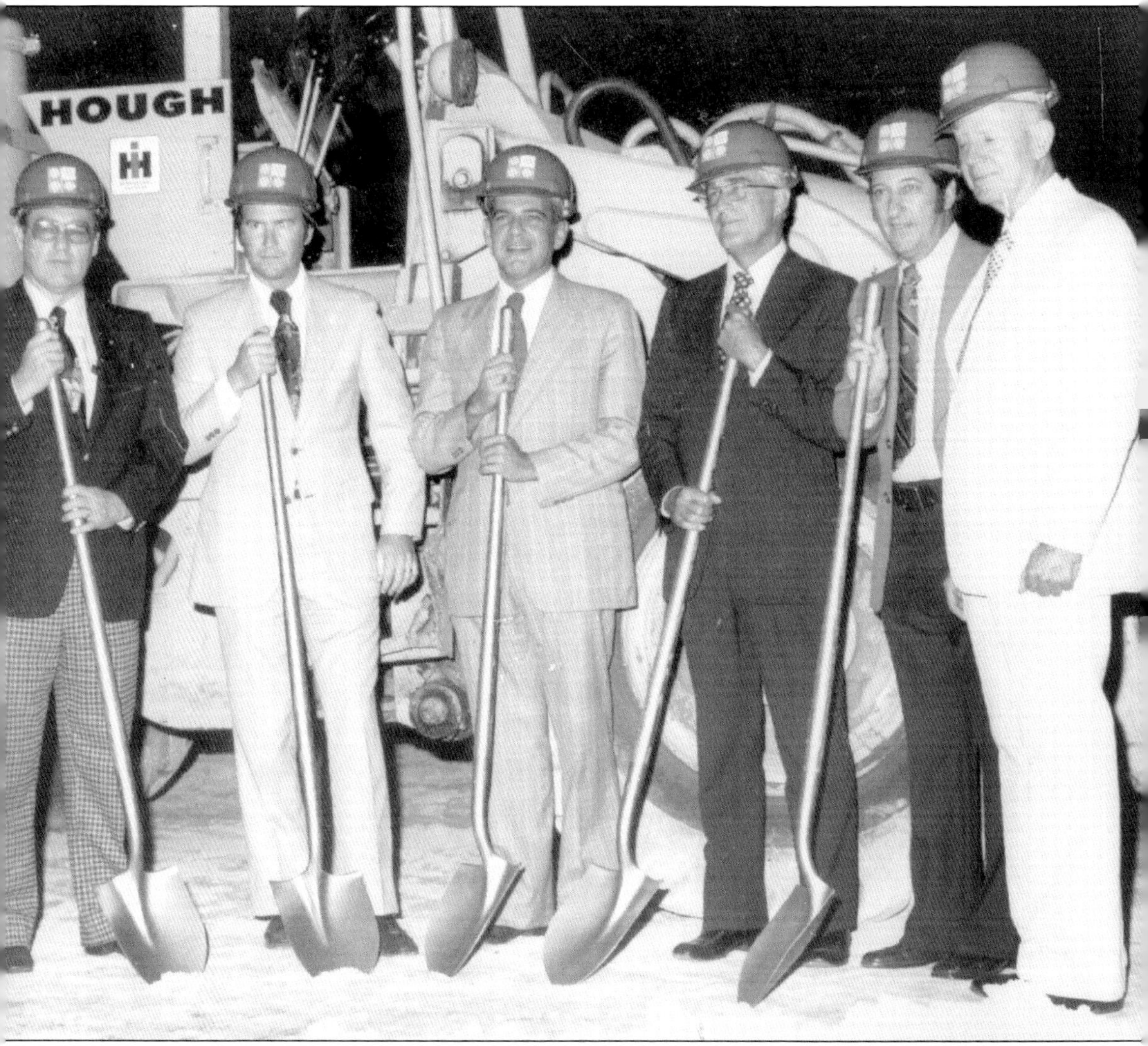

PLANT CITY WELCOMES HILLSBOROUGH COMMUNITY COLLEGE TO TOWN. The groundbreaking ceremony for the first permanent building for Hillsborough Community College's Plant City Campus included, from left to right, John Bouseman, Fred Kirons, Dr. Morton Shanberg, Hilman Bowden, Dick Elston, and Frank Moody. The Plant City Campus is situated on a 93.5-acre site on Park Road, one mile south of Interstate 4. The Plant City Campus of Hillsborough Community College offers a full range of university transfer, career/technical courses, and a large variety of continuing education courses. This campus also contains the college's horticultural greenhouse, the Florida Studies Center.

Four

BUSINESSES

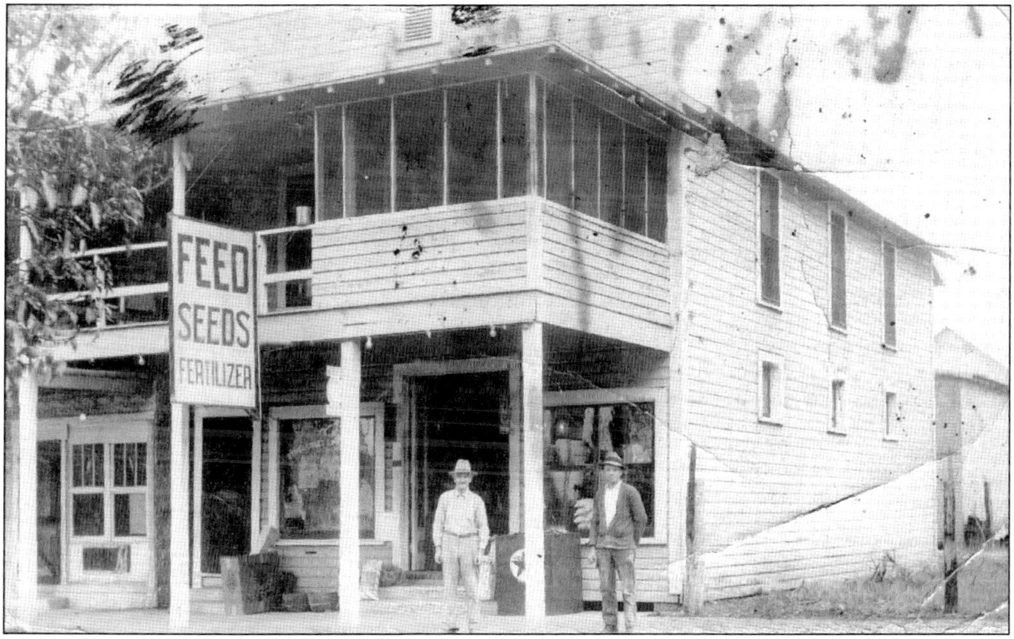

HAINES STREET STORE SELLS FEED, SEEDS, AND FERTILIZERS. Plant City's agricultural community was served by stores that sold feed, seeds, and fertilizers. Local truck farmers grew vegetables that were harvested and taken to the local farmers' market every day. Some of the crops grown were beans, corn, potatoes, squash, and peas.

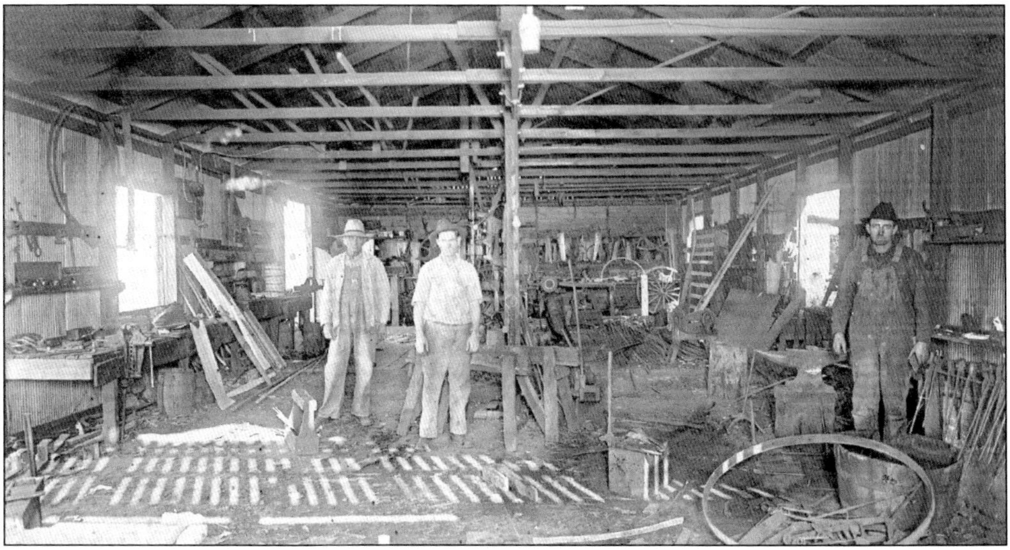

Blacksmith Shop, Established in 1883. Pictured from left to right are brothers R.L. Berry, James O. Greene, and Wilbur O. Greene. The blacksmith shop was located at the southeast corner of Collins and Alabama Streets. The business was established in 1883 by their father and uncle, James A. and Arnold W. Greene, expert carriage- and wagon-makers. They could set four tires on a buggy or wagon in 30 minutes using a cold tire setter. The old-fashioned way could take several hours. Their stationery read "Greene & Co., Carriage and Wagon manufacturers, Repairing Neatly Done."

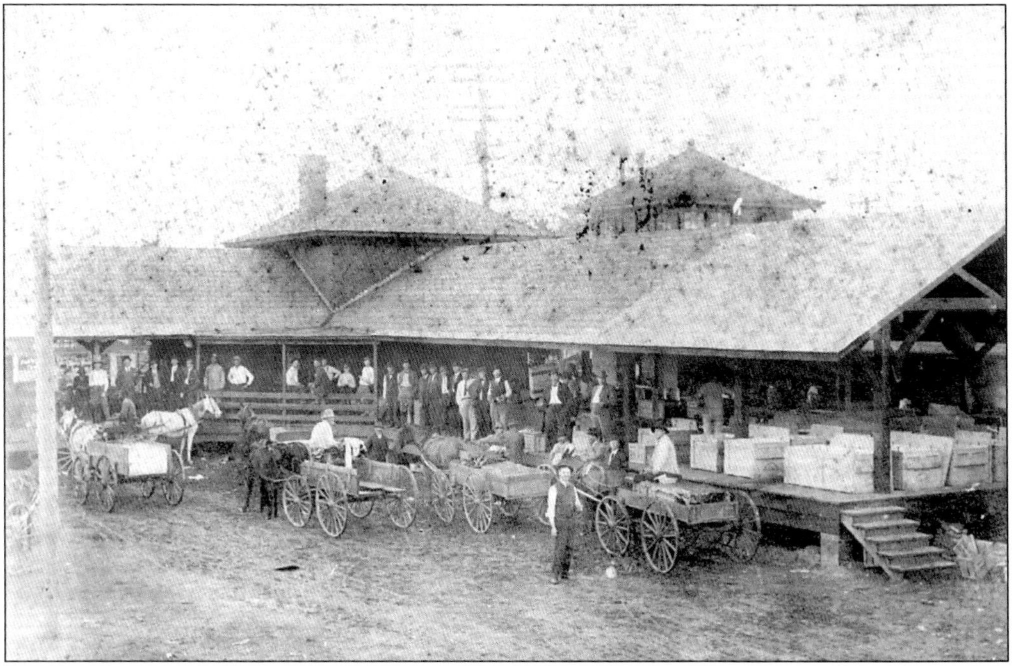

Produce Being Brought to Market, 1910. Local farmers and growers brought their fruits and vegetables to the shipping platform in wagons. The rooflines of the Express Office (left) and Union Station (right) can be seen. Trips to the market were made every few days to keep the vegetables fresh. (Courtesy of EHHS R.M. Morgan Collection.)

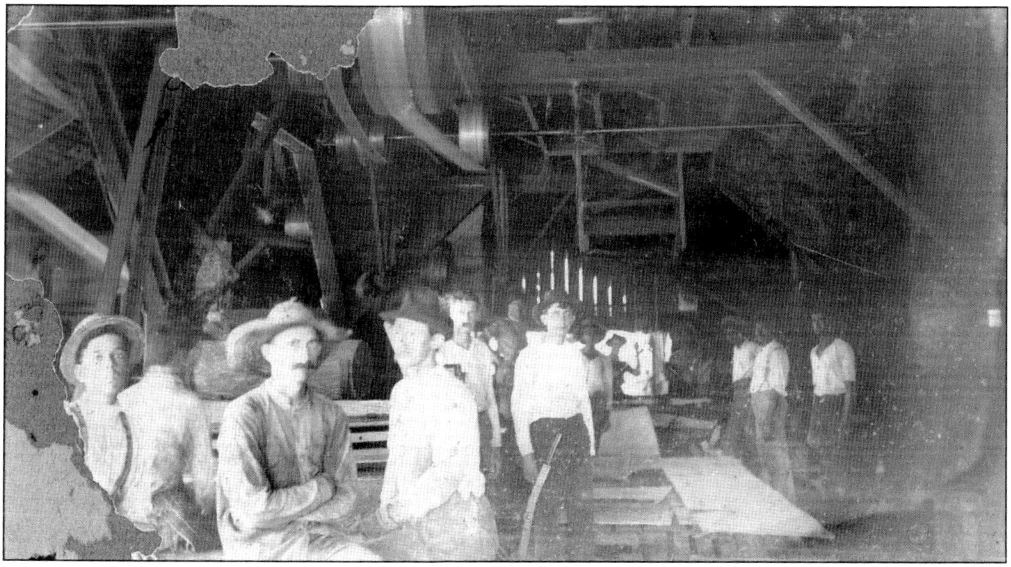

Taking a Break at the Local Sawmill. Workers at the local sawmill take a break during their shift at the mill. Local lumber of pine, oak, and other woods were brought to the sawmill for cutting and preparing for use in construction. Many local buildings were built of lumber that was processed at the local mills.

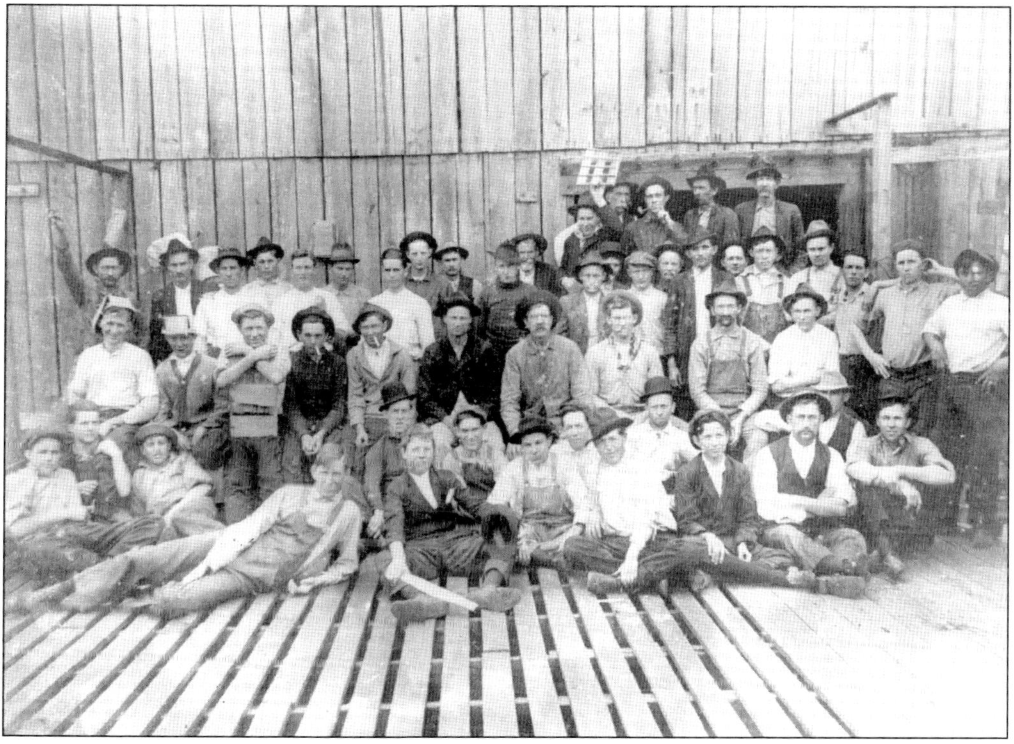

Warnell Mill Basket Department, c. 1898 or 1899. The Warnell Mill Basket Department made crates, hampers, and baskets for packaging fruits and vegetables in the farmers' packing sheds. Identified in the photo is Dunlop Bailey, with a stick in his hand. Other workers chose to wear a strawberry basket as a hat or a crate as a shirt.

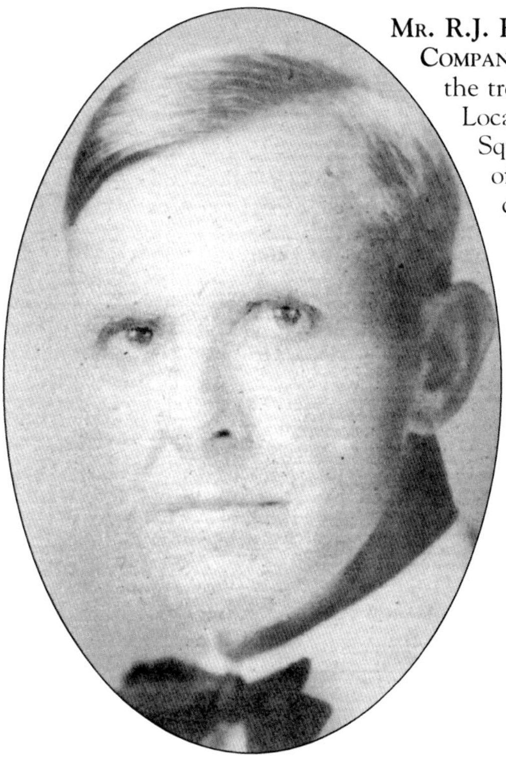

Mr. R.J. Ritter, President of the Plant City Brick Company. During World War I, Plant Citians supported the troops with the purchase of Liberty Loan bonds. Local supporters The East Hillsborough Flying Squadron exceeded their quota by thousands of dollars and won the silver Loving Cup in a county-wide drive. R.J. Ritter served as the manager of the Flying Squadron. The Loving Cup, engraved with the 38 names of the squadron members, was donated to the East Hillsborough Historical Society by William Reece Smith Jr.

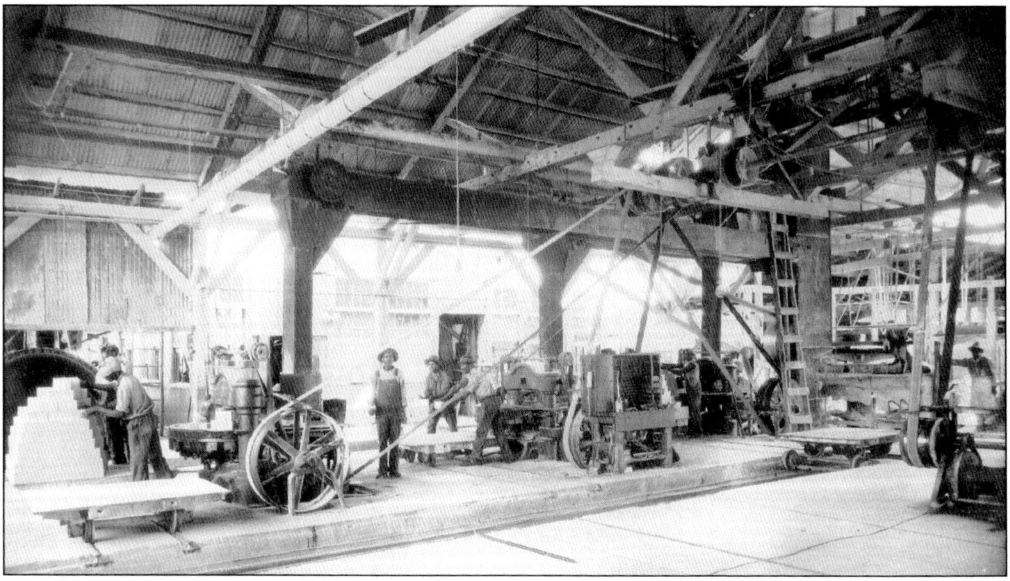

Plant City Brick Company, 1920. R.J. Ritter, president of the Plant City Brick Company, is proud that the company has taken great strides in its work of expansion and in the making of sand lime brick. All sand used is local material, obtained from its own properties. The bricks are placed under tremendous pressure before being subjected to high-pressure steaming. Building storefronts used the more decorative red or blonde bricks, while the sand bricks were used for the building side and exterior walls. Some of the walls' thicknesses would be up to 16 inches, adding strength and stability to the use of the sand bricks.

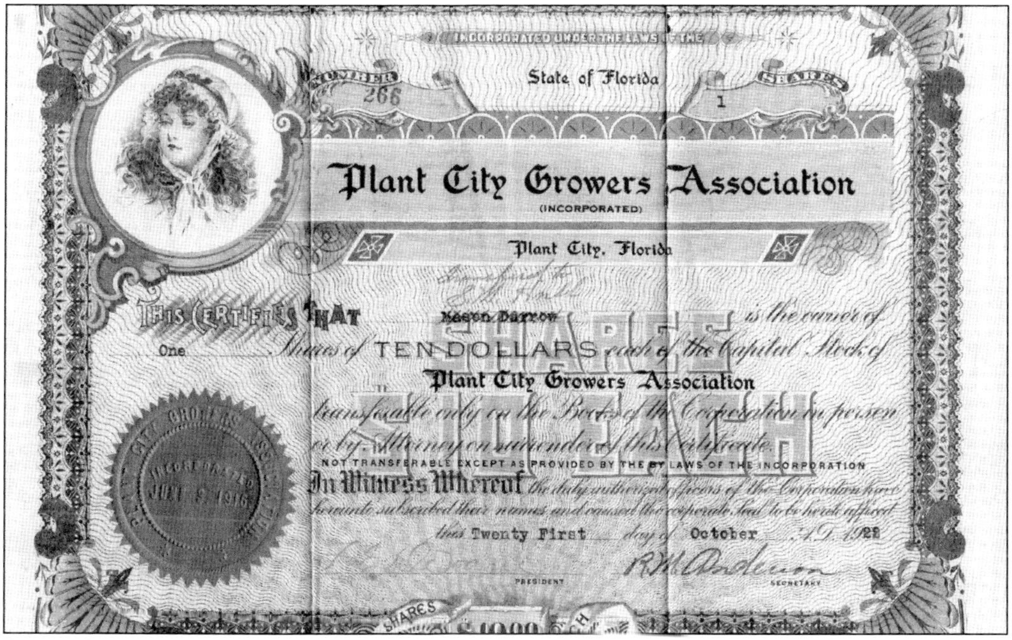

PLANT CITY GROWERS ASSOCIATION STOCK CERTIFICATE NO. 266. Issued to Mason Darrow and transferred to S.M. Hull, the certificate was originally issued on October 21, 1922. The shares were valued at $10 each. The Plant City Growers Association was organized on June 17, 1916, with 150 grower members, for the purpose of marketing strawberries and spring vegetables. The association was founded by Frank E. DeVane, president; H.E. Galyean, secretary; and directors J.W. Bradford, A.A. Ellis, L.W. Wilder, C.C. Wiggins, J.E. Johnson, and I.J. Simms.

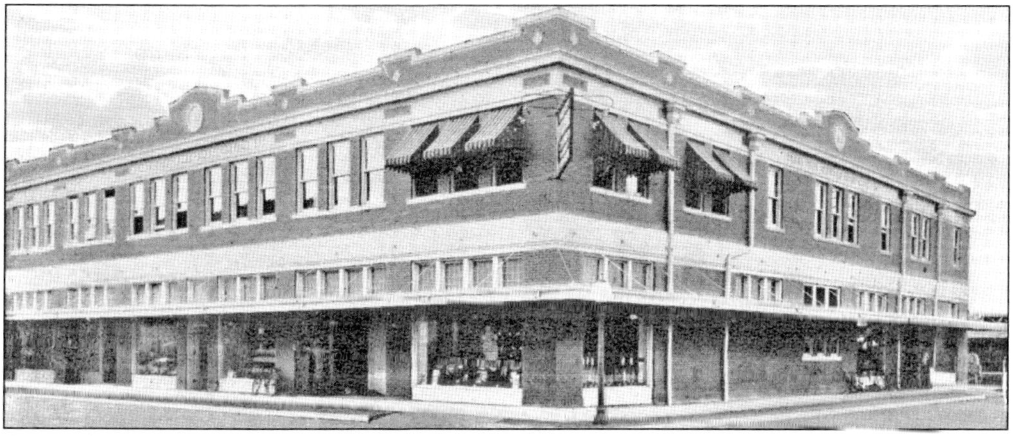

PLANT CITY GROWERS ASSOCIATION BUILDING. The Plant City Growers Association (PCGA) was expanded in 1921 by building a two-story store and office building at North Drane and Palmer Streets. Mr. W.D. Marley, manager, conducted the opening on a Saturday. A grocery and farm supply store were in operation on the Palmer and North Drane Streets corner for many years. The building was demolished for parking for downtown. The PCGA built a vegetable packing house at North Drane and the Atlantic Coastline Railroad and operated it for many years. When the packing house was closed, a store was opened where corn was ground into meal and grits, and a hammer mill was used to make cow feed from whole corn and velvet beans.

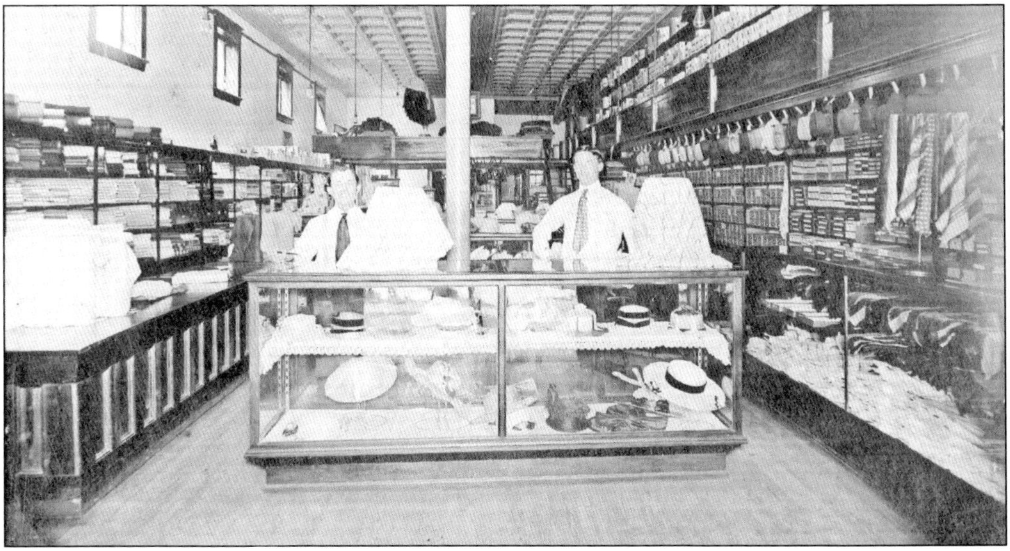

STRICKLAND BROS., PLANT CITY'S BIGGEST AND BEST DEPARTMENT STORE, APRIL 1916. The brick Strickland Building was constructed in 1911 by Thomas Marion Strickland at a cost of $23,000. The dry goods department offered the finest for everyday needs. Mr. Thomas Strickland was the proprietor of the Strickland Bros. Store. The capable workers in the store were George Cassels, Margaret Peace, H.E. Mower, ? Bugg and ? Ement. The store offered a fine line of men's hats, shoes, and ties for Plant City's menfolk. The ladies' ready-to-wear department was located on the second floor. The store went out of business in 1925, and the building was offered for sale at $100,000. Tampa investors C.T. Jordan and H.J. Turner purchased the building for $80,000 and opened a hardware store.

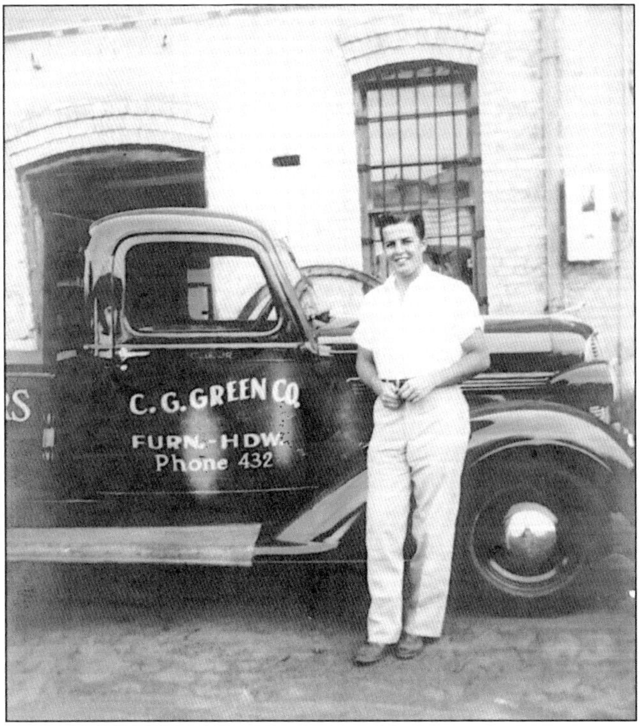

C.G. GREEN CO. FURN.–HDW. C.G. Green, of Live Oak, came to Plant City in 1922 and bought the second-hand furniture and household goods business of George E. Faison. The store was located on South Collins Street next to the railway line. Locals could give C.G. Green Jr. a call for free local delivery on furniture or hardware at phone number 432. Green was a charter member of the board of directors of the First National Bank of Plant City, organized in 1956.

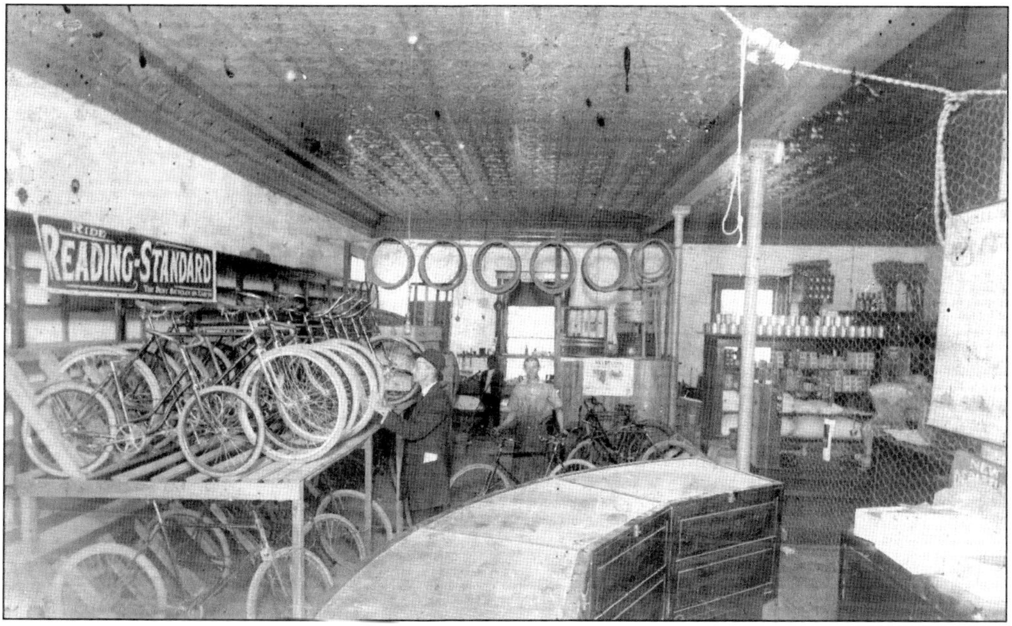

RIDE READING-STANDARD, THE BEST BICYCLE ON EARTH. J.W. Simmons Bicycle Shop was located in the Simmons Building at the northwest corner of Collins and Haines Streets. Later, it was Arthur Tickels Shop. Bicycles were used for general transportation and for grocery, newspapers, pharmacy, and dry goods store deliveries.

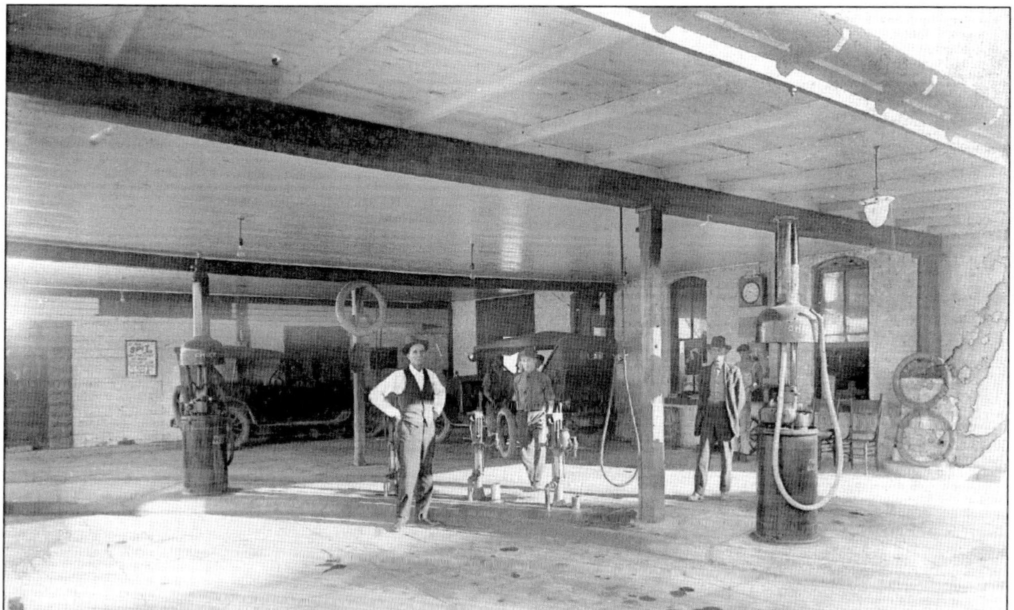

WAVERS FILLING STATION, FEBRUARY 10, 1920. As more cars came to Plant City, additional gas or filling stations came also. You could stop and visit for a while in the chairs out front, but please read the sign. "If You SPIT On the Floor at Home Then We Want You to SPIT On It Here Cause We Want You to Feel at Home." They sold the Chief brand of filtered gasoline. The clock reads 4:47. Posted in the window is a football poster supporting the local high-school football team.

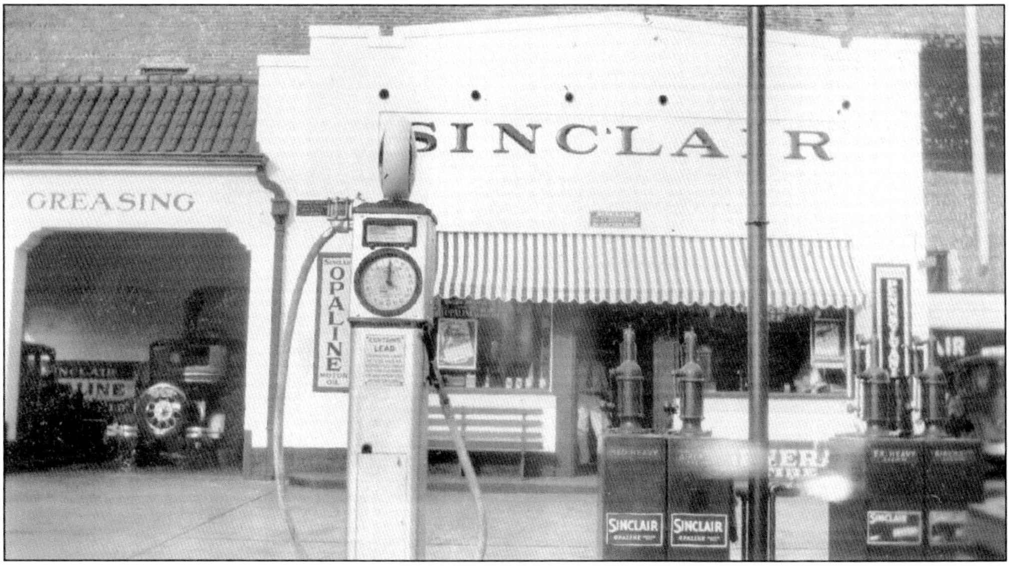

SINCLAIR STATION, OPERATED BY RUSSELL ROGERS. Located in the heart of town at the intersection of Collins and Reynolds, this station later became a Shell jobber. Those were the days of full-service gas stations. With every purchase of a tank of gas, the attendants checked under the hood for oil and water levels and belt conditions, checked the tires for good air pressure, and washed the windshield. That's full service with a smile. W. Reece Smith purchased this Sinclair agency from Jake Miles in 1934.

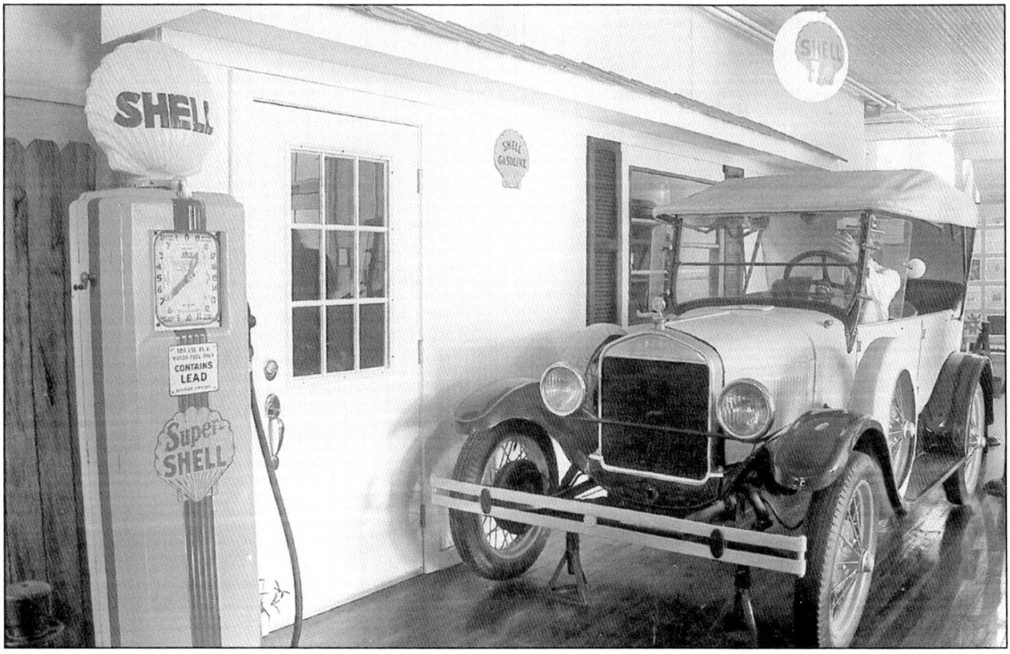

NINETEEN-TWENTY-SEVEN FORD MOTEL T (MODIFIED A). Located in the lobby of the 1914 Plant City High School, this car was once owned by one of Plant City's finest doctors, Dr. Frank Chambers. His family donated the car to the East Hillsborough Historical Society, and it has since been part of an exhibit in the main entry hallway. He was an alumnus of Plant City High School, Class of 1941, and practiced medicine in Plant City. (Courtesy of John Briggs.)

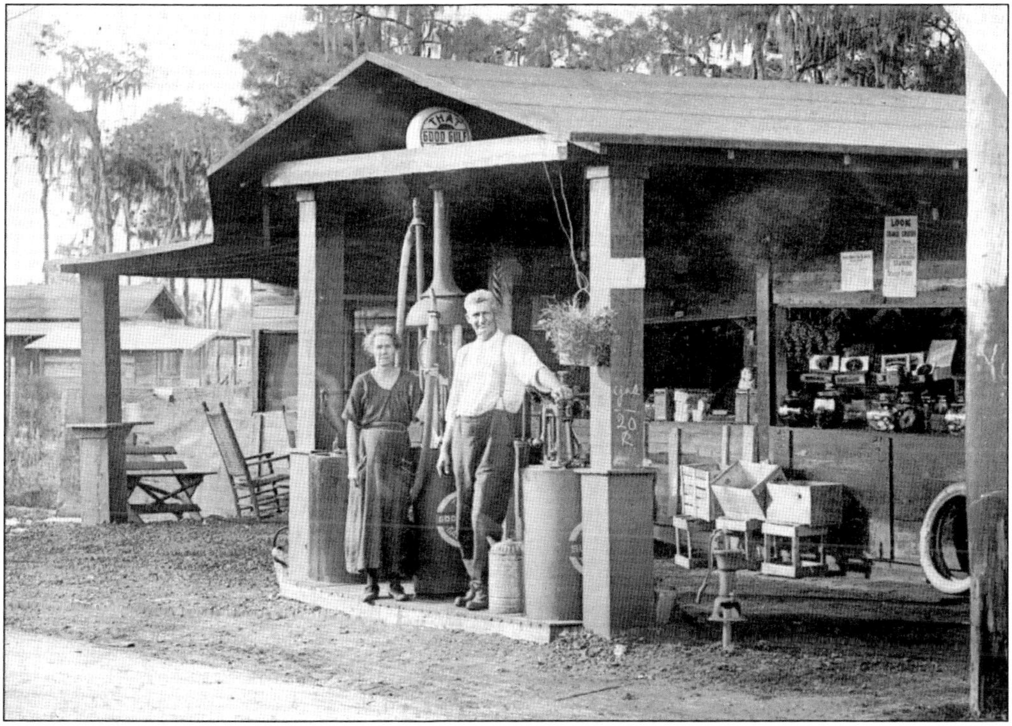

HENRY STORE, CORONET ROAD. Ed Henry and his wife, Appie Waters Henry, stand in front of their store and station, located on Coronet Road in Plant City. Mr. Henry was a carpenter by trade and built houses in the community. Mrs. Henry's niece, Lorraine Collins Barnes, remembers living in one of the houses he built. (Courtesy of Lorraine Collins Barnes.)

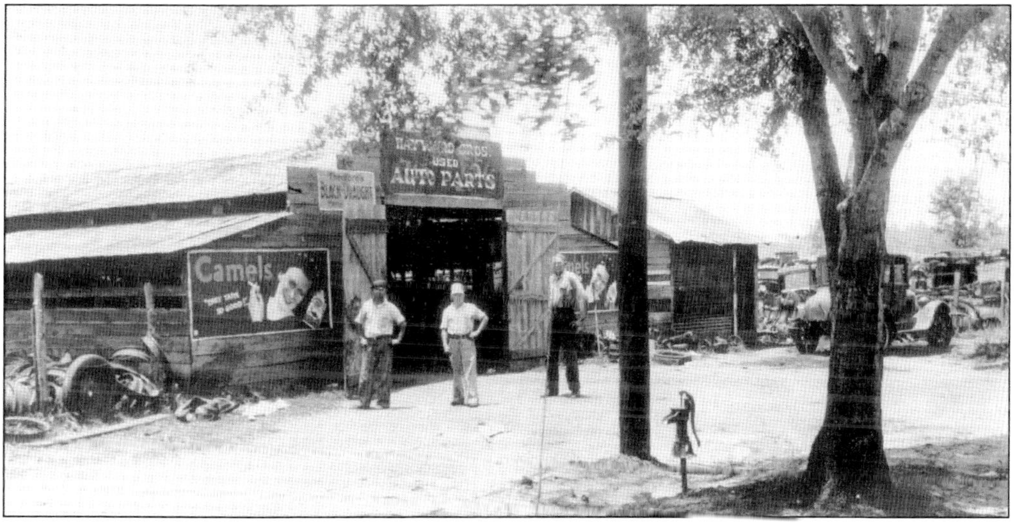

HAYWARD AUTO PARTS, KNIGHTS, C. 1930. Brent and Vance Hayward operated this garage on State Road 39, approximately three miles north of Plant City, Florida. John Cleveland Hayward and Emma J. Hayward lived north of the large residence of Plant City physician Dr. McGuire, which still stands today. The garage was torn down when the property was sold in February 1947 to Dr. McGuire to settle Emma J. Hayward's estate. Pictured from left to right are John Rice, Pat Robinson, and Vance Hayward. (Courtesy of James B. Hayward.)

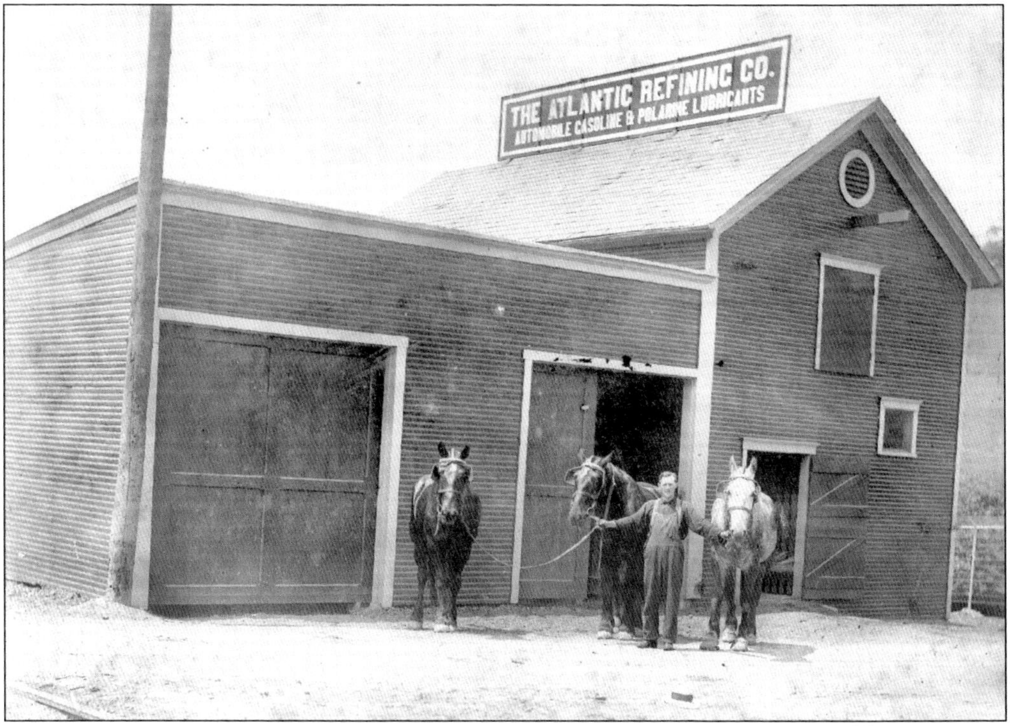

THE ATLANTIC REFINING CO. The Atlantic Refining Co. sold "Automobile Gasolines & Polarine Lubricants." If you have mules or horses, why do you need gasoline? And what was a polarine lubricant?

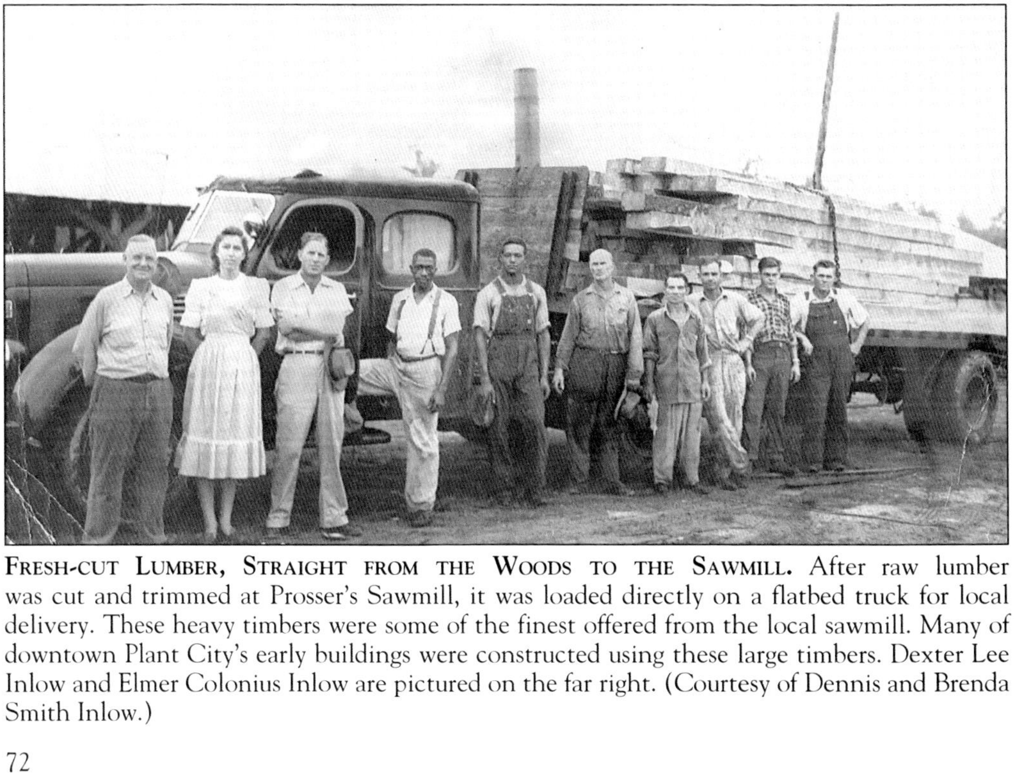

FRESH-CUT LUMBER, STRAIGHT FROM THE WOODS TO THE SAWMILL. After raw lumber was cut and trimmed at Prosser's Sawmill, it was loaded directly on a flatbed truck for local delivery. These heavy timbers were some of the finest offered from the local sawmill. Many of downtown Plant City's early buildings were constructed using these large timbers. Dexter Lee Inlow and Elmer Colonius Inlow are pictured on the far right. (Courtesy of Dennis and Brenda Smith Inlow.)

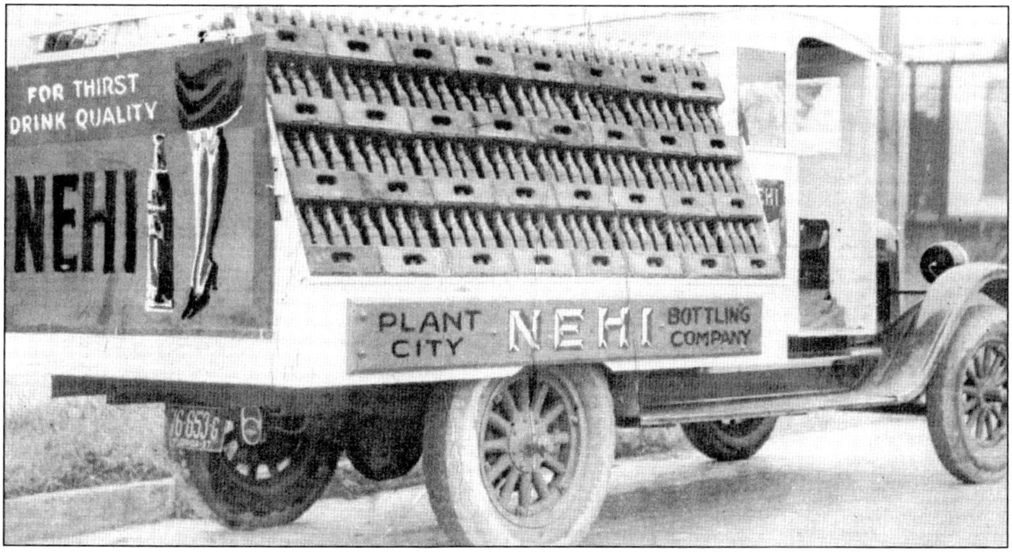

For Thirst Drink Quality Nehi. A delivery truck for the Plant City Nehi Bottling Company plant, located on East Reynolds Street, is pictured here. The local plant supplied a good number of distributors with quality Nehi from the popular tall bottle. In June 1929, the Nehi Bottling Company relocated to a new, brick building owned by Smith and Ryals on South Collins Street.

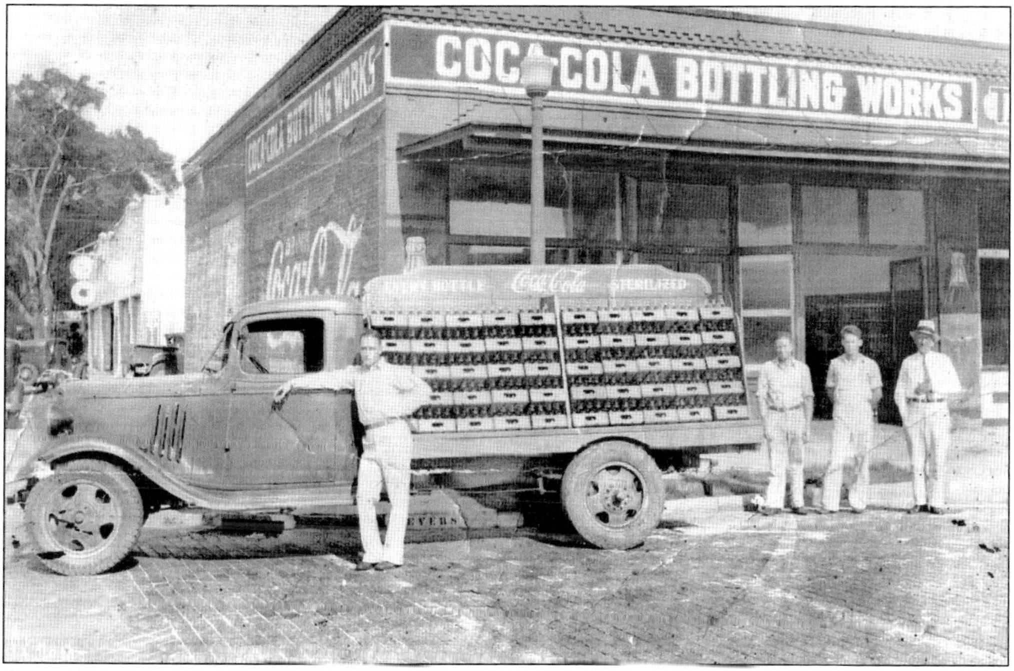

Coca-Cola, Every Bottle Sterilized. One of the fastest-growing concerns in Plant City in 1927 was the Coca-Cola Bottling Works. Mr. J.W. Henderson was the proprietor and manager. For the first two years, he did all the work and made deliveries in a wagon drawn by a gray mule. A new building was built at East Baker and Pennsylvania Streets in November 1939. Pictured from left to right are Ray Lominac, Jesse Wright, Wallace Wilson, and J.W. Henderson (owner), c. 1930s. (Courtesy of Bill and Betty Wilson.)

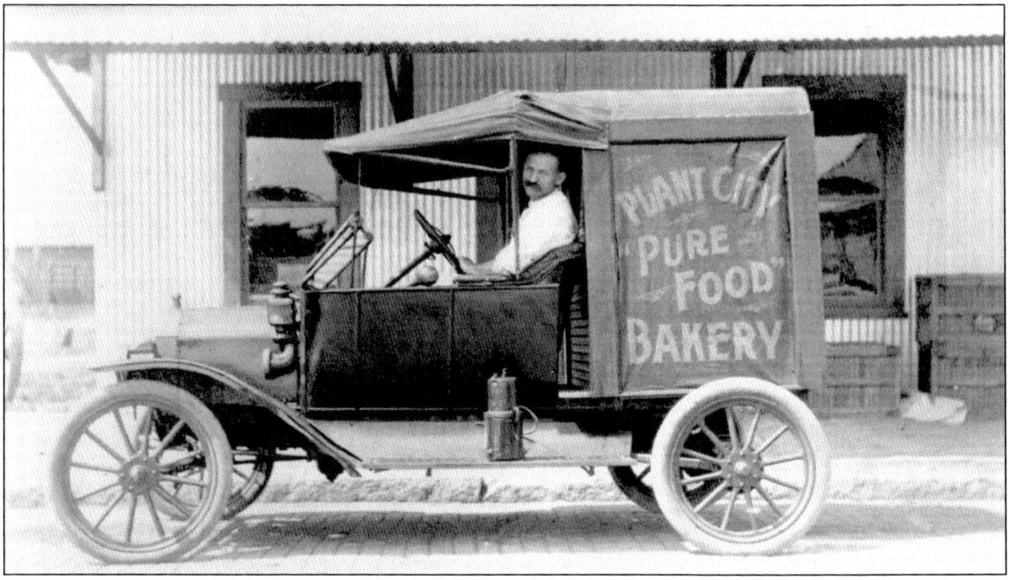

PLANT CITY "PURE FOOD" BAKERY C. 1915. Charles Rokus Bohner Sr., owner of Plant City's first bakery, is ready to make a delivery of his fresh baked goods in his 1914 Model T Ford. The Model T had a carbide gas generator mounted on the running board and gas headlights. The bakery was located on South Collins Street across from Knotts Hardware.

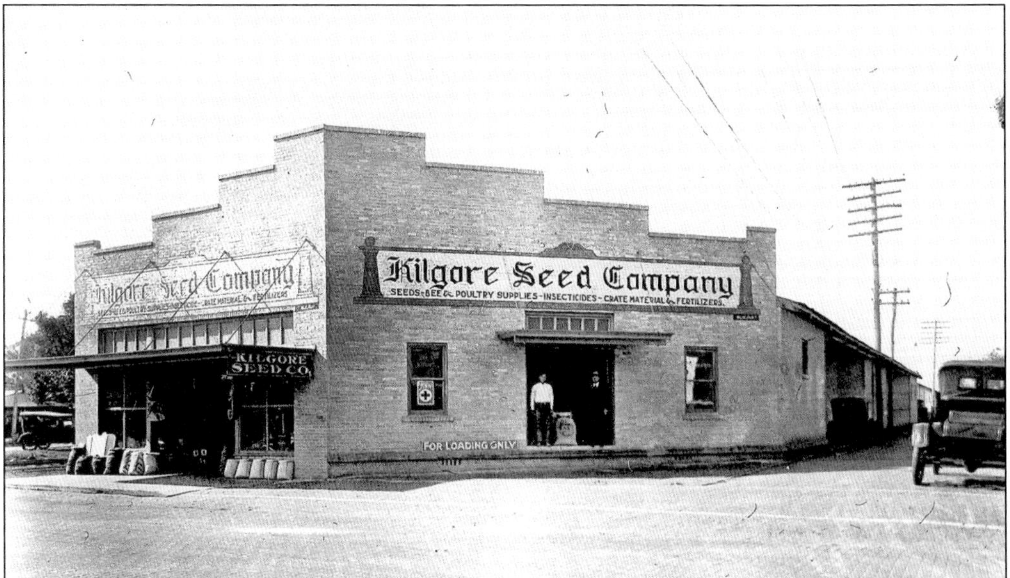

KILGORE SEED COMPANY. With headquarters and main offices in Plant City, Kilgore Seed was the largest concern of its kind in Florida and among the leaders in the South. With its volume of business showing tremendous increases each year, the Kilgore Seed Company also opened branch stores in Plant City, Palmetto, Moore Haven, Wauchula, Sanford, Vero, and Canal Point. This location served as the main office building of the Kilgore Seed Company, House of Quality and Service. Mr. H.M. Kilgore was president of the Kilgore Seed Company and served as the president of the Southern Seedman's Association. The Plant City branch store of the Kilgore Seed Company sold crates, seed, and Bradley Fertilizers.

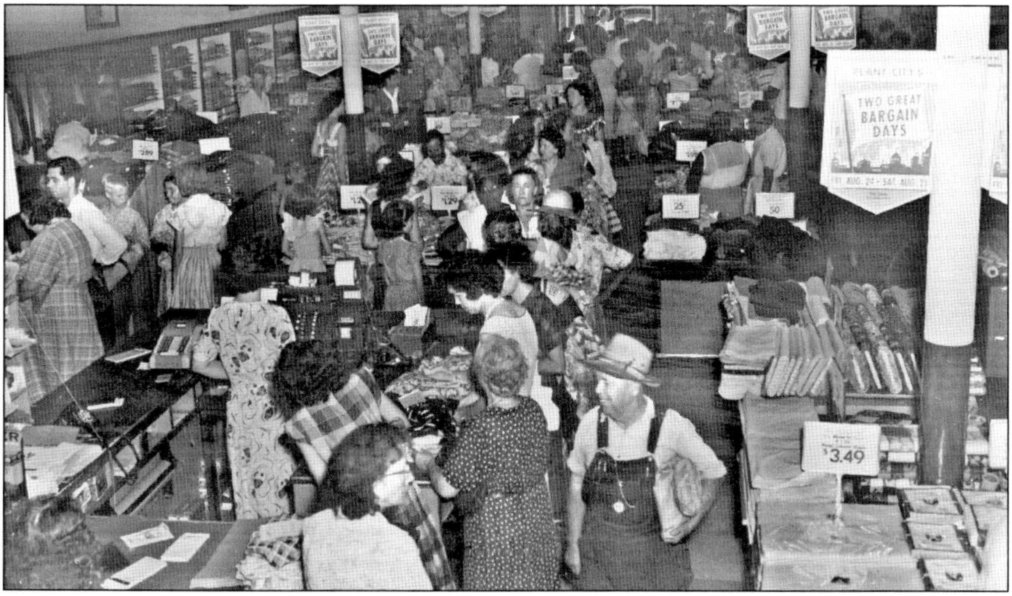

PLANT CITY'S TWO GREAT BARGAIN DAYS, FRIDAY, AUGUST 24 AND SATURDAY, AUGUST 25. Everyone came to town to shop the great bargains at Black's Department Store. Shoppers flocked to the super sale looking for a bargain. What a great time to do your back to school shopping! (Courtesy of Arcade Studio.)

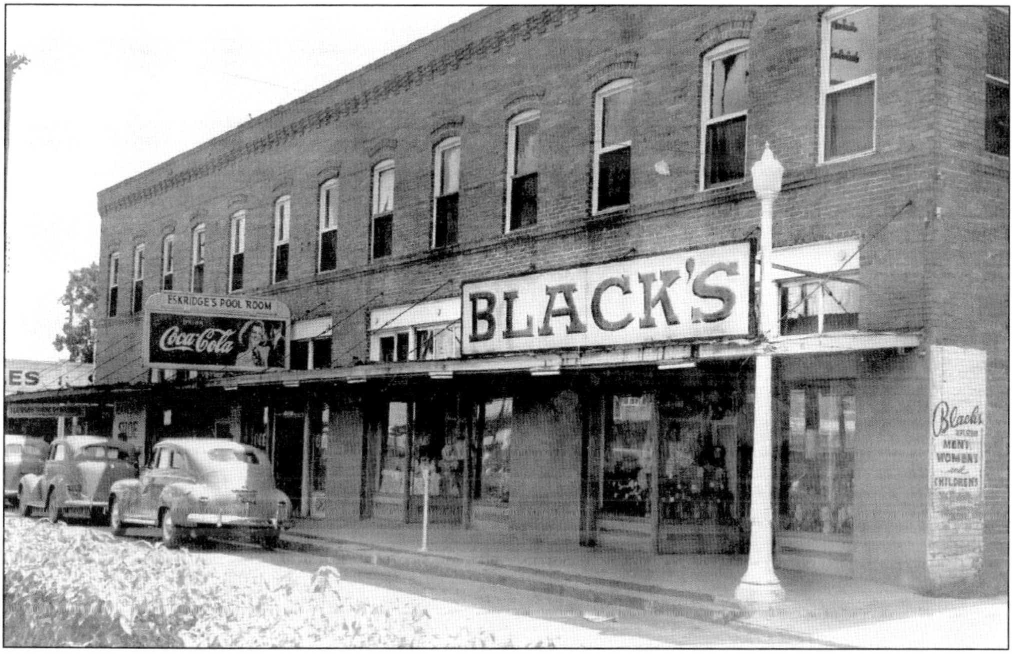

BLACK'S DEPARTMENT STORE. Mr. William Black and his wife, Lillian Black, were the owners of Black's Department Store, located at the corner of South Drane (J. Ardens Mays Boulevard) and Palmer Streets. The store was awarded the "Window Shopping Night" award by the East Hillsborough Chamber of Commerce during the Christmas season in the years 1954 to 1957. Their mechanical displays in the street-front windows of the store were quite elaborate. Located next door to Black's was Eskridge's Pool Room.

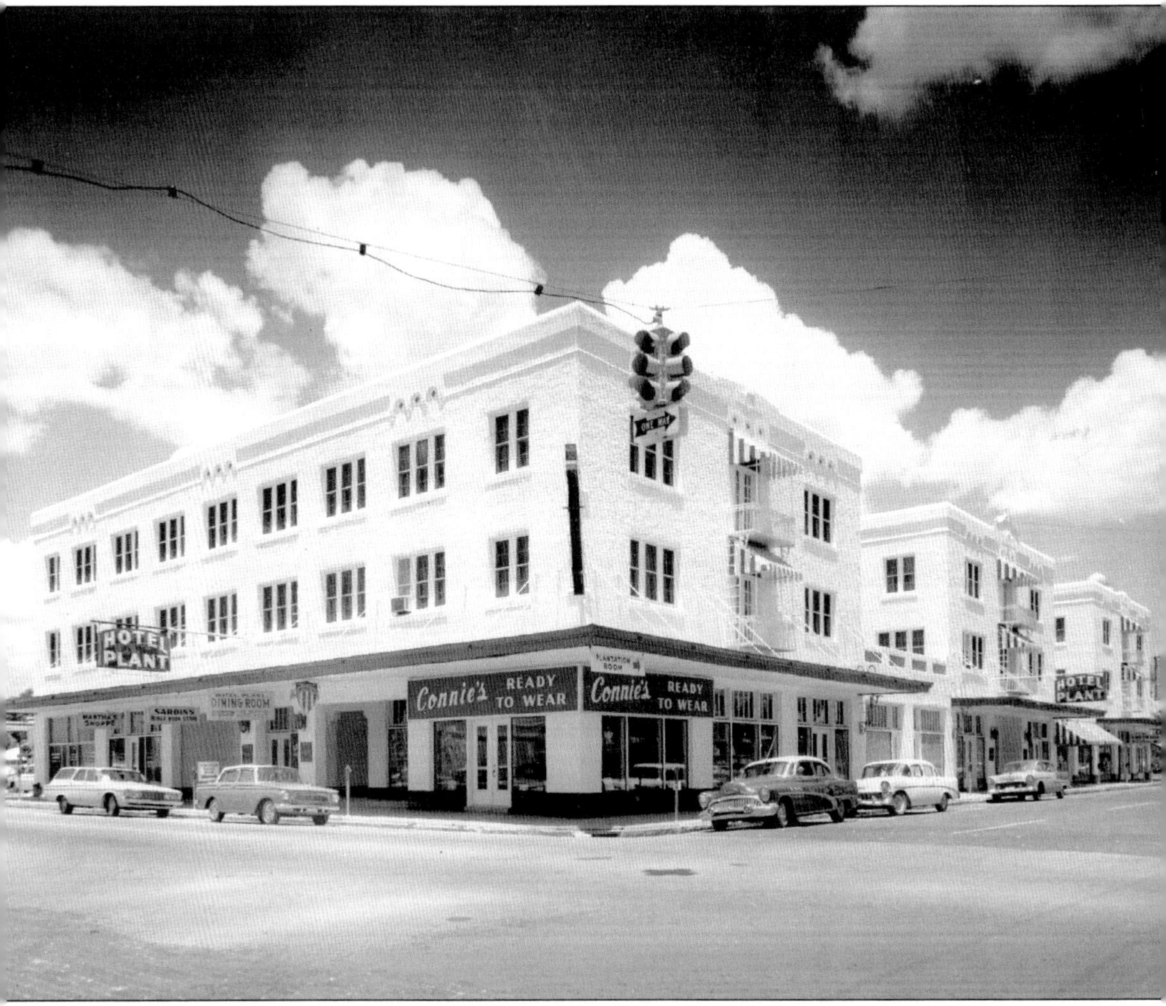

HOTEL PLANT BUILT IN 1925. The Hotel Plant had 100 well-appointed and comfortably furnished rooms, each featuring a private bath. The Plant, since its opening on Armistice Day 1926, was a popular stopping place for both transient and resident guests. It was "home sweet home" to Miss Martha Robinson, who lived there for 26 years, and Mrs. Lena Duyck, who resided there for 20 years. The dining room of the Hotel Plant served the choicest of seasonal foods throughout the year. The kitchen, one of the most modern in all the South, featured a complete menu serving orange, tomato, grapefruit, or prune juice for breakfast. Your evening meal could be finished in Plant City style, with a serving of strawberry shortcake with whipped cream. Connie's Ready to Wear, one of Plant City's finest ladies' dresses shops, was located on the ground floor at the southeast corner. Martha's Shoppe, Sardin's Bible Book Store, and T.M. & W.L. Tyling (real-estate brokers who sold homes, farms, and groves) also occupied rental space on the street-front floors. After the 1929 stock market crash, the community hotel promoters were unable to pay interest on the mortgage, and the mortgage was foreclosed. An insurance company operated it until 1942, when it was bought by Mr. and Mrs. Ben Rawlins, Mrs. Rawlin's mother Mrs. Susan Alice Hipp, and Mrs. Hipp's son C.H. Moorman. Among the VIP guests were Sen. Park Trammell and Florida governors Fred Cone, Fuller Warren, Dan McCarty, Millard Caldwell, and Spessard Holland, who became a U.S. senator also.

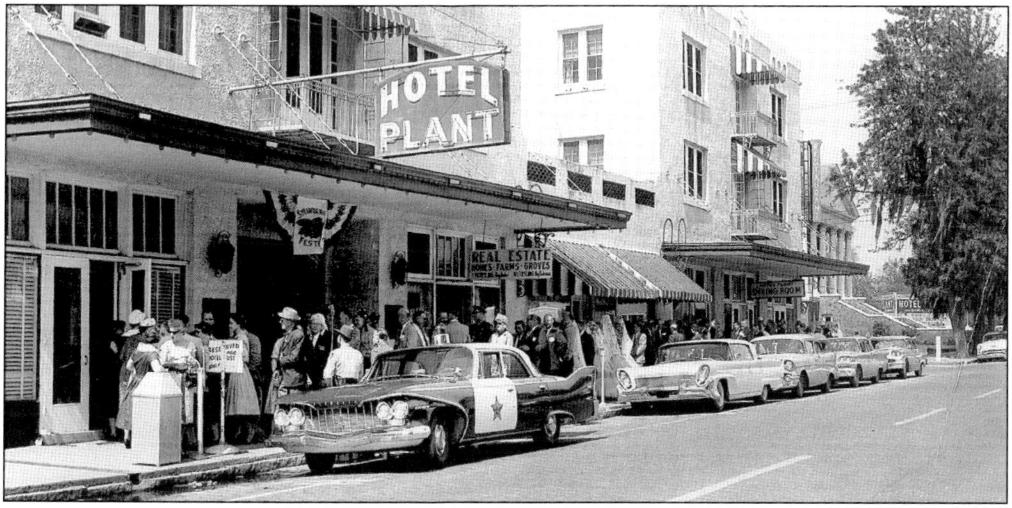

Hotel Plant Festival Luncheon. The Tampa Electric Company hosted the annual reception during Festival Week at their offices in the Hotel Plant until the company built a new office building on Haines Street. For many years, the parade kick-off reception was held under a tent at Tampa Electric Company's Haines Street location.

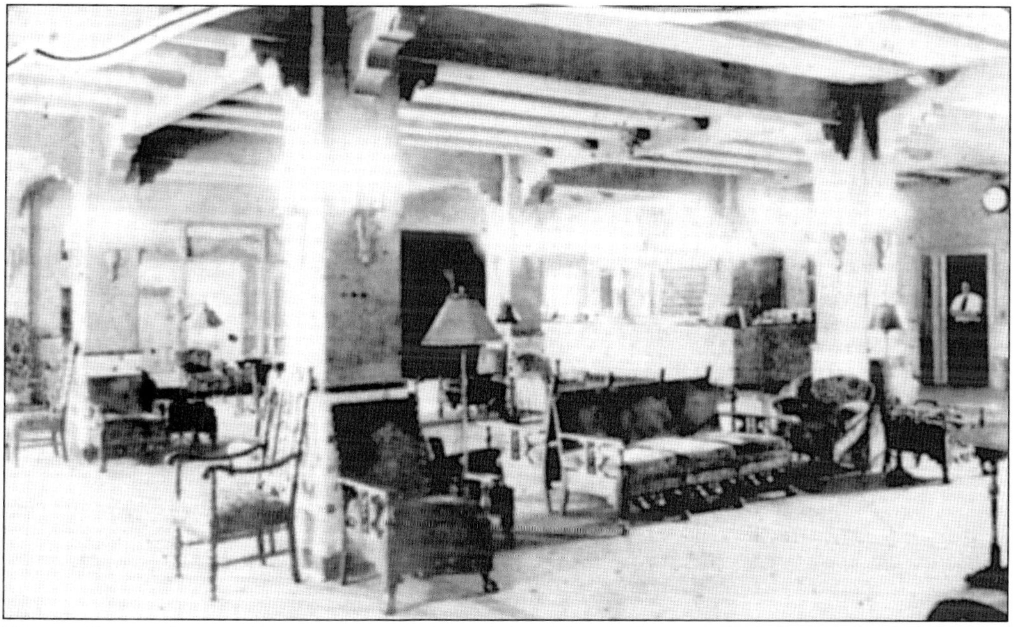

Hotel Plant Lobby. The inviting lobby of the Hotel Plant was where guests and visitors found the atmosphere most desirable for comfort and conversation. The Plant's lobby and sun parlor above it were popular among local social club members as an ideal meeting place. Lights from the new 100-room Hotel Plant beckoned a welcome for a gala reception to celebrate the opening of the hotel, which cost over one-half million dollars. Guests toured the structure and sipped punch, while Plant City women served as hostesses in showing off the sparkling rooms. Brides held their wedding reception in the dining room of the hotel. The hotel was a haven in times of disaster. During hurricanes, owner Ben Rawlins opened the doors to more than 300 families, filling all the rooms and using the lobby and halls as sleeping quarters. Free meals were served to the evacuees.

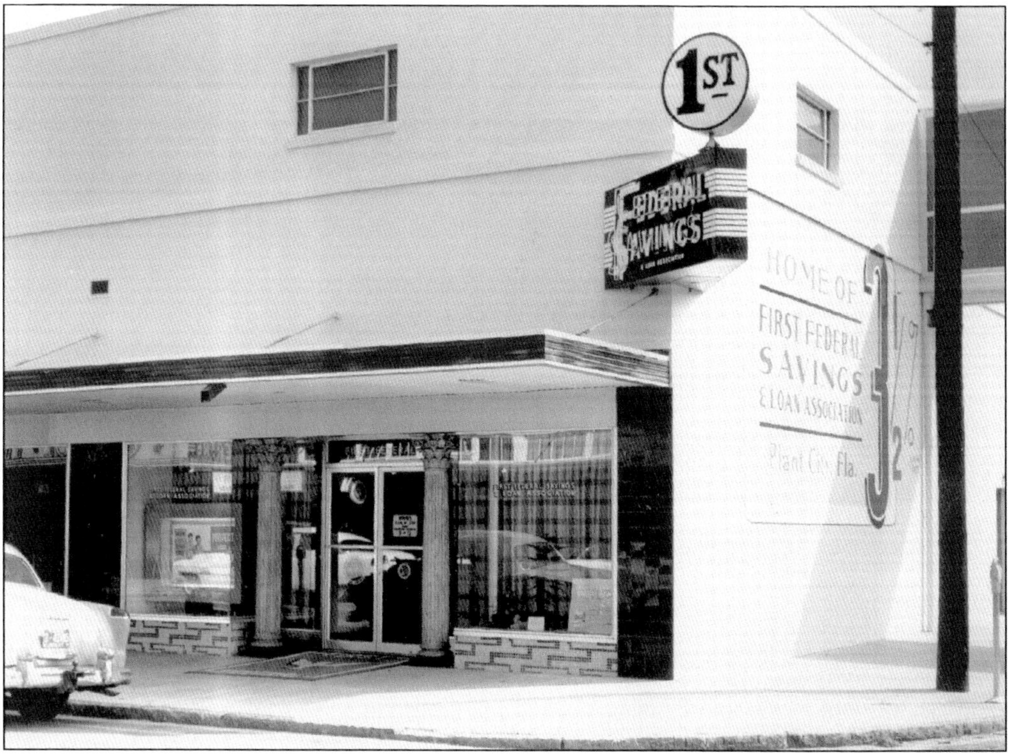

FIRST FEDERAL SAVINGS AND LOAN ASSOCIATION, PLANT CITY. An open house was held at the Reynolds and Evers Streets location of the offices of the local savings and loan association on June 25, 1957. The sign from this location was moved and installed when the construction of the new facility was completed in 1960.

YOU ARE CORDIALLY INVITED

TO ATTEND THE

OPEN HOUSE

AT

OUR NEW HOME

111 WEST REYNOLDS STREET

TUESDAY, JUNE 25, 1957 9:00 A.M. TO 8:00 P.M.

FIRST FEDERAL SAVINGS AND LOAN
ASSOCIATION OF PLANT CITY

OPEN HOUSE CELEBRATION FOR NEW HOME OF FIRST FEDERAL SAVINGS AND LOAN ASSOCIATION OF PLANT CITY. Friends and customers received engraved invitations to the all-day open house reception. This location served the institution from 1957 to 1960. Interest rates were stable enough that they could be painted on the side of the building—3.5 percent in 1958.

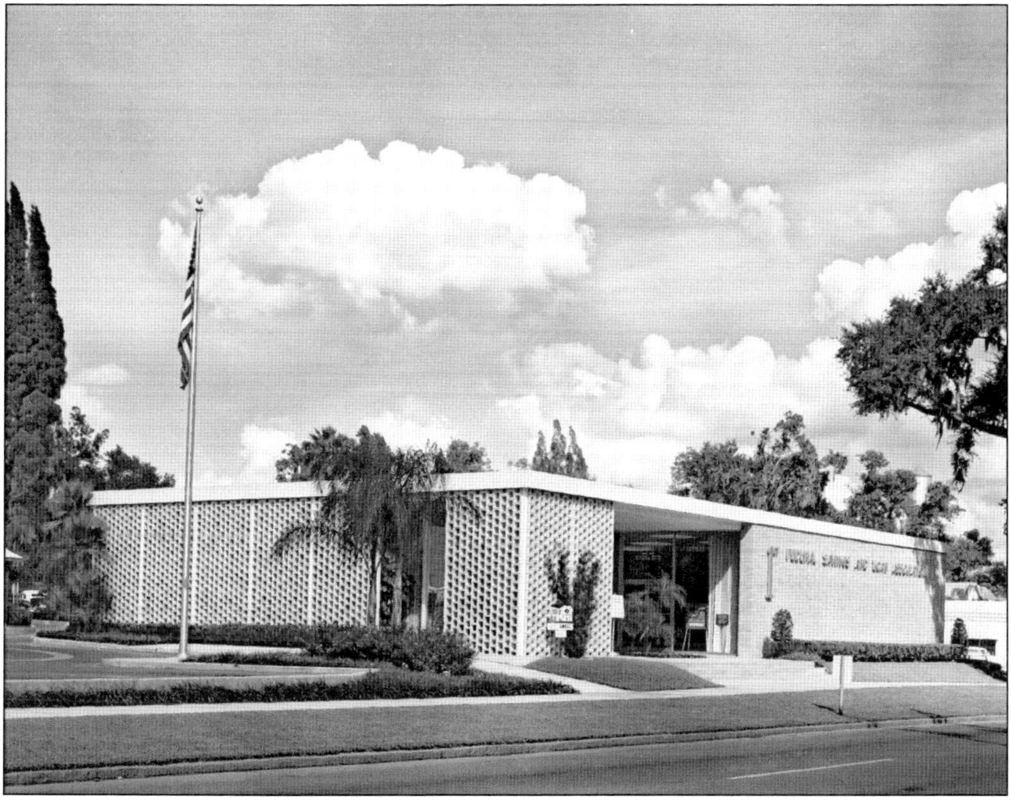

First Permanent Association Office on Baker Street. The 4,500-square-foot office building was designed by Pullara and Watson of Tampa, architects and engineers. This original structure, opened in December 1960, is still part of the remodeled building today. (Courtesy of Bill Friend's Studio.)

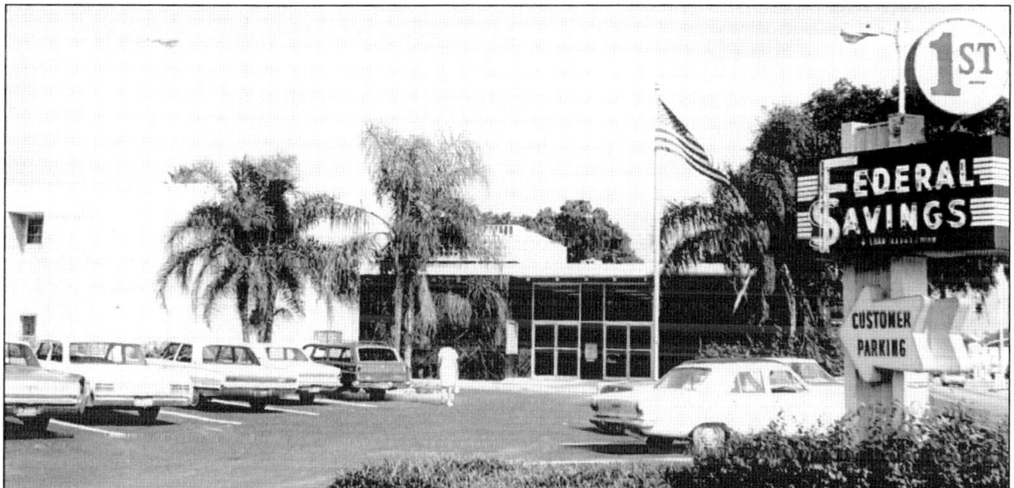

First Federal Savings and Loan Association, Remodeled in 1969. Striving to fulfill the needs of its customers, the offices were remodeled in 1969. This office remained unchanged until 1983, when the facility received a remodeled facelift.

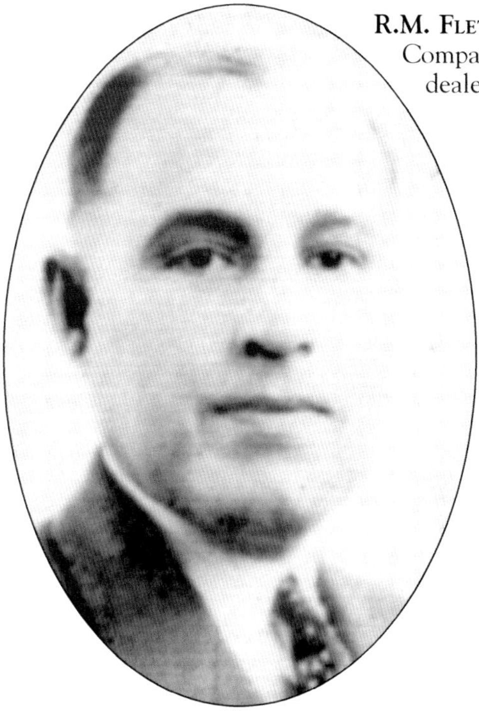

R.M. FLETCHER. Mr. Fletcher operated the Fletcher Motor Company in Zephyrhills, Florida, as well as the Ford dealership in Plant City, seen opposite.

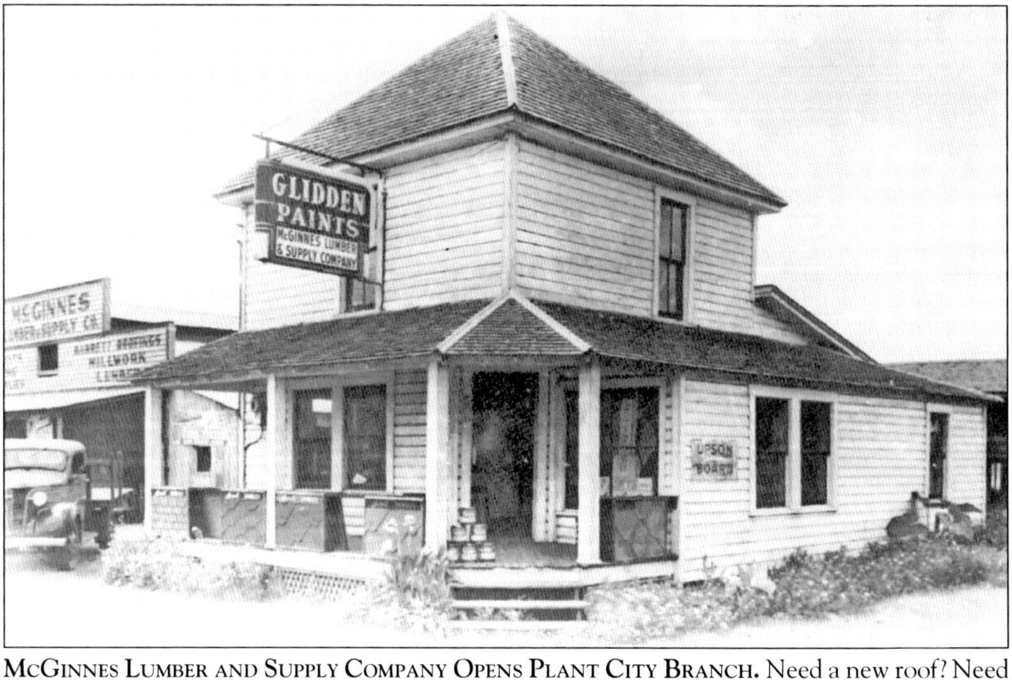

McGINNES LUMBER AND SUPPLY COMPANY OPENS PLANT CITY BRANCH. Need a new roof? Need a paint job or a new door? Whatever your construction needs, McGinnes Lumber Company can supply it. They carried Barrett roofing, Upson boards, custom millwork, paint, and kit homes. The family-owned McGinnes Lumber Company has served the Plant City community since 1936. The business was sold to Stock Lumber Company in the late 1990s, but many of the longtime managers and employees are still there.

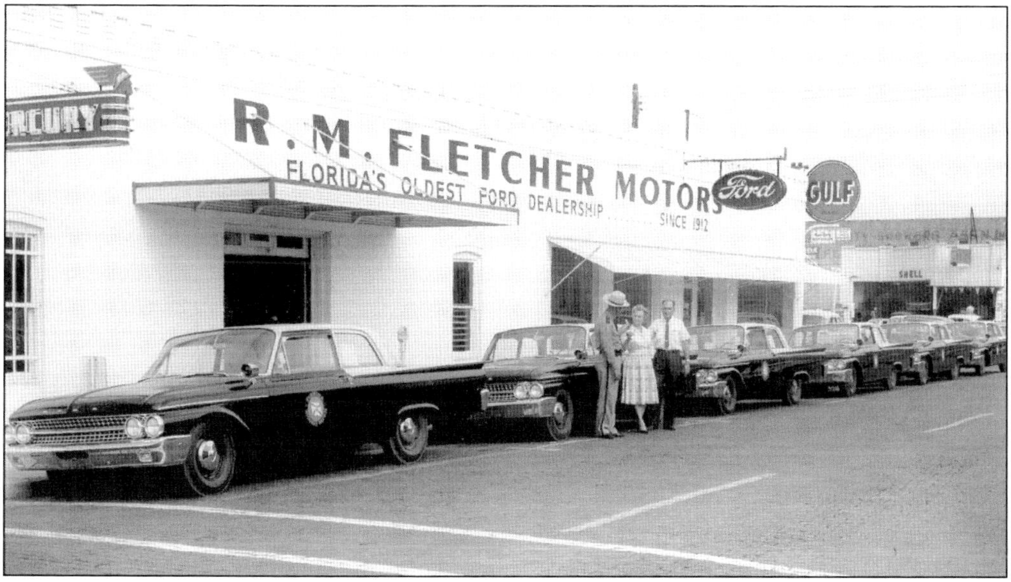

R.M. FLETCHER MOTORS, FLORIDA'S OLDEST FORD DEALERSHIP SINCE 1912. Mrs. Nita Fletcher presents the keys to the new fleet of cars for the Florida Highway Patrol. Fletcher Ford supplied the fleet cars for the Florida Highway Patrol for many years. Located on Palmer Street, Fletcher Ford was the local Ford and Mercury dealership. Seen in the background are the Reynolds and Palmer Street Gulf Service Station, the Shell Station, and the Plant City Growers Association, which faced Palmer Street. (Courtesy of Bill Friend's Studio.)

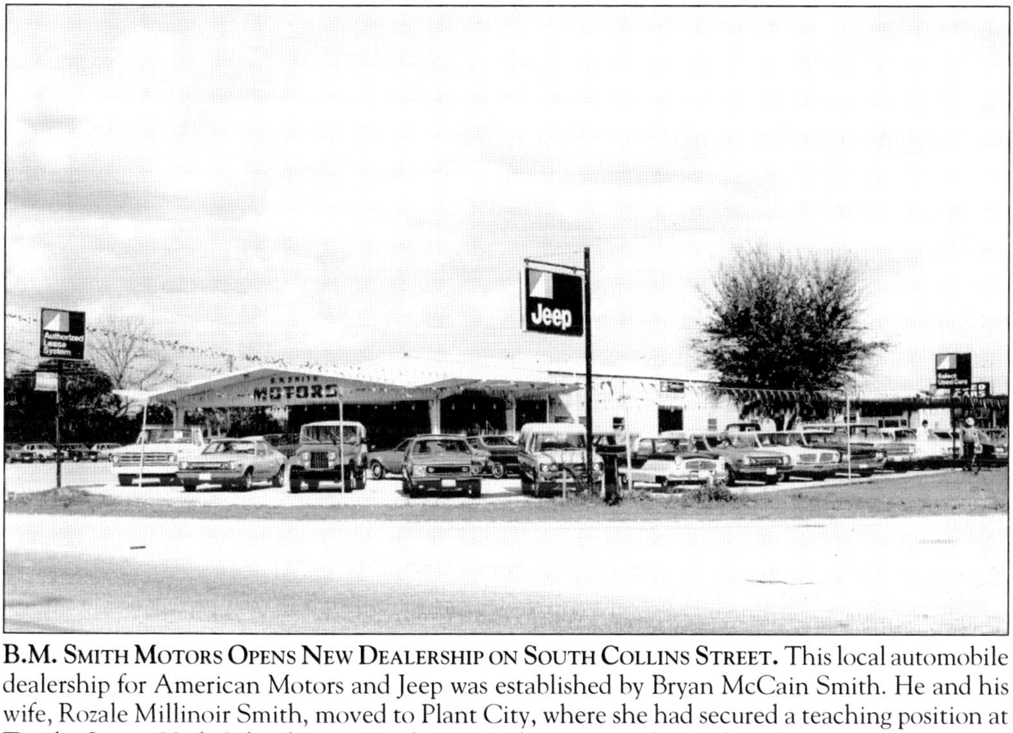

B.M. SMITH MOTORS OPENS NEW DEALERSHIP ON SOUTH COLLINS STREET. This local automobile dealership for American Motors and Jeep was established by Bryan McCain Smith. He and his wife, Rozale Millinoir Smith, moved to Plant City, where she had secured a teaching position at Tomlin Junior High School in 1934. They were the parents of B.M. (Mac) Smith Jr. and Robert Patrick (Pat) Smith, both of whom have made Plant City their hometown.

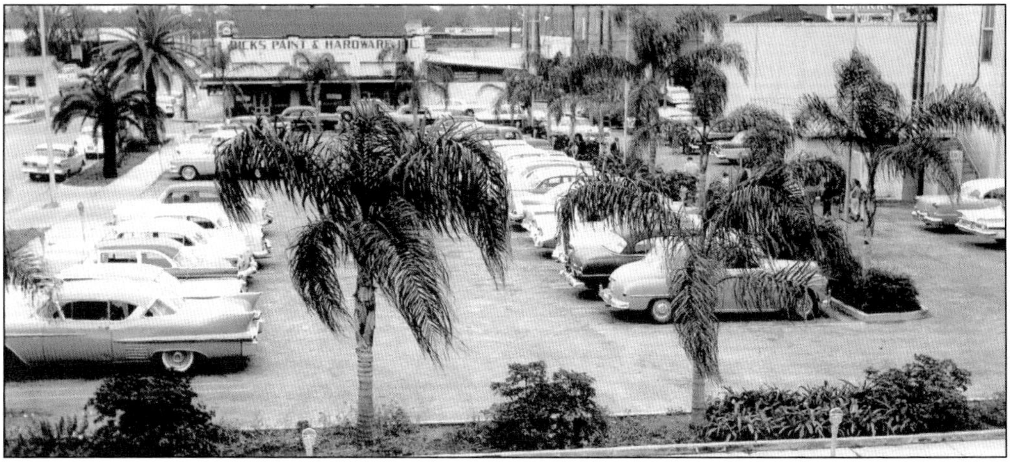

THE CITY OF PLANT CITY'S DOWNTOWN MUNICIPAL PARKING LOT. Located at the corner of Mahoney and Evers Streets, the new parking lot, with metered spaces, served shoppers for the downtown stores. The perimeter of the parking lot was landscaped with palms and granite curbing. The small building with a railed rooftop was used for outdoor events. Dicks Paint and Hardware was located in the building at the corner of North Collins and Mahoney Streets. J.R. Dicks Jr. had purchased the building from J.A. Miles in 1945.

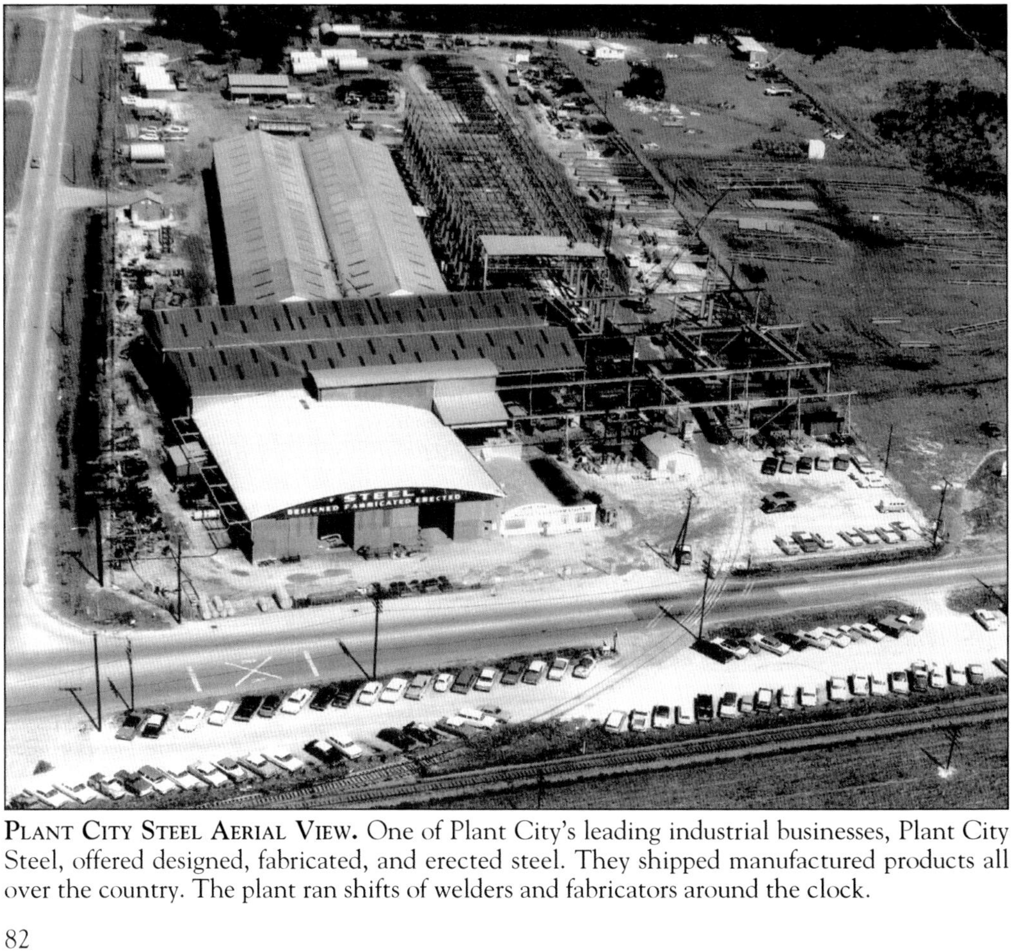

PLANT CITY STEEL AERIAL VIEW. One of Plant City's leading industrial businesses, Plant City Steel, offered designed, fabricated, and erected steel. They shipped manufactured products all over the country. The plant ran shifts of welders and fabricators around the clock.

Five

HISTORIC BUILDINGS

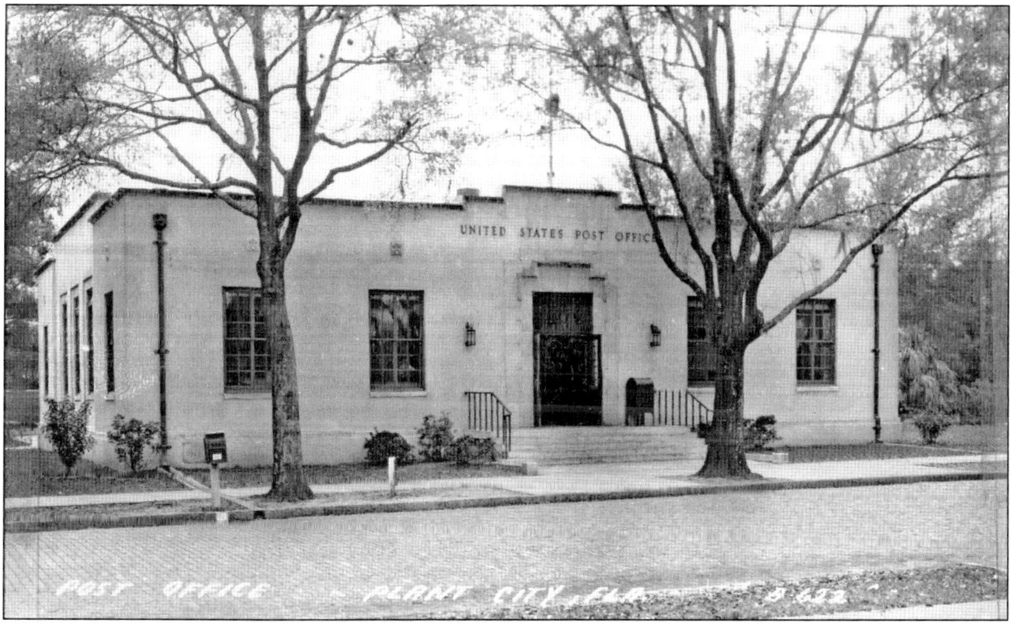

UNITED STATES POST OFFICE. Mrs. Mamie E. Barnes was the postmaster when the post office moved into this federal building, located at Reynolds and Wheeler Streets. (Courtesy of Anna E. "Nancy" Simmons Duffield, 1975.)

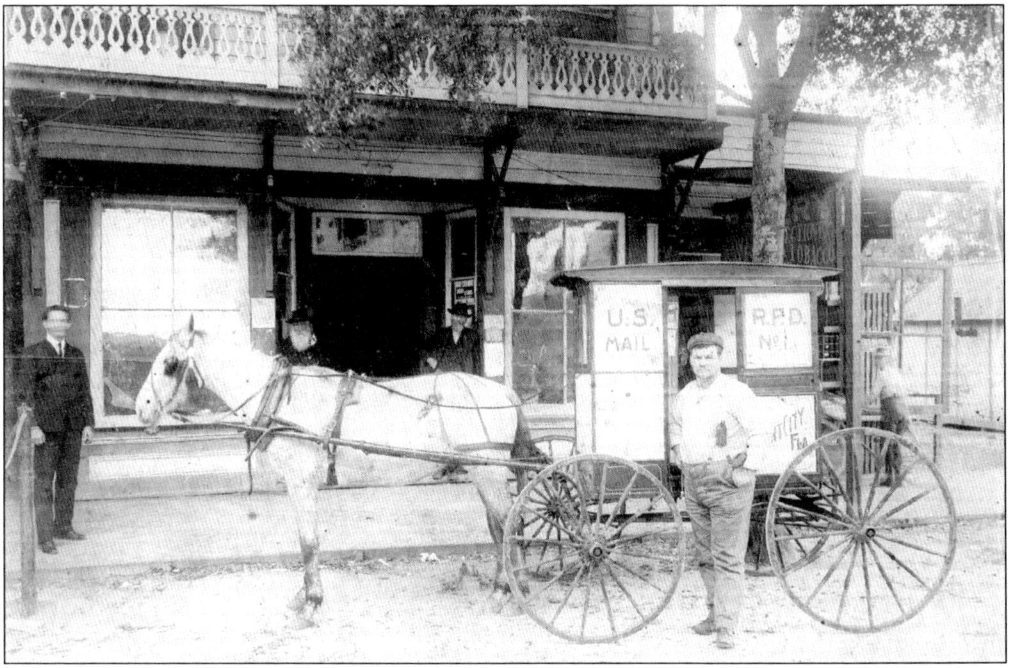

M.F. TILLMAN, FIRST RURAL MAIL CARRIER. M.F. Tillman, Plant City's first rural mail carrier, is pictured in front of the post office at the northeast corner of Reynolds and Collins Streets in 1903, shortly after rural delivery began. Mr. E.B. Trask was the postmaster.

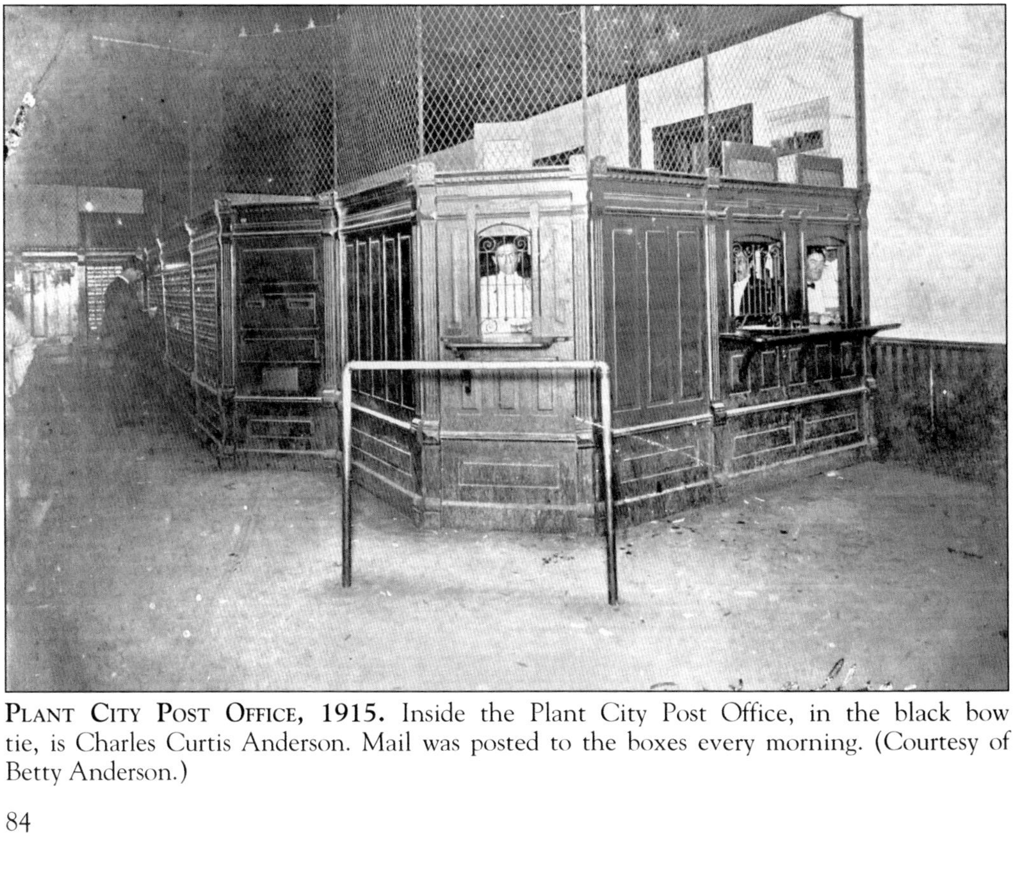

PLANT CITY POST OFFICE, 1915. Inside the Plant City Post Office, in the black bow tie, is Charles Curtis Anderson. Mail was posted to the boxes every morning. (Courtesy of Betty Anderson.)

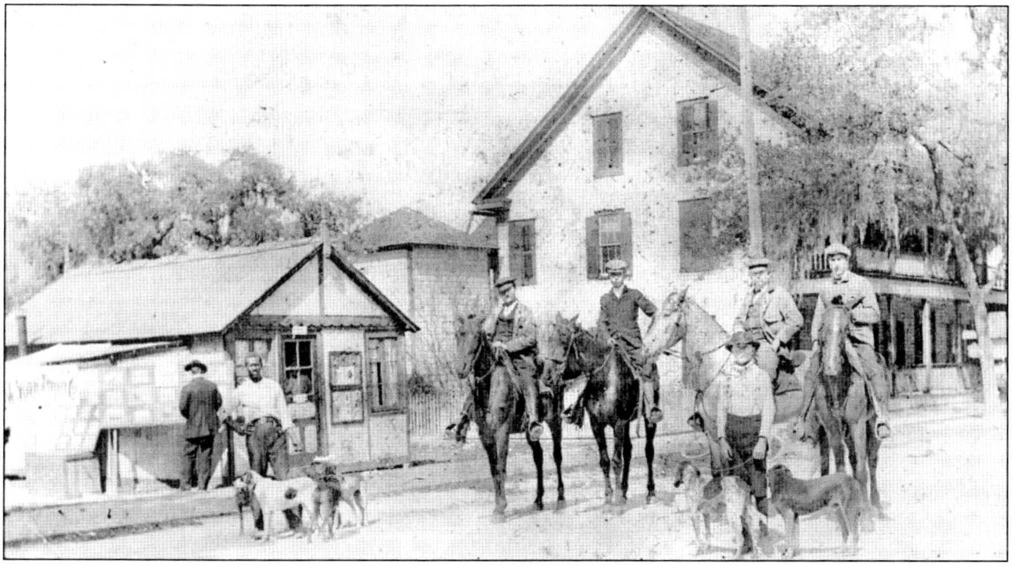

STREET SCENE OF LOCAL MEN ON HORSEBACK WITH THEIR HUNTING HOUNDS, 1897. Ready for a hunt, these men have gathered up their finest hounds and paused for the photographer in front of the New York Photo Studio on Reynolds Street. Beyond is a partial view of the old Tropical Hotel, located on the site of today's Lee Building.

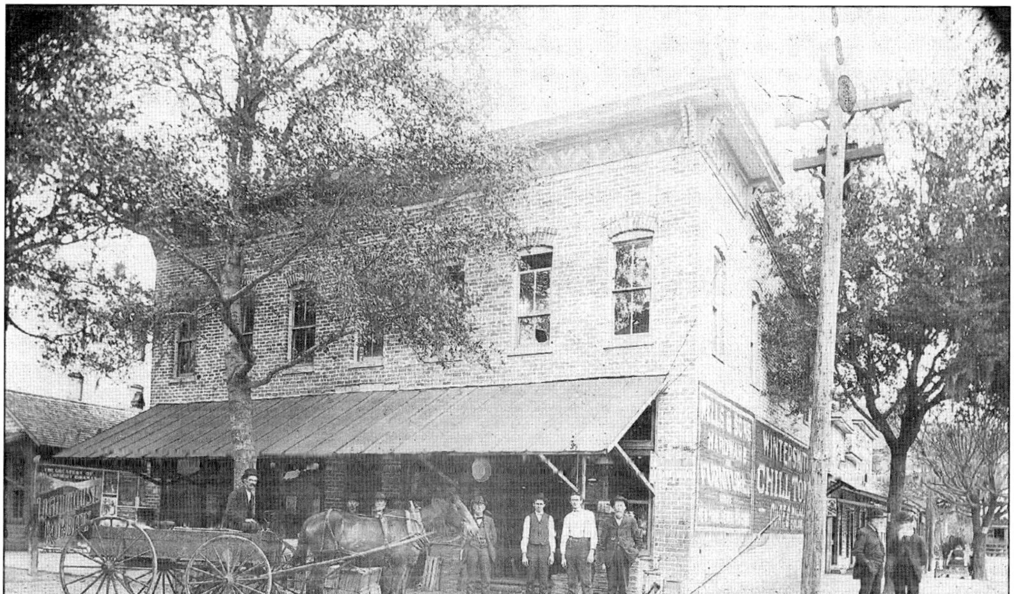

WELLS & SONS HARDWARE AND FURNITURE STORE. Wells & Sons was located at the northeast corner of Collins and North Drane Streets. Pictured from left to right are Fred Fisher (in wagon), G.W. Huntsman, William Wells, John Graham, and G.W. Wells (proprietor); (at the side of the store) Col. J.L. Young and Dr. A.M. Barns.

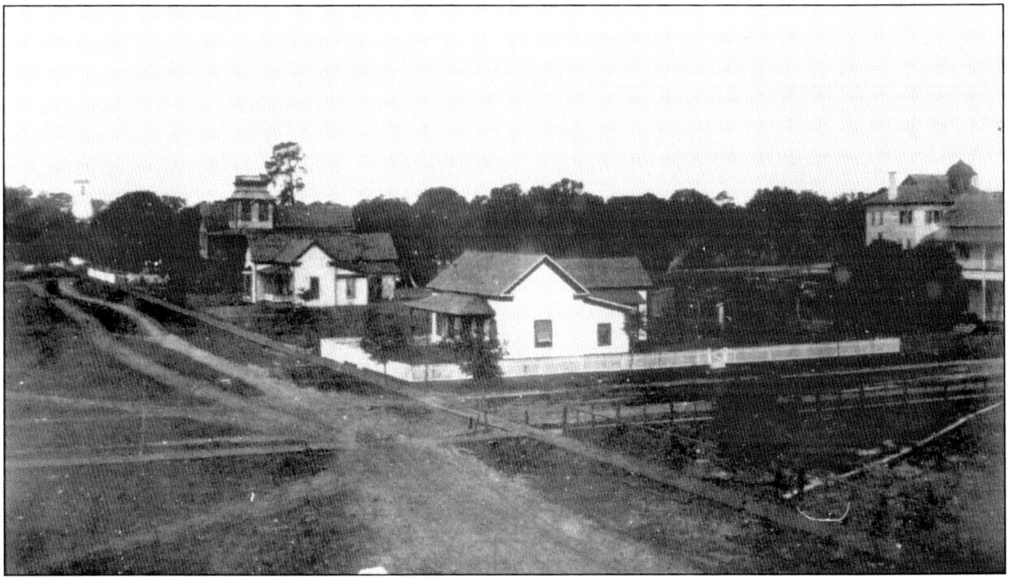

Plant City's Early Neighborhoods. Shown is a view of the downtown residential area when the streets were dirt and the sidewalks were made of wooden planks. Typical homes were of the frame vernacular style with front porches. Picket fences were used to keep the stray livestock from making themselves "at home."

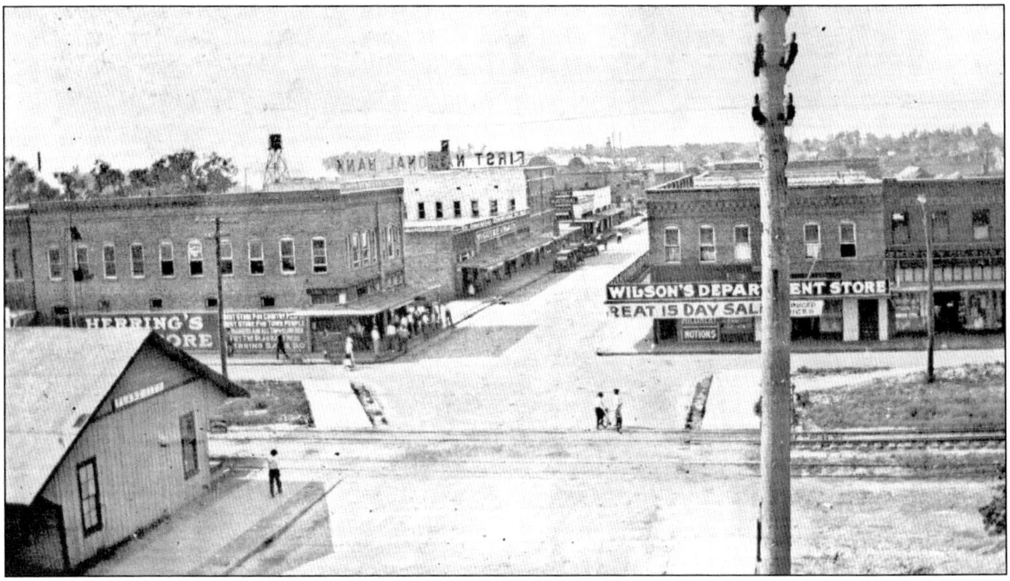

Coastline Depot at the "A" Tracks. Looking south on Collins Street at the Coastline Tracks, Herring's Drugstore is on the left. To the south of Herring's is McGuire's Store, whose slogan was "We Guarantee Everything We Sell," and First National Bank is seen at the far left. The bank was later moved farther west on Haines Street to a newly built building. The sign painted on the side of the Herring's Drug Store building reads, "Best Store For Country People, Best Store For Town People, Strangers And All Traveling Men, Get The Glad Hand Here, Herring Says So." The sign on the top of the front facade reads, "Plant City Business College." On the right is Wilson's Department Store, who was having a great 15-day sale. The chamber of commerce was located in the two-story building west of Wilson's.

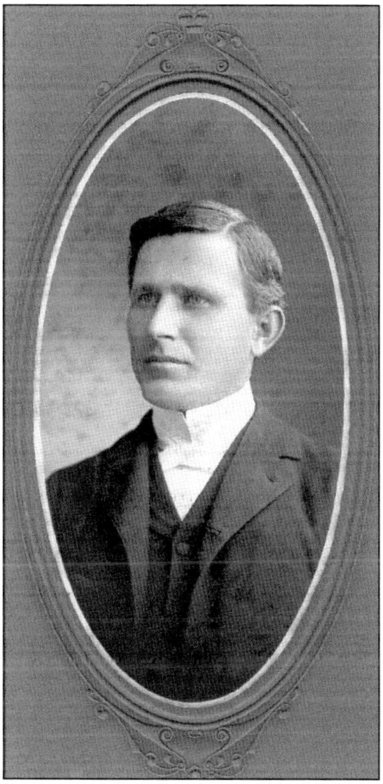

GEORGE BENJAMIN WELLS, BORN MAY 5, 1848, DIED MAY 15, 1934. Born in Plant City, George Benjamin Wells became a well-known lawyer who served in the Florida House of Representatives and also as town clerk, mayor, and city attorney of Plant City. He was the son of George Washington Wells, born in Georgia in 1843, and Mary Jane Drew, born in Tampa in 1850. George and Mary Jane were married in Madison County, Florida, in 1864. Their other children were Mary Jane Wells, who married Dr. John Clarence Knight, and sons Walter Charles, Sheldon Cornelius, and William Jason Wells. George W. Wells was one of the pioneer merchants of Plant City. Wells & Sons Hardware, formed in 1897, carried steel, tin, iron, farm implements, furniture, coffins, caskets, and burial robes. They offered everything required for the rites of burial and funeral ceremonies. (Courtesy of Morasl, Tampa, Florida.)

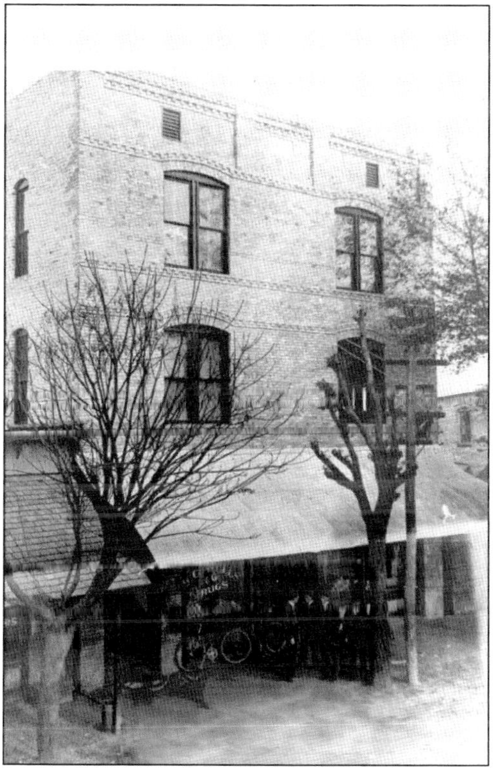

WELLS BUILDING, BUILT IN 1904. This three-story masonry vernacular structure features double-hung sash windows with decorative brick around the windows, frieze, and parapets. In November 1939, young lawyer James D. Bruton Jr. located his law offices on the second floor and remained there for years. For many years, the building was a part of Hooker's Department Store and Thorp's. Currently owned by John and Betty Briggs, the building is used by John as an artist studio/gallery and retail space. A graduate of Florida State University with a Master of Fine Arts, John is an Ohio native and has been featured on the ABC *Good Morning America* show, *American Artist Magazine*, *Art News*, *Artists and the American Landscape*, and numerous other publications. He was awarded an NEA Artist-In-Residence Fellowship, Dupont Foundation Purchase Award, and other honors and recognitions. His work is represented in New York City and the throughout the South.

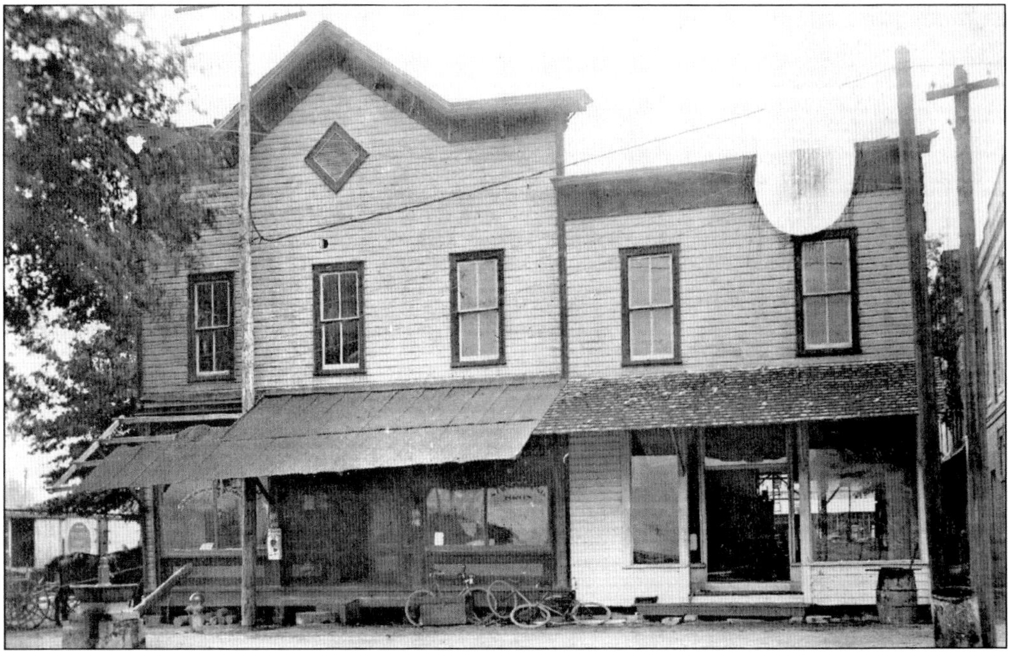

EARLY STRICKLAND STORE. Located at the northwest corner of Collins and North Drane Street West is the first building built by the Strickland Brothers for their dry goods store. The office of the telephone company is on the right. The front store canopy and roof were made of wooden shakes. Bicycles were a popular mode of transportation and were used for delivery. Although downtown was serviced by electricity, street paving was still a few years away. The wooden structure was moved to make way for the new, brick building. It was eventually demolished.

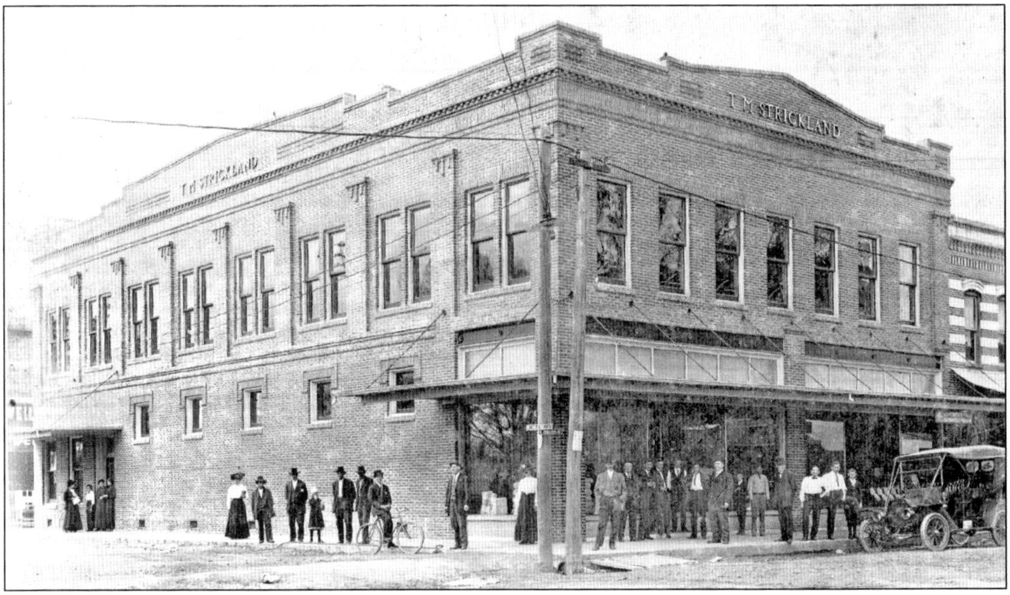

T.M. STRICKLAND BUILDING, BUILT IN 1910. A handsome new brick building was constructed by T.M. Strickland on the site of the early Strickland store and telephone office. Automobiles had come to Plant City and were a convenience welcomed by many.

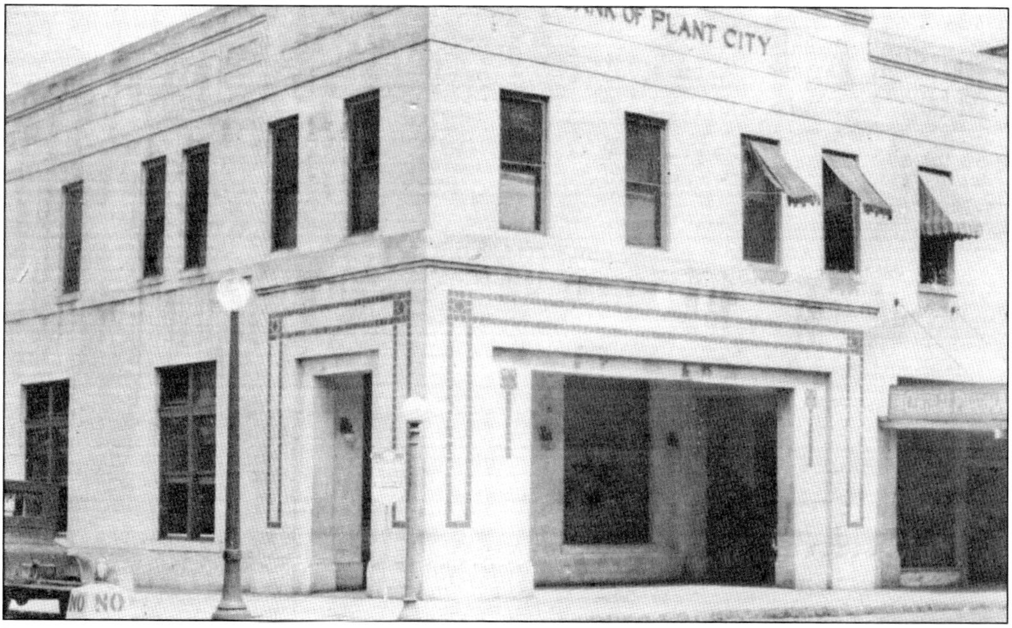

BANK OF PLANT CITY. Chartered in 1906, the bank opened its offices in a two-story building just south of the Wells Building on Collins Street. In 1919, the Bank of Plant City moved to the southeast corner of Collins and Reynolds Streets. Officers were Pres. Wm. Schneider, Vice Pres. E.W. Wiggins, Vice Pres. W.J. McDonald, cashier R.M. Morgan, and assistant cashiers S.E. Youngblood and A.L. Hall. Directors were Dr. L. Bize, J.E. Cassels, D.H. Laney, McDonald, Morgan, Schneider, H.H. Root, W.C. Wells, and Wiggins.

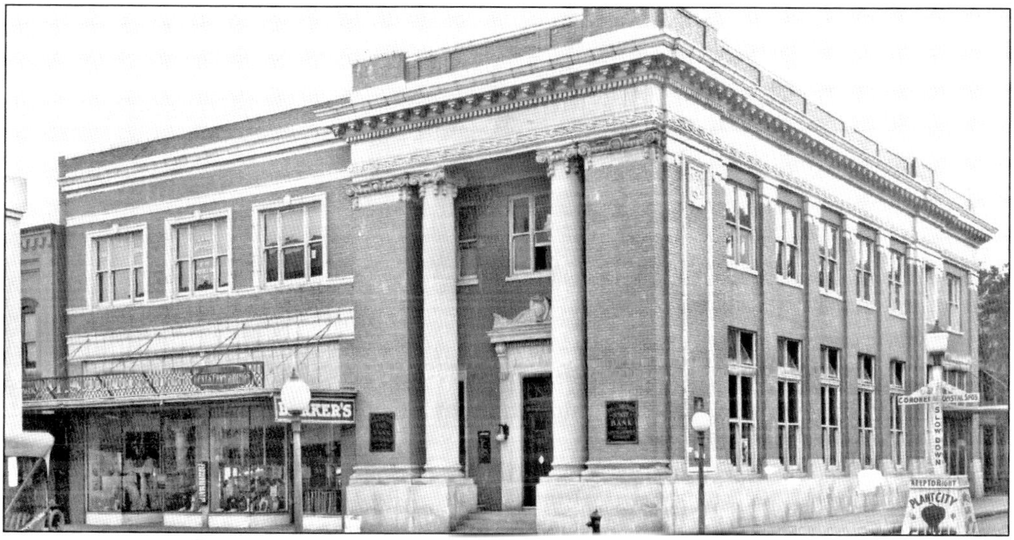

HILLSBORO STATE BANK. Constructed in 1914, this building is individually listed on the National Register of Historic Sites. The yellow brick building with terra-cotta detailing embodies certain features of the Beaux-Arts style. A double-door entranceway is set in a classical surround and has the words "Hillsboro State Bank" engraved in the frieze of the entablature. Officers were Pres. J.L. Young, Vice Pres. M.E. Moody, Vice Pres. E.T. Roux, Vice Pres. S.E. Mays; cashier T.E. Moody; and assistant cashier A.R. Boring. The directors were Young, M.E. Moody, Roux, P.A. Merrin, Mays, Dr. C.T. Young, and T.E. Moody.

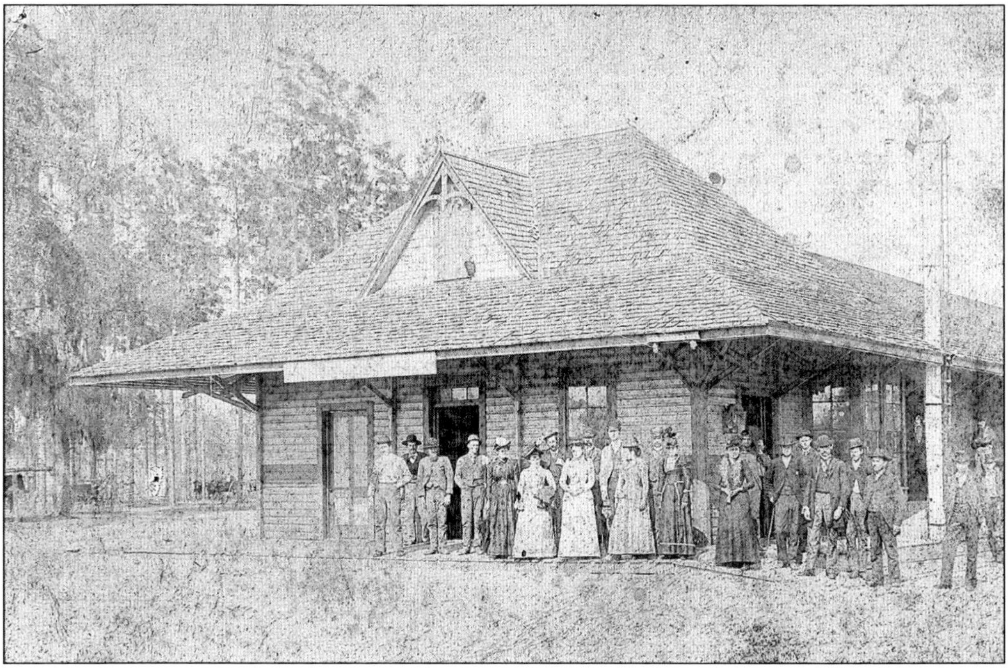

RAILROAD STATION, PLANT CITY. This is one of the earliest photos of the train depot in downtown Plant City. Rail travel and delivery was vital to the community. The daily mail came in on the morning train along with shipments of dry goods, hardware, and furnishings for the local stores.

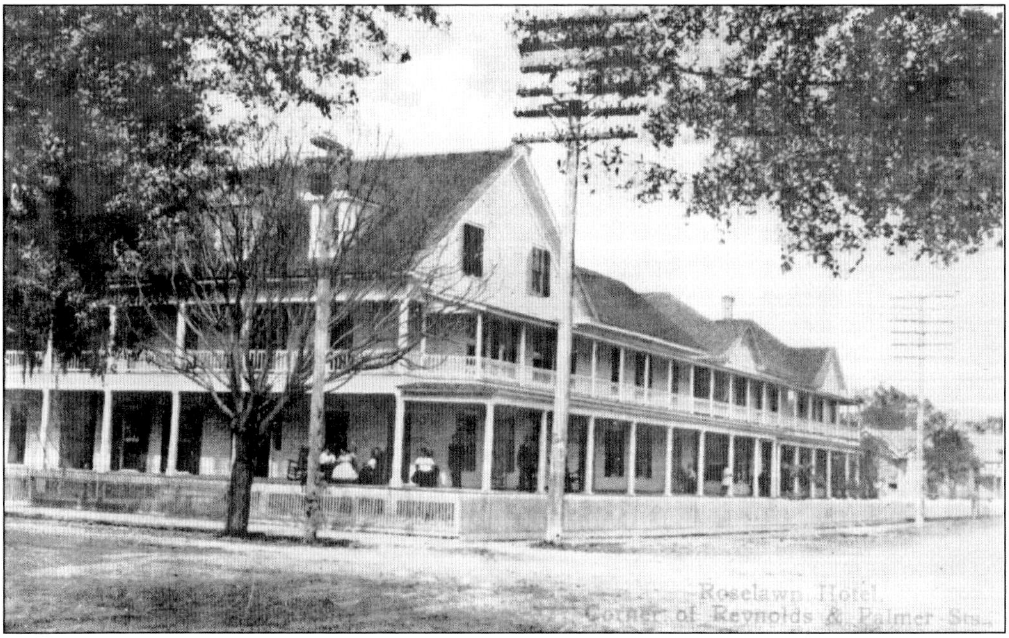

ROSELAWN HOTEL, CORNER OF REYNOLDS AND PALMER STREETS. The original structure, built in 1888 as the Tropical Hotel and owned by Mr. W.F. Burts, was enlarged and remodeled by his daughter, Ella Burts Strickland Crum, and renamed the Roselawn Hotel in 1908. It was Plant City's most fashionable hotel and the site of many social occasions.

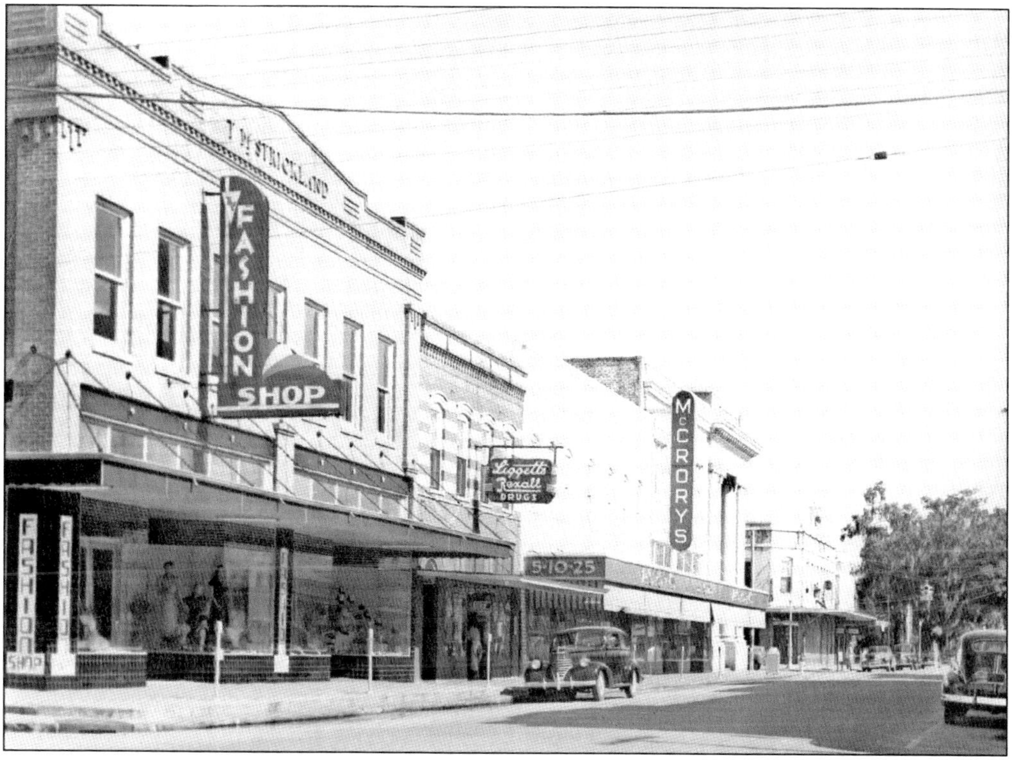

THE FASHION SHOP, LIGGETT'S REXALL DRUGS, AND McCRORY'S 5-10-25. The T.M. Strickland Building enjoyed many long years as a downtown shop for family apparel. The interior features a mezzanine. The McCrory's building had entrances on both Collins and Evers Streets. A luncheon counter with both counter and booth-style seating was a favorite eatery for downtown visitors and employees. Plant City's McCrory's closed its doors on January 26, 1985, having been a fixture in downtown Plant City since June 20, 1918.

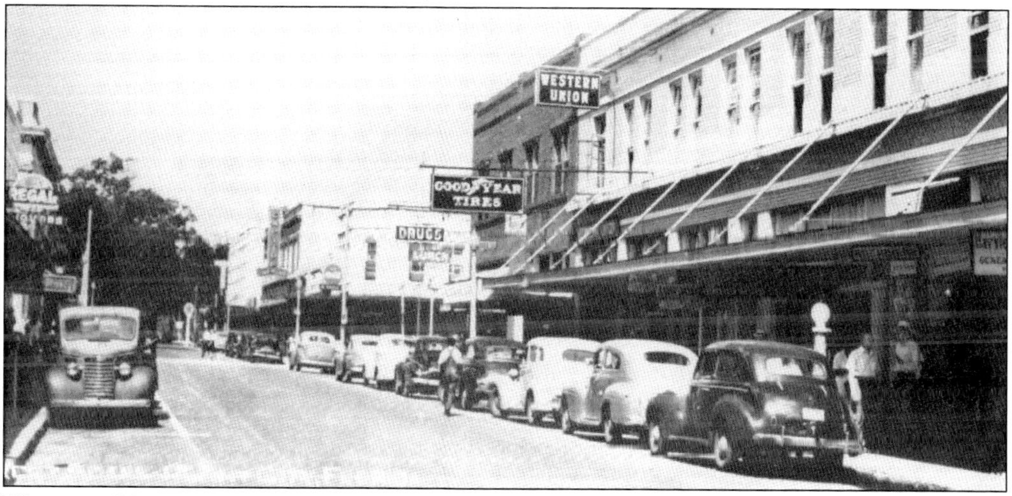

WESTERN UNION, GOOD YEAR TIRES, MAGNOLIA PHARMACY, AND THE CAPITOL THEATER. Reynolds Street, looking west from Palmer, was a busy area of downtown, handling two-way vehicle traffic. The Western Union telegraph office served as the source of communication for many citizens. Harvley's Appliances sold every machine you needed for your home.

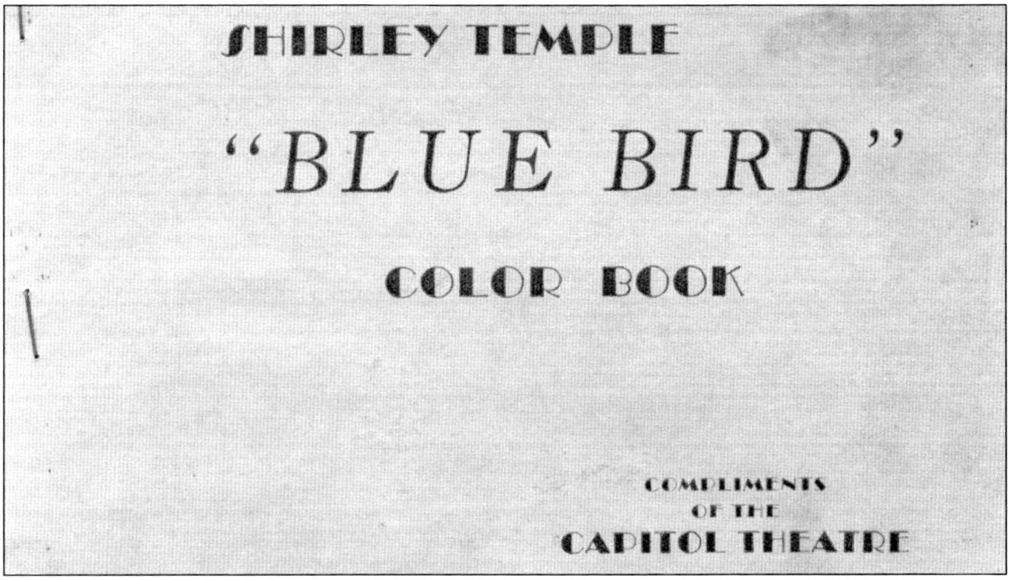

SHIRLEY TEMPLE WAS A STAR WITH PLANT CITY'S CHILDREN. Themes from Shirley Temple movies were featured in a coloring book given out to children visiting the Capitol Theater. The "Blue Bird" of happiness gives everyone a smile on their face and a whistle on their lips. Movies cost 10¢, and the air conditioning was a fan blowing across a 400-pound block of ice. After seeing the movie, local kids stopped off at the soda fountain for a 5¢ strawberry soda.

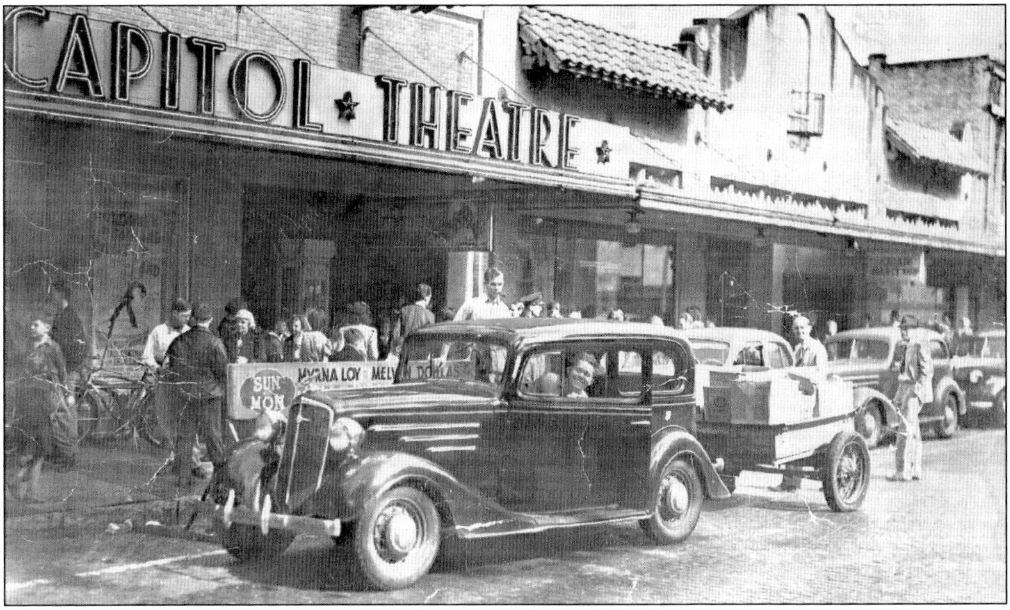

CAPITOL THEATER MOVIE SCREEN FEATURES MYRNA LOY AND MELVIN DOUGLAS. The red-brick carpet was rolled out to welcome movie-goers for the showing of popular movies with the latest from Hollywood. The grand opening was held on Saturday, March 6, 1924. In July 1933, Dr. C.T. Young and M.E. Moody, owners of the Young & Moody Building housing the Capitol Theater, purchased the fixtures of the movie house. The downtown theater served the community until the 1960s. The theater space was converted to retail, and Tatum & Johnson Store, Inc., Plant City Travel, a beauty salon, and a jeweler were located there.

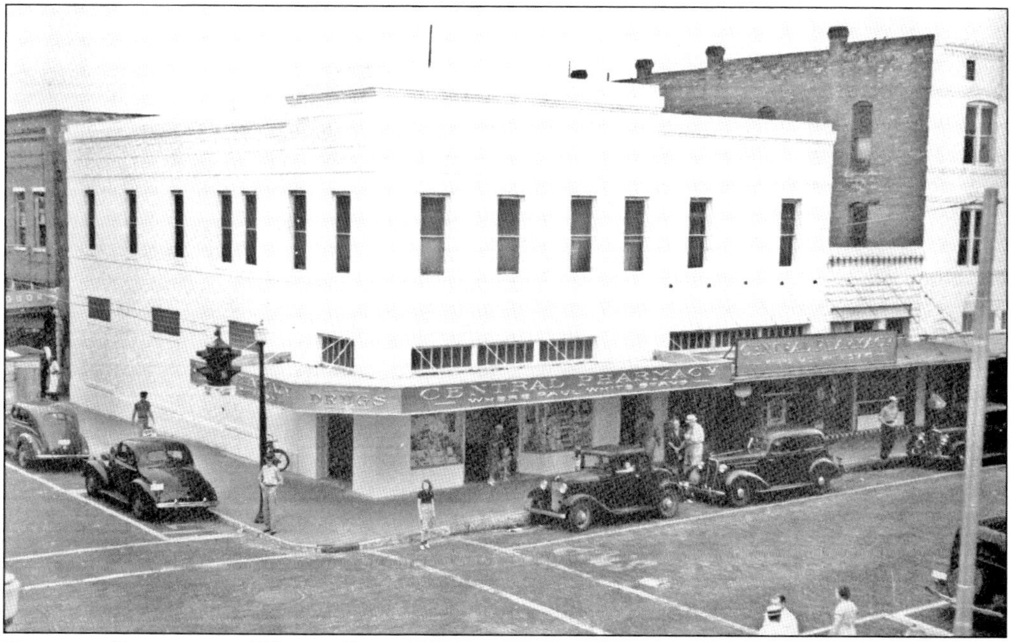

CENTRAL PHARMACY—WHERE PAUL WHITE STAYS. This is a comforting marquee for your pharmacist to post. Always on call for your families' needs, Paul White filled many prescriptions. The upstairs was the location for the Plant City Hospital, which closed when the new South Florida Baptist Hospital opened on December 29, 1953.

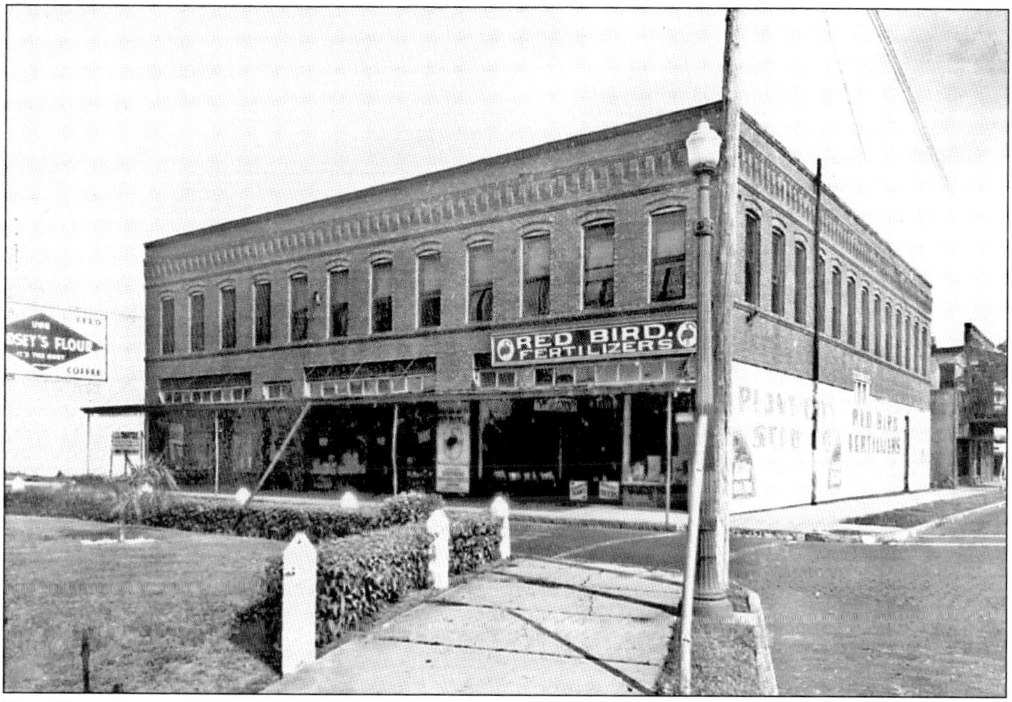

RED BIRD FERTILIZERS. Located at Evers and J. Arden Mays Boulevard, this building has been home to city offices, Plant City Seed Company, Plant City Appliances, and the *Courier*, and is now an antiques shop.

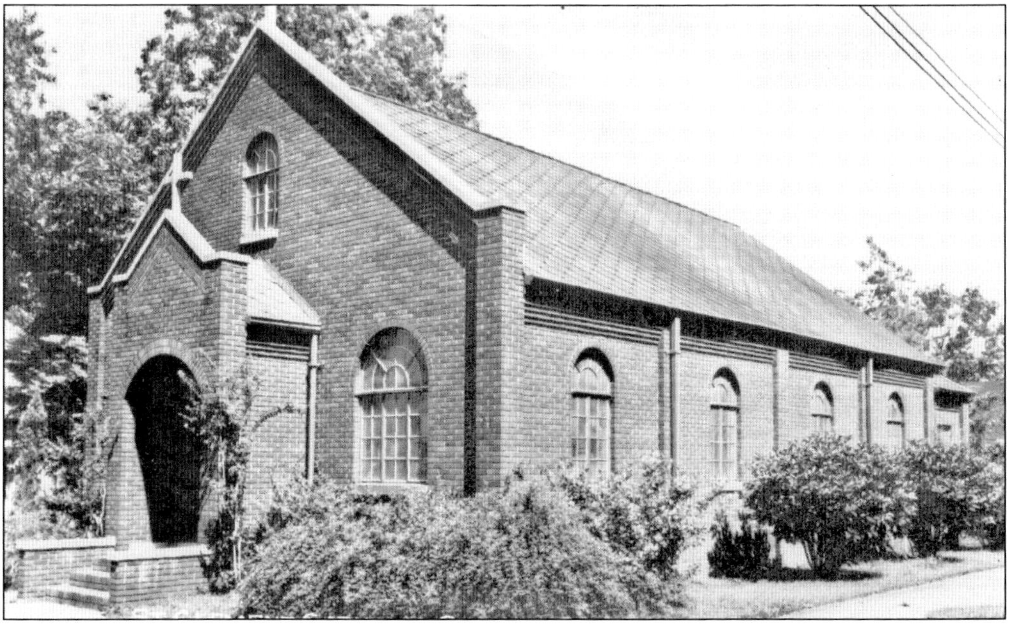

St. Clement Catholic Church, Plant City. Originally called Holy Name of Jesus Mission, this church and its parishioners first met in the West Baker Street home of Mrs. Thomas Surrency. A new church was constructed and mass was celebrated in May 1931. A new fellowship hall was built on Alexander Street in 1976. The stained-glass windows from the 1931 red brick building were moved to the new site. When a new sanctuary was built in the 1990s, the windows were once again moved and placed in their permanent home. Iglesia de Dios Pentecostal Movimiento Internacional now owns the Baker Street property and continues to hold church services in the building.

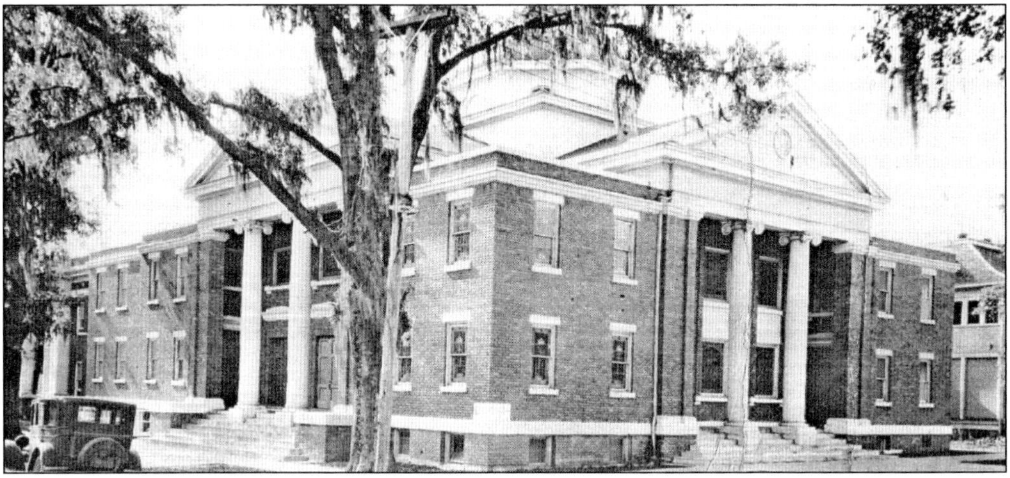

First Baptist Church, Plant City. Completed in the fall of 1923, the building is the cornerstone of the northeastern section of the downtown historic structures. It is a classical revival–style structure and features two colossal porticos that overlook Collins and Baker Streets. An octagonal dome surmounted by lanterns caps the building. The building is owned by the Cornerstone Center, Inc., a non-profit organization dedicated to the preservation of the property. The original stained-glass windows and dome ceiling are elements of design that give the building a unique character.

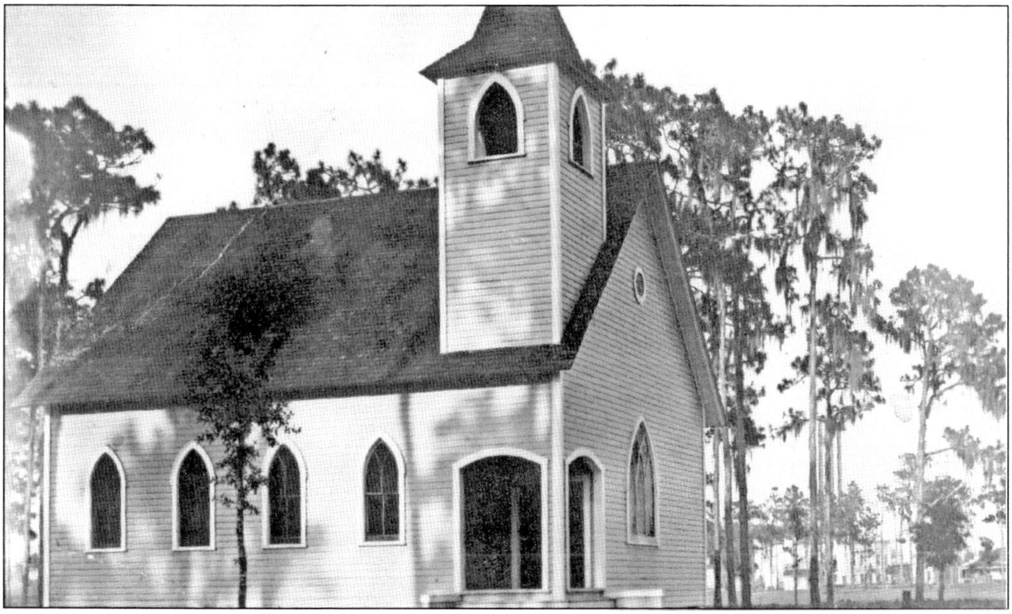

Associated Reformed Presbyterian Church, Coronet, Florida. Located across from the Bungalow, this small church building was built for the employees of the Coronet Phosphate Company. The building was torn down in the 1930s. According to *Coronet: "Life In The Backsquare," A Personal Reminiscence* by Wallace W. Prophet, the pews from the church were salvaged and are in use at the 1912 Methodist Church building at Knights.

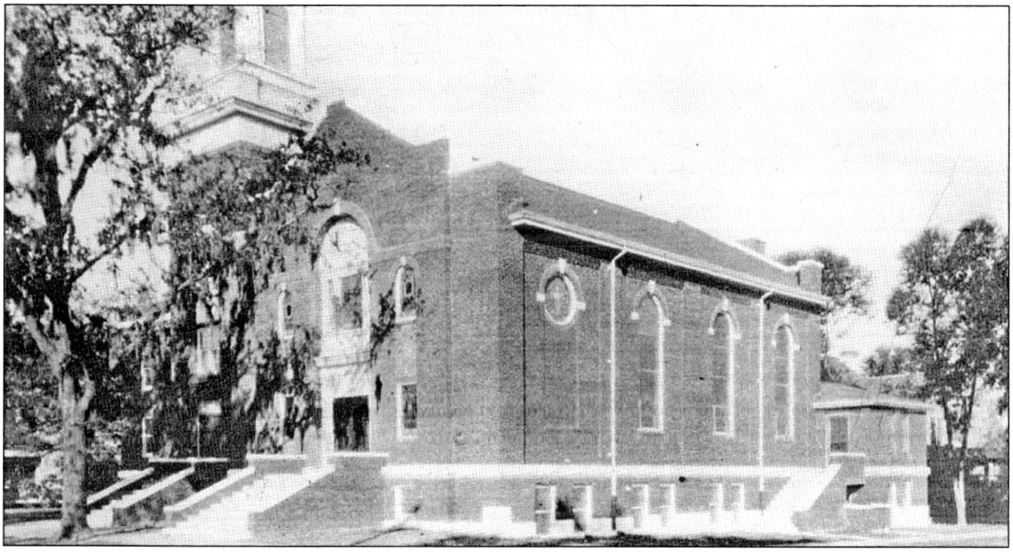

First Presbyterian Church, Plant City. Located on West Reynolds Street, the main structure of the present Romanesque revival–style church was completed in 1925. Costing $65,000 including furnishings, the building was described in the newspapers as a structure of "Colonial and Spanish architecture, made of oriental tapestry brick trimmed with stucco and Tennessee limestone and lined with Georgia red brick and hollow tile." The Manse, the residence of the pastor, was moved from the church property on Reynolds Street to a vacant lot on North Collins Street in the residential historic district and continues to be one of Plant City's finest historic homes.

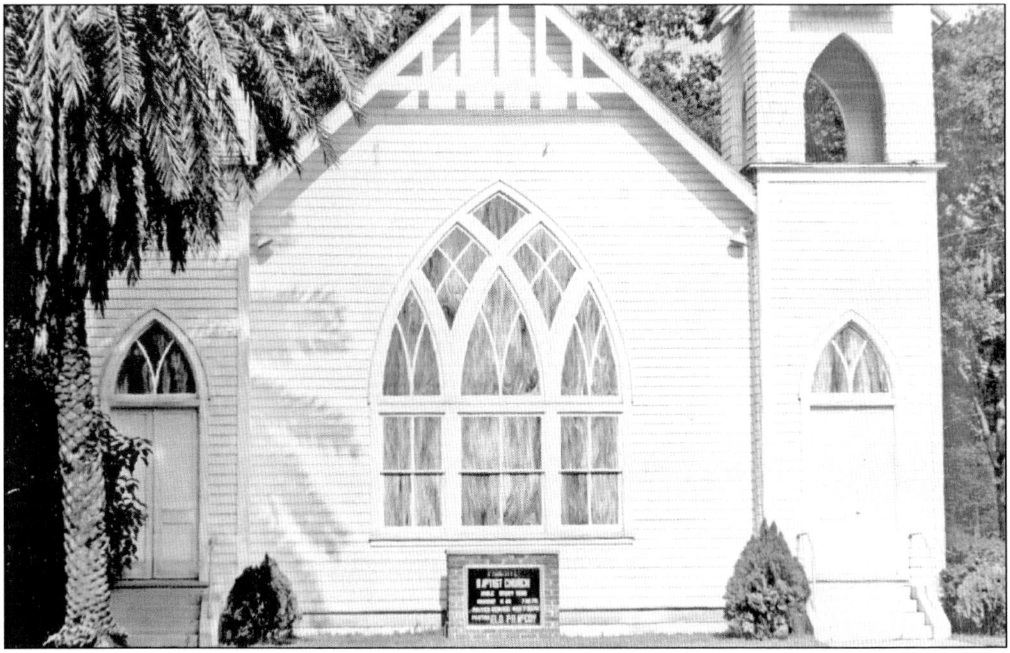

Primitive Baptist Church. Built in 1917, this Gothic vernacular structure is the oldest building still used for religious worship at its original site. Its simple design is of one room with a central aisle and twin steeple towers on the east front. A large, pointed-arch window filled with Gothic tracery and stained glass, along with the two towers, are the main features. The upper portions of the two towers are pierced on all four sides by pointed arches of equal size, unglazed. Small hipped roofs cap the towers. Entrances are located between the base of each, and the arched windows serve as transoms. The sides feature five-pointed arched, stained-glass windows. Primera Iglesia Bautista la Fe holds church services in this historic building.

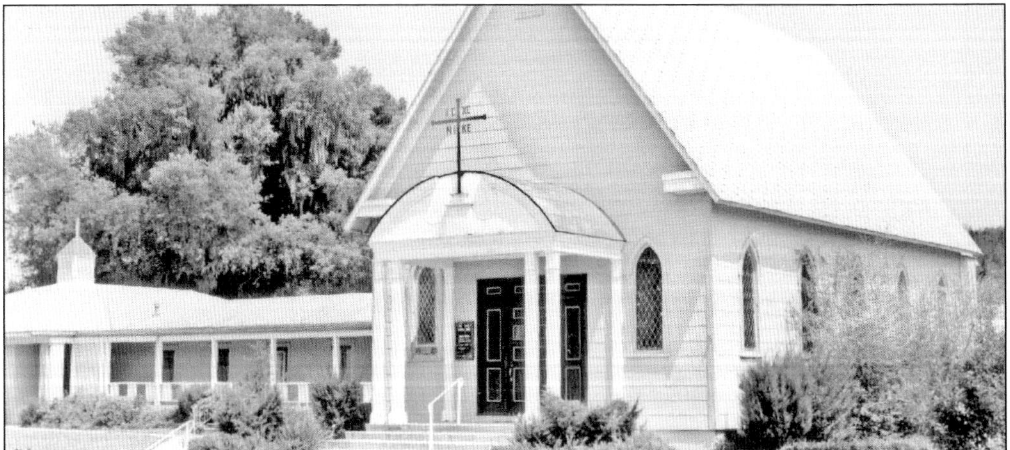

St. Peter's Episcopal Church, Plant City. In 1889, the Episcopal Church purchased property on the southeast corner of Wheeler and Mahoney Streets, which would become the original site of the parish for St. Peter's Episcopal Church of Plant City. The current nave, built on that site in 1908 by builders Krutz and Krutz, was moved to its present location at Mahoney and Carey Streets in 1953. A bell tower and balcony were added and the exterior remodeled to a Gothic revival style of vertical planks of board-and-batten finish in the 1980s.

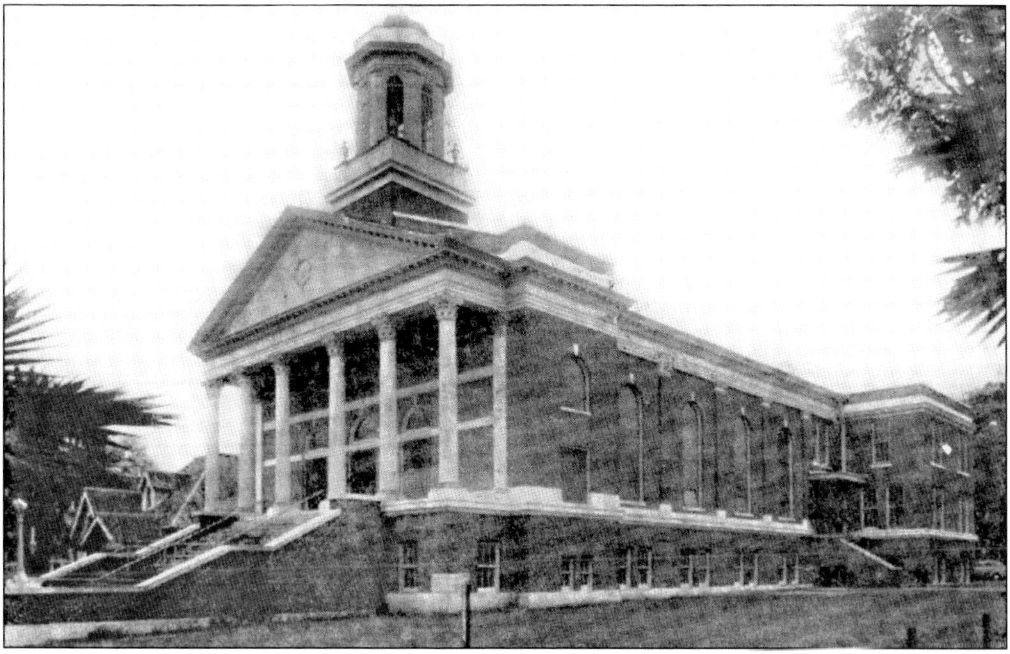

FIRST METHODIST CHURCH, PLANT CITY. The cornerstone for First Methodist Church, built by local contractor Chester C. Carlton, was laid in 1924, but the sanctuary was not completed until 1926. This large, classical revival–style church occupies an entire city block. The front facade of the three story structure includes a five-bay colossal portico with Corinthian columns and a tall octagonal cupola. Many of the stained-glass windows were moved from the 1901 Methodist church building at the corner of Reynolds and Wheeler Streets and were installed in the narthex and sanctuary of the new church. A new pipe organ was purchased for the sanctuary at a cost of $15,000 when construction was completed. Taking two years to complete, the massive structure stood as a symbol of all that is good and pure in the city.

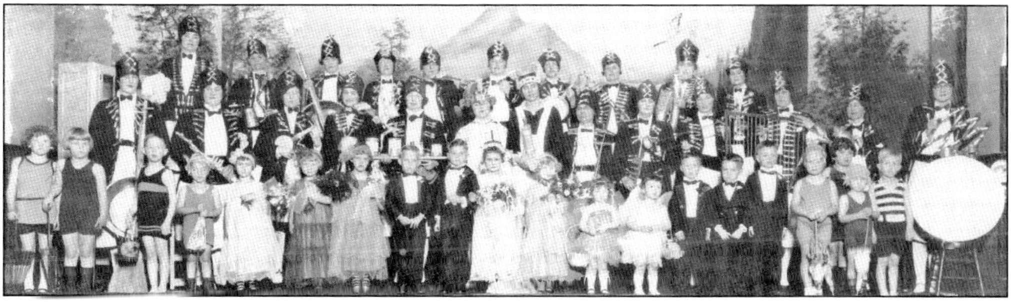

THE BRIDAL PARTY, FIRST METHODIST CHURCH. Included in this photo are bride Catherine Fletcher; groom Burke Lay; bridesmaids Ruth Boring, Edna Ruth Peacock, and Florence Green; best man John Morgan; groomsmen Jimmy Waters, Murrel Bailey, and Harry Carlton; flower girls Grace McRae and Cecille McColpin; Kitchen Band members Sybil Strickland (director), Mary Collins Roux, Mrs. L.C. Hull, Wilma Hague, Inez Friday, Yvette Tardiff, Rhoda Chapman, Jane Forehand (kindergarten teacher), Mrs. Tom Lay, Mrs. J.A. Pearce, Mrs. L.K. Helms, Mrs. H.E. Hayes, Margaret Wilson, Mrs. G.W. Haven (pianist), Mrs. B.H. Sanchez, Mrs. C.B. Root, Mrs. Fredrica Dowling, Mrs. H.S. Moody, Mrs. Bun Tyner, Mrs. Hoyt Chapman, Mrs. Earle Youngblood, Miss Rhoda Chapman, Mrs. Louis Parish, Miss Lucy Cone, Mrs. E.T. Roux (class teacher), Mrs. W.J. Holton (class president), and Mrs. Virgil Murphy (accompanist). (Courtesy of Gene Thompson.)

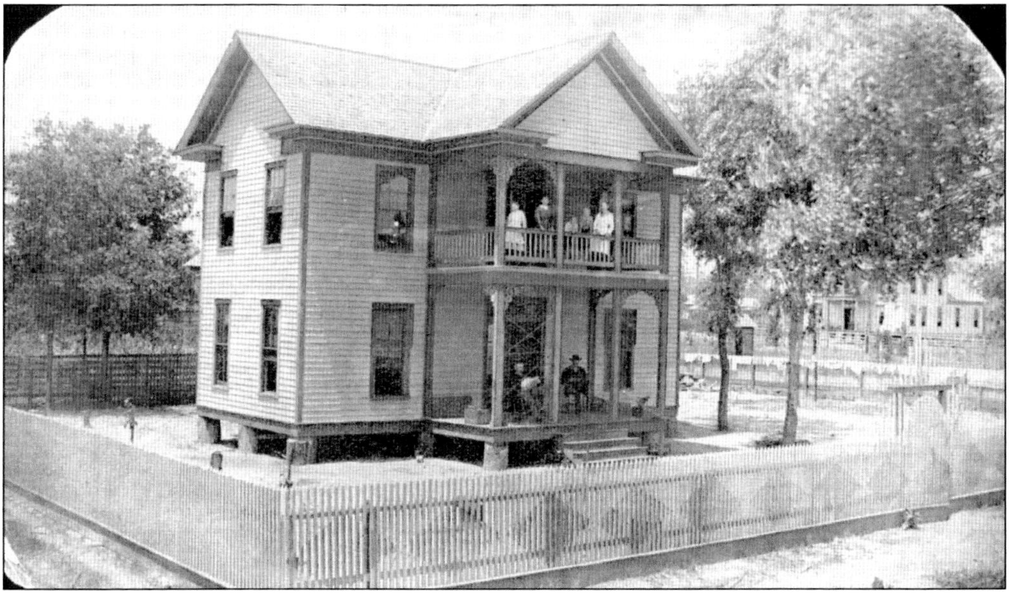

Picket Fences Enclosed Early Homes in Plant City. Good fences make good neighbors. Not only did picket fences make good neighbors, but they also enclosed early homes to keep out hogs and other loose animals that roamed the streets. Pictured is the home of Mrs. James Taylor Evers on Haines Street.

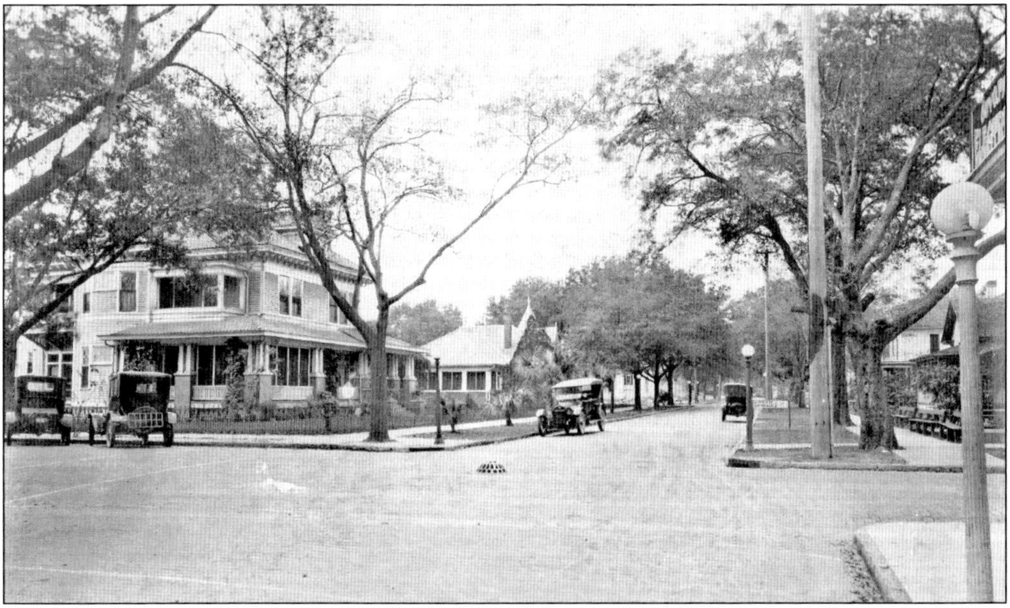

Home of Col. James L. Young, Built 1904. This classic Victorian is of the Colonial revival/ American foursquare style. It was originally built at the corner of South Evers and Reynolds Streets. The home features more than 7,000 square feet of living space in its two and a half stories, including a parlor, formal dining room, family room, breakfast room, kitchen, six bedrooms, three baths, and wrap-around porch. (Courtesy of Leavitt Photo Co., Plant City; established 1921.)

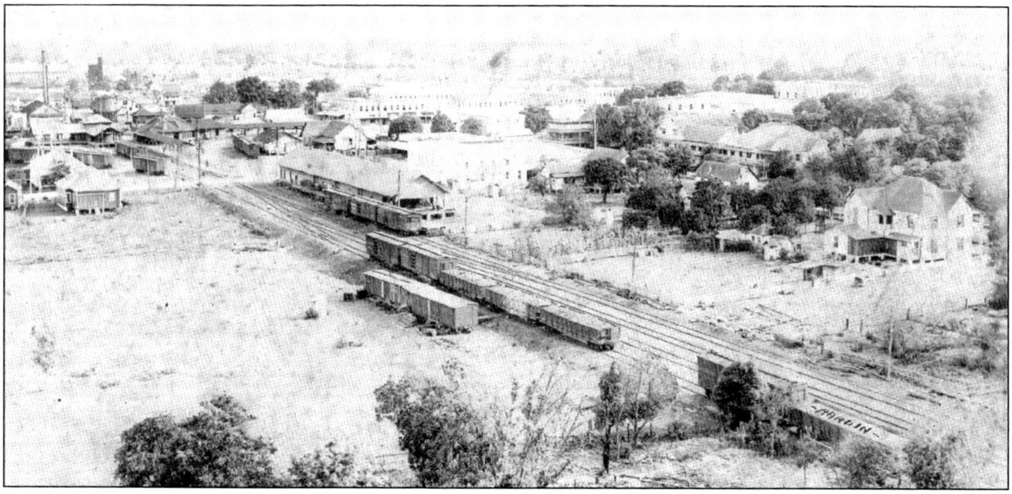

Plant City from the Water Tower. In a view looking southwest across town after 1914 from the town water tower, Warnell Lumber & Veneer Co.'s mills are seen in the left background. Baker Street had not yet been extended east across the tracks. This view clearly defines what was considered to be the limits for the incorporated city.

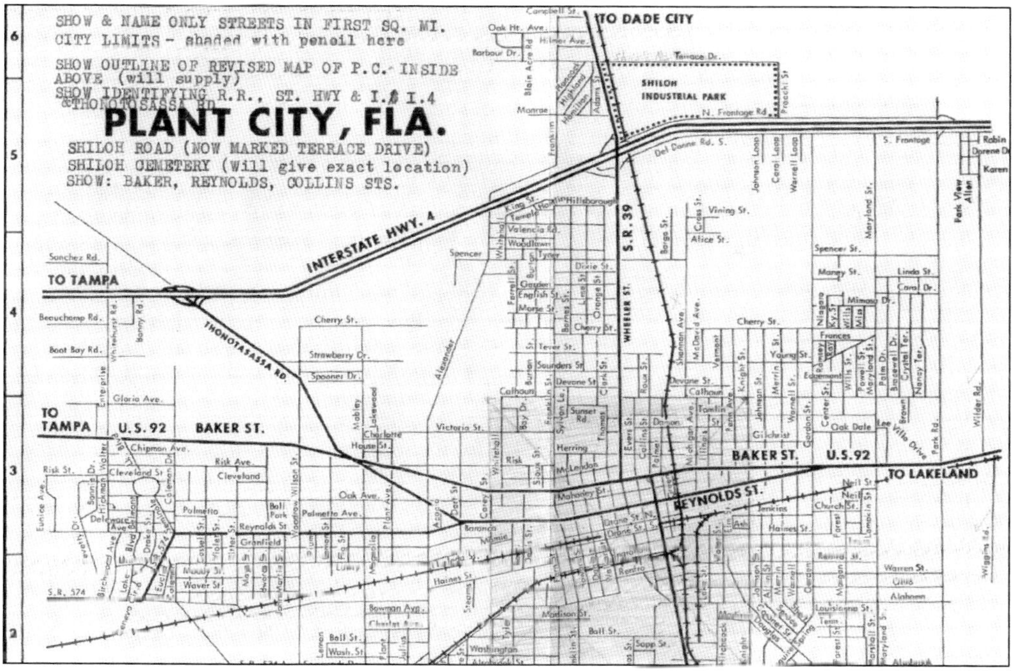

Map of Plant City, Florida. Plant City's community has seen many changes. Interstate Highway 4 borders the north limits of the city. Plant City Airport and Industrial Park, along with the Shiloh Industrial Park, serves the industry sectors. Plant City is a town built around the railroads, which control the downtown traffic patterns. Even though Plant City is no longer serviced by passenger rail, the rail line that brings materials and goods is busy throughout the day and night. The coal train serves the Lakeland Power Company, the Tropicana train travels with orange and other juice concentrates, and car carrier units travel from the Port of Tampa to destinations throughout the state and the Southeast. Always be prepared for a stop at the railroad crossing!

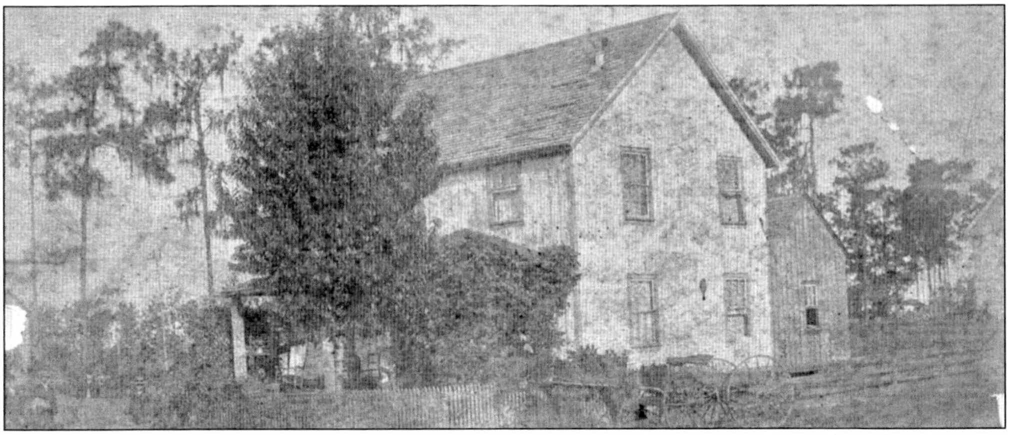

Home of George W. Wells, Haines Street, c. 1894. Considered to be on the edge of town, this was the wooden, two-story home of George W. Wells, town clerk in 1887. A horse and buggy is parked at the fence edge. Mr. Wells was one of the more prosperous businessmen in the community. His active leadership in the community led to a firm foundation upon which Plant City has continued to build. (Courtesy of W.J. Wells.)

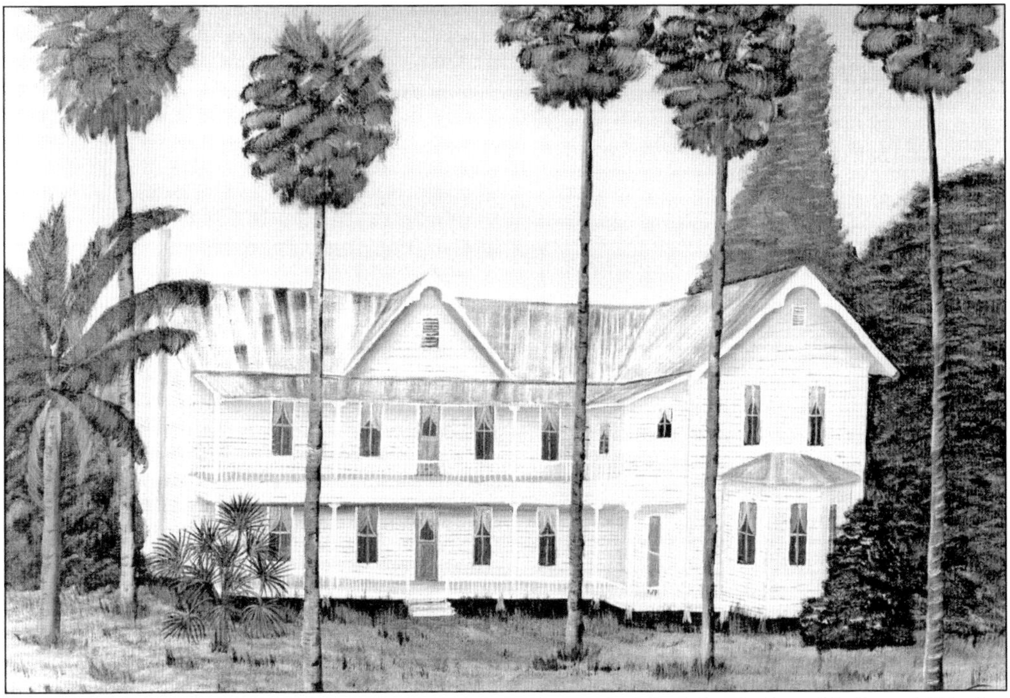

McDonald Homestead, Hopewell, Florida. Built in 1903 by John Robert McDonald II, this two-story, wood-frame house is a fine example of early 20th-century picturesque vernacular architectural style. It borrows from Queen Anne and other Victorian influences and demonstrates a sense of elegance in a rural setting and a presence of aesthetic values. The double-tiered gallery is richly detailed with turned posts and balustrade brackets and a decorative barge board on the end gable. The McDonald family, led by John Robert McDonald, arrived in the Hopewell area (then known as Callsville) in 1870 from Morgan County, Alabama. He gave two acres of his land for use as the site of the Hopewell Baptist Church in 1886. His son, Walter "Preacher" McDonald, served as pastor for more than 50 years. (Courtesy of Jack Gibbs.)

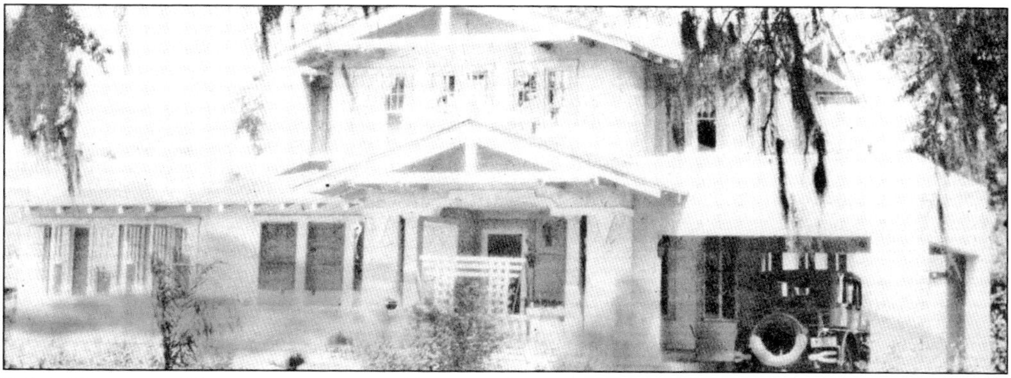

R.M. Fletcher Home, located on Palmer Street. This stucco, two-story home was built by local contractor R.M. Fletcher for his family home. The property was purchased by the First Baptist Church for expansion, and the home was moved to North Merrin Street. Although the porte cochere was not restructured with the move and restoration, the front porch remains a prominent feature of the home. Having been moved to another of Plant City's older neighborhoods with brick streets, the home continues to offer a feel of historic character.

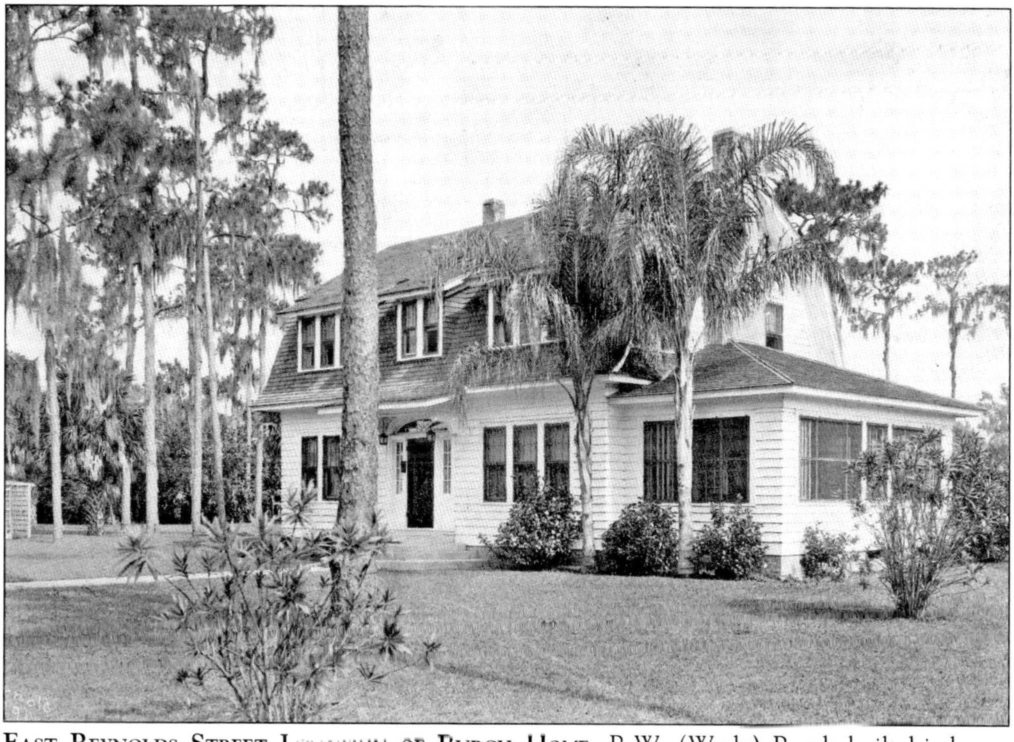

East Reynolds Street Location of Burch Home. R.W. (Wade) Burch built his home in 1922 on East Reynolds Street. Later, Dr. J. Edgar Austin's family made their home in the spacious two-story Colonial home surrounded by well-groomed grounds amidst whispering pines and flowering azaleas. The home became the center for many social events. Guests admired the massive second-floor bedroom that stretched across the front of the house; they chatted in the big living room and sun porch and dined by candlelight in the formal dining room. Sitting vacant for a time, the home was purchased and relocated in 1972 to North Knight Street. Situated on a large lot with draping oaks and a serene and peaceful landscaped setting, the home still has all its original historic charm. (Courtesy of Eloise Austin Cameron.)

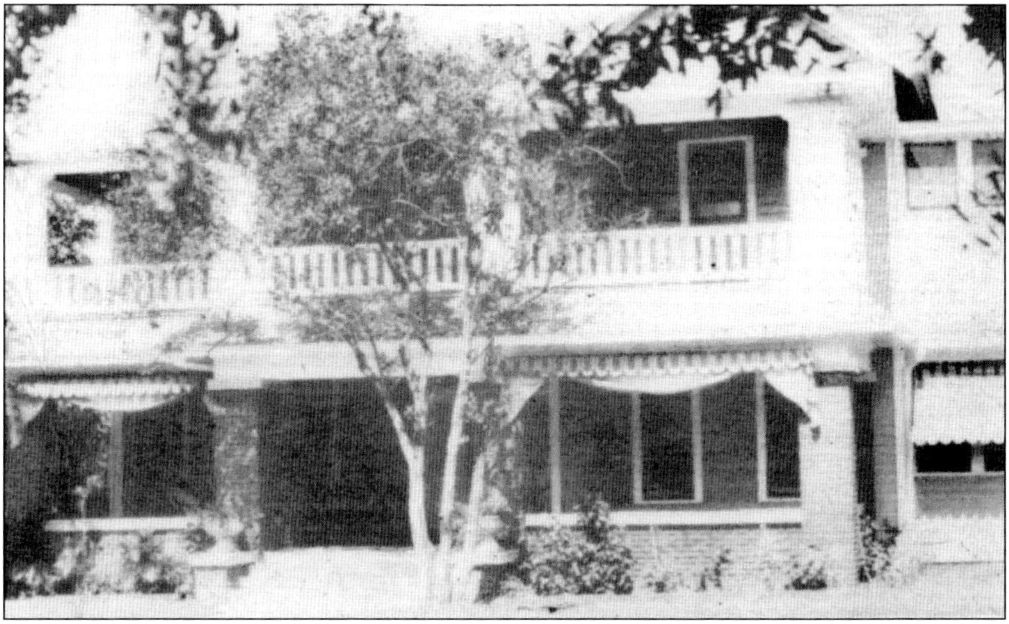

W.B. Herring Home, North Evers Street. Early Plant City had a generous share of substantial homes. Ever since the founding of Plant City as a small village, there has been the predominant desire of its people to build good homes and to build them well. No expenses were spared with the construction of Plant City's early homes. All the modern conveniences were installed. The downtown homes were within an easy walk of shopping and business matters. Attending church on Sunday morning was an easy and relaxing stroll for the entire family. This home was moved from a Baker Street location to it North Evers Street site. It has since been demolished.

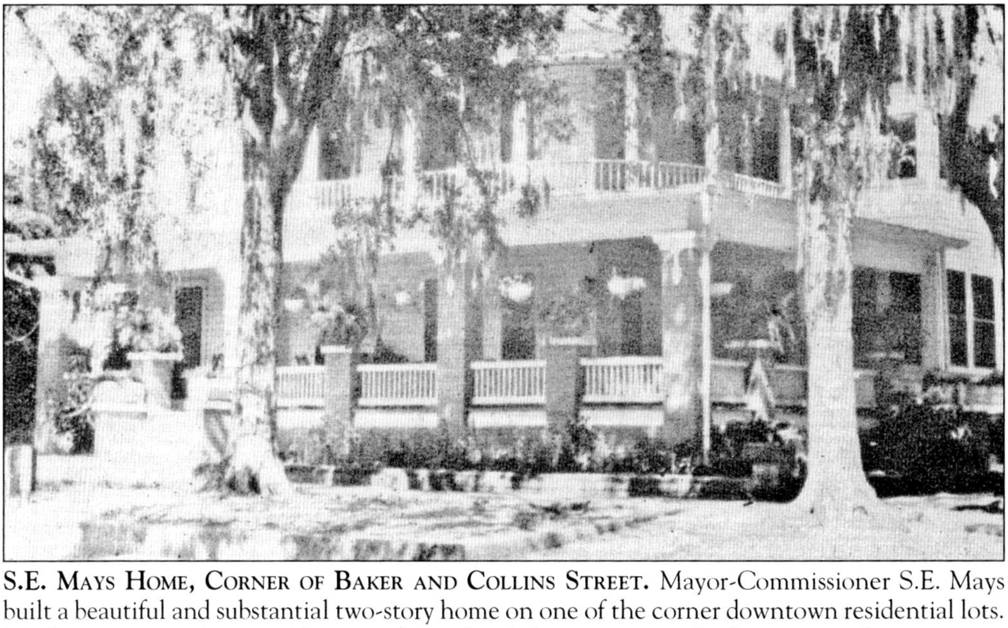

S.E. Mays Home, Corner of Baker and Collins Street. Mayor-Commissioner S.E. Mays built a beautiful and substantial two-story home on one of the corner downtown residential lots. The home was a private residence and rental unit for many years. Its large square footage seems a bit overwhelming for a family residence.

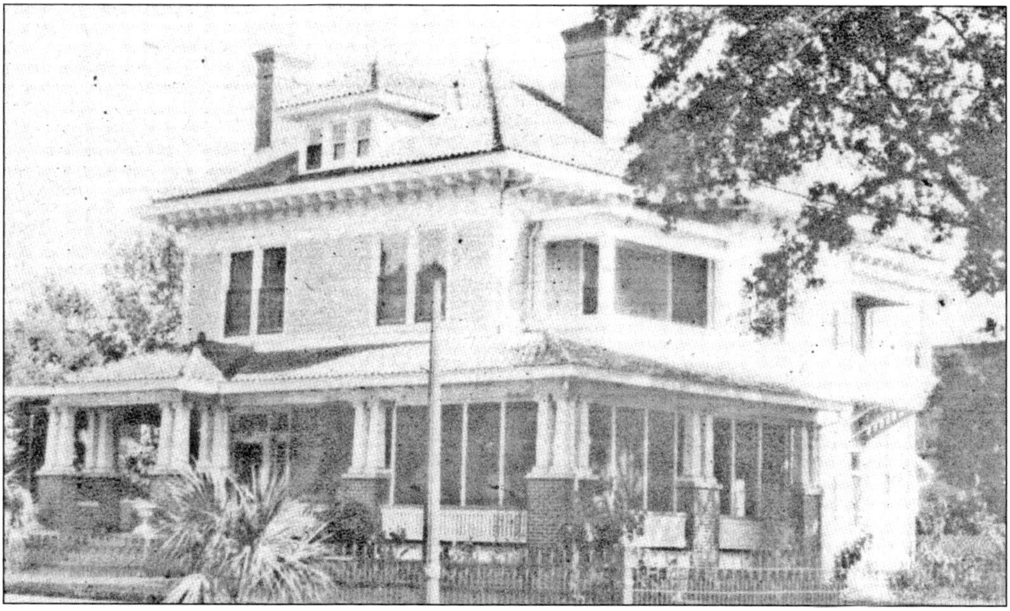

Young Home, Moved to West Baker Street. The expansion of the business section of the downtown area created a need for vacant lots. The large Victorian home of Colonel Young was relocated to West Baker Street in the 1950s. The house was split in two and transported by truck. The second-story sleeping porch has been removed, but other details remain. The home is included in the Downtown Plant City Residential Historic District.

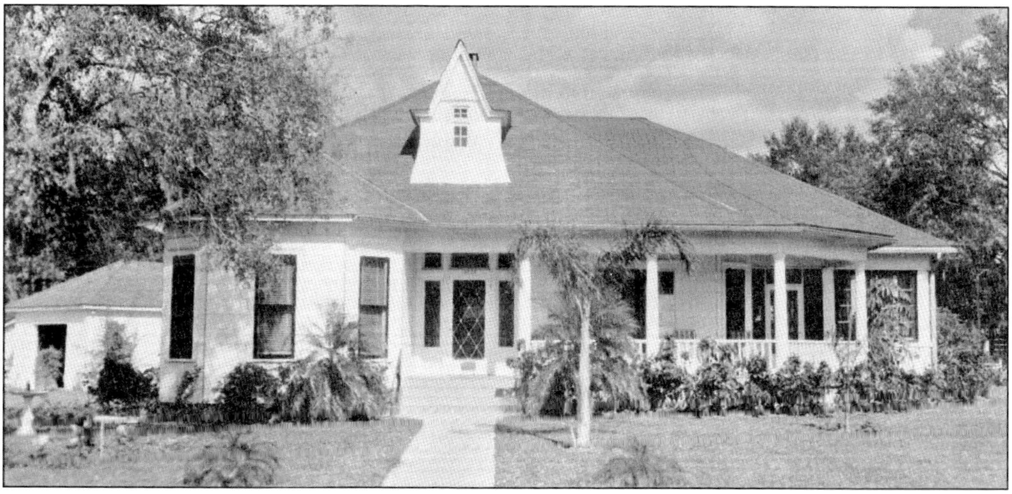

New Location for the Home of Albert and Annie Hammerly Schneider at Gilchrist and Merrin Streets. The newlywed couple moved into their just-finished home at Reynolds and Wheeler Streets in 1902. A narrow wooden sidewalk led up to the elegant Queen Anne cottage that Schneider had built for his bride. The Schneiders, who had one of the first victrolas in town, opened their home for townspeople to enjoy Victrola musicales and concerts. Sometimes attended by as many as 75 people, the events included someone giving a brief biographical sketch of the composer and the performing artists before the group listened to the recording. The sun-porch wicker furnishings were a gift to Mrs. Schneider from Albert for one of their early anniversaries. The home remains a fine example of Queen Anne–style architecture. (Courtesy of Bill Friend's Studio.)

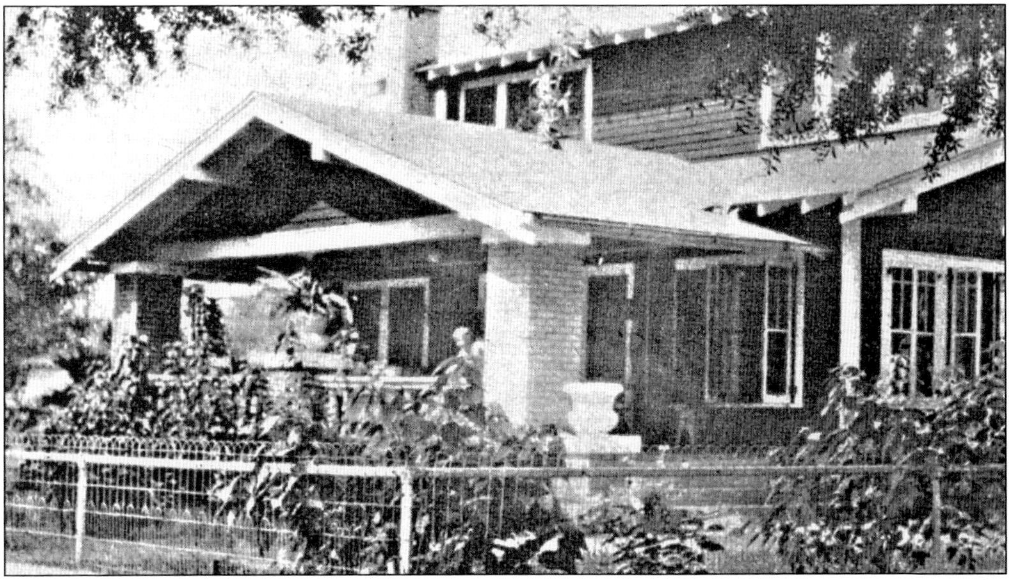

HOME OF J.W. BOOTH, WEST BAKER STREET. Built in 1921 by J.W. Booth, owner of the Plant City Machine and Iron Works, this Craftsman bungalow home has three bedrooms and two baths and was built for $3,500. Defining elements include the low pitched, intersecting gables, a recessed side-facing gable, exposed rafter ends, and the original metal shingle roof. The substantial feeling of this bungalow is supported by its roof braces and wide, square brick piers. The green-colored heart cypress wood siding is stained, as was traditional with bungalows of this period.

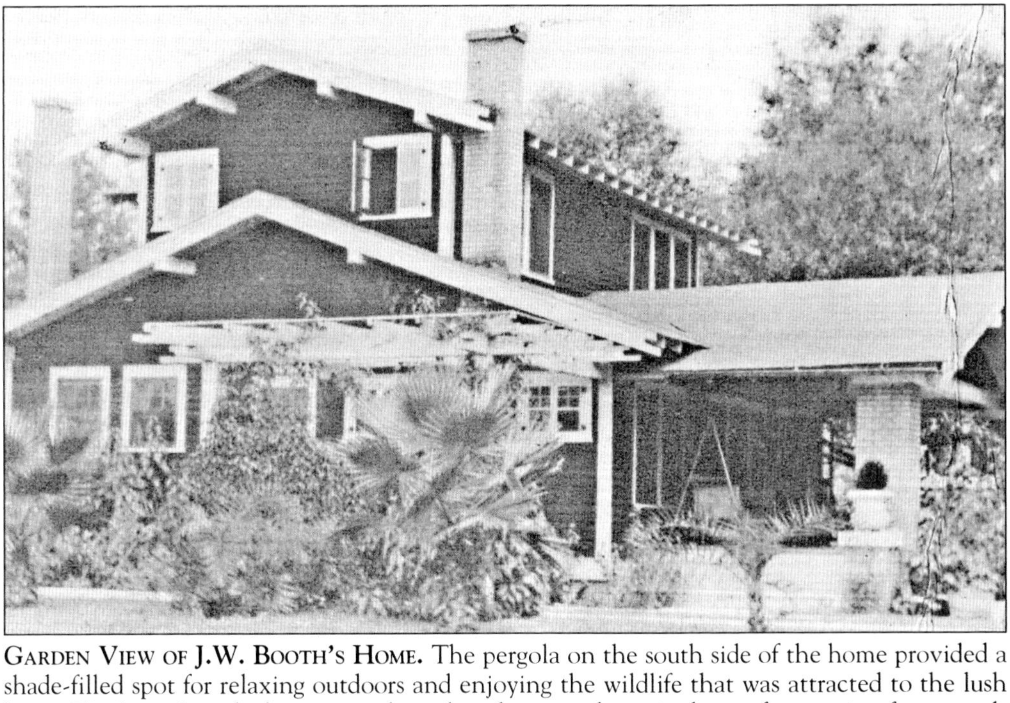

GARDEN VIEW OF J.W. BOOTH'S HOME. The pergola on the south side of the home provided a shade-filled spot for relaxing outdoors and enjoying the wildlife that was attracted to the lush lawn. The home's wide front veranda with a deep overhang is the perfect setting for a porch swing. The welded wire fence is part of the original landscape.

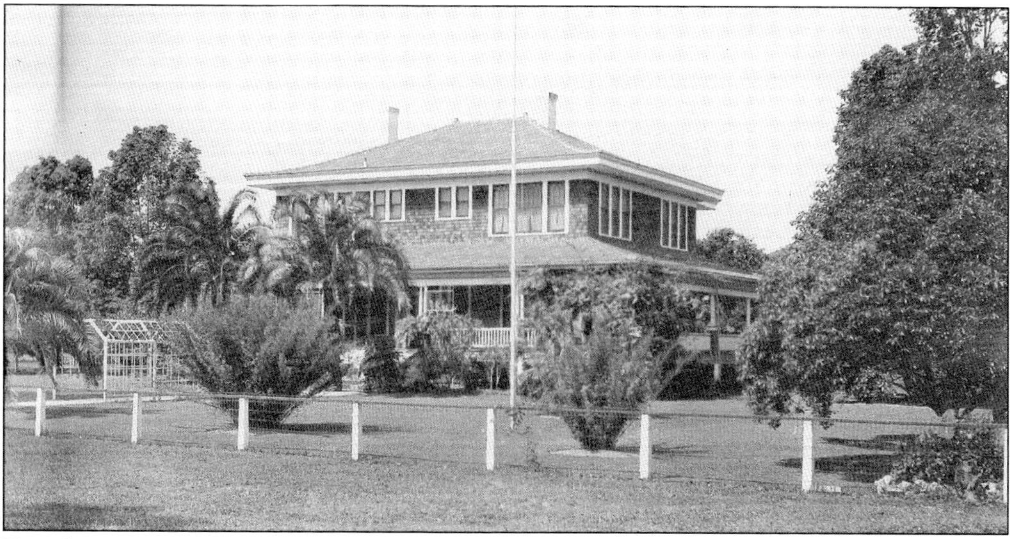

THE CORONET BUNGALOW, CORONET, FLORIDA. Built in the early 1900s, the Bungalow was first used as a residence for the mine operator. A second story was added in 1916, and the building was used as a temporary home for visiting executives to the Coronet Phosphate Co. The 4,000-square-foot building, with more than a dozen rooms, contains six bathrooms and five fireplaces, a double stairway, and a large veranda that has been converted to a private residence. Bells were in each room to call the servants, who lived in three small homes on the estate.

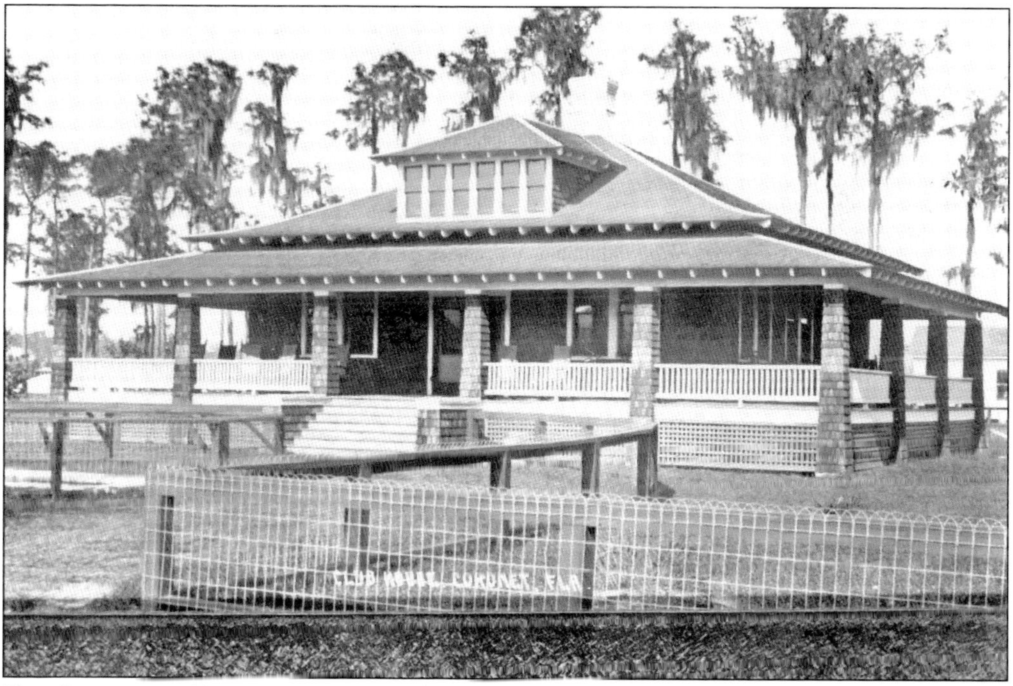

THE CLUBHOUSE, CORONET, FLORIDA. The company built and maintained a delightful clubhouse for the use of its employees. The club was the social center of the community. All kinds of entertainments—meetings, dances, socials, ice cream festivals, and bazaars—took place in the clubhouse. The main room has a big fireplace, a piano, and big easy chairs. A well-furnished library is available for study.

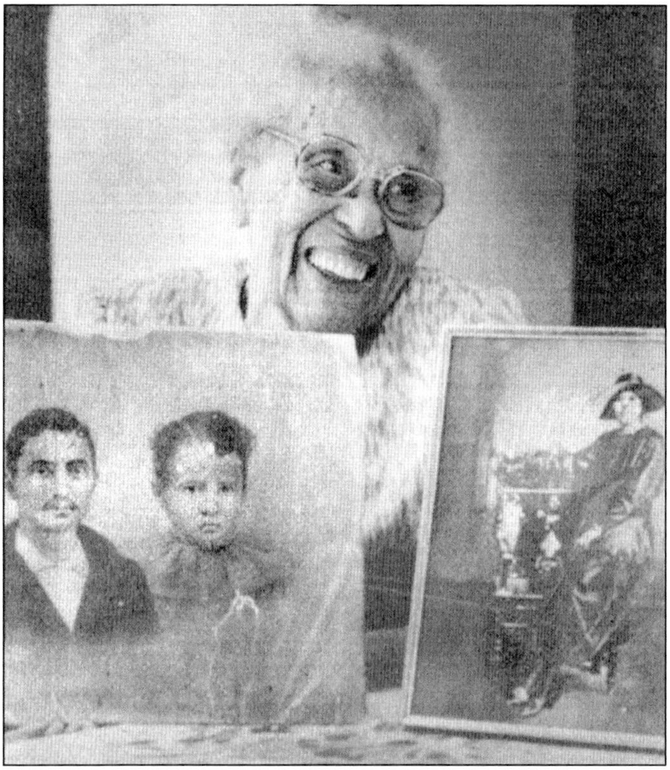

The Bing Family. Mrs. Janie Wheeler Bing operated the Bing-Washington House in the Lincoln Park section of Plant City during segregation, when African Americans were not allowed to stay at white hotels or eat at white establishments. The house served visitors and local residents until 1975. James Washington, grandson of Mrs. Bing, and the Improvement League of Plant City, Inc., have formed a partnership to restore the property and create a museum depicting the area's African-American heritage of the early 1900s. The Bing-Washington House, a local landmark in Plant City, is individually listed on the National Register of Historic Places.

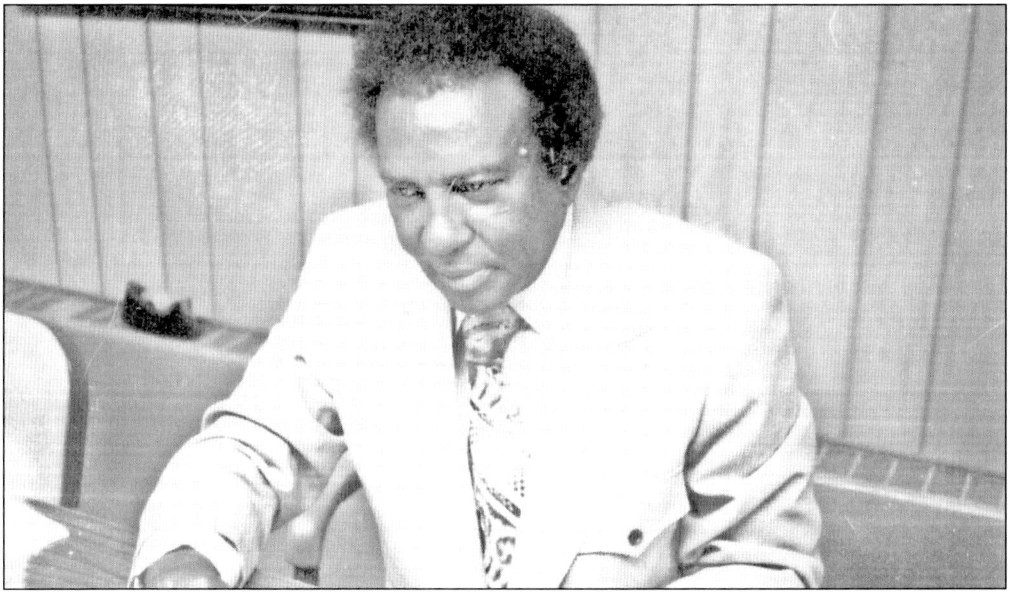

E.L. Bing of Plant City—Outstanding Educator and Community Member. Mr. Bing was born in Plant City and attended Lincoln School. He was principal of Marshall High School from June 1954 until 1967, when he was made director of federal projects. His successful plans for the county's busing program, in connection with desegregation, became a forerunner for the nation. He served as an advisory member of the Florida Desegregation Center, University of Miami.

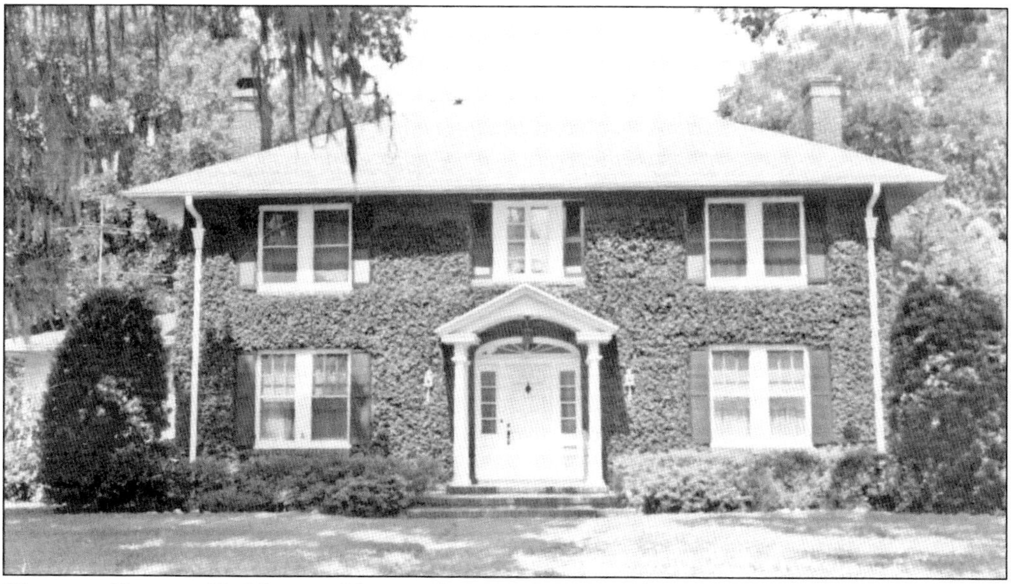

Home of Thomas E. Moody, North Collins Street. The Moody home, built c. 1924, is of the formal Georgian revival style. This red brick residence has a pedimented portico with Doric columns and a distinctive entry with a fanlight and sidelights. The south side of the house features a solarium typical of that period. The home was built by local craftsman Chester Carlton at a cost of between $12,000 and $13,000. Thomas Edwin Moody Jr. came to Plant City in 1901 and married Anna Herron. They had four children. Mr. Moody organized the Moody and Moody Insurance Company in 1903 and became president of the Hillsboro Bank in 1945, remaining in that position until his death in 1948.

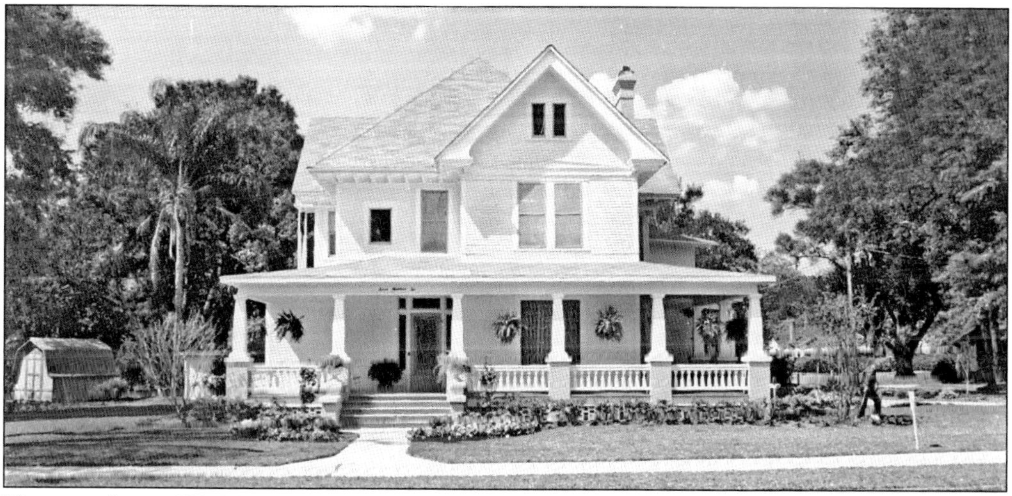

Home of James W. Meldrim, West Reynolds Street. In 1913, local lumber magnate James Wynn Meldrim instructed builder J.P. Moser to spare no expense with the architectural details. The Queen Anne–style home includes influences of the Colonial revival style. The wrap-around veranda features tapered square wood columns atop brick piers and turned balusters, and it conveyed the warmth and hospitality of the "Old South." Stained glass and marble and architectural millwork have been restored and retained with recent renovations to the home. An original carriage house for the family's buggy was located to the rear of the property.

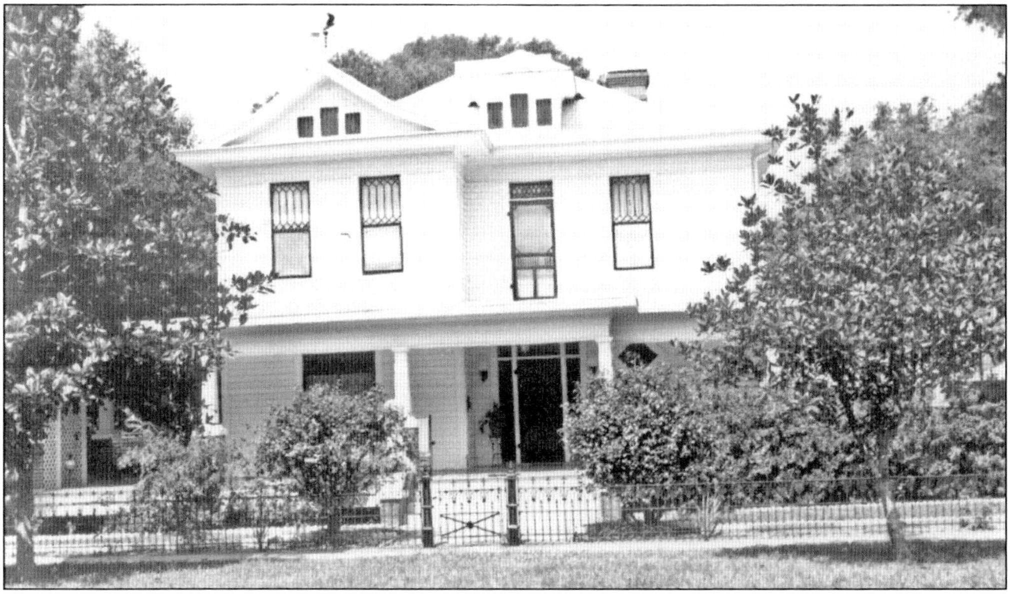

Home of John Chapman, North Collins Street. This two-story house, built in 1910, is one of the largest and most impressive historic residences in Plant City. Displaying a blending of Victorian and Colonial revival elements, its original cost was $4,500. The house has a hipped roof, which contributes a decorative effect along with decorative and stained-glass windows. A 10-bay veranda wraps the house on three sides. The porch roof is supported with square, wood columns on brick. Mr. Chapman died in January 1911, and his funeral rites were conducted from the parlor of his handsome home. The black wrought-iron fencing is accentuated with the large concrete lions poised on the front steps.

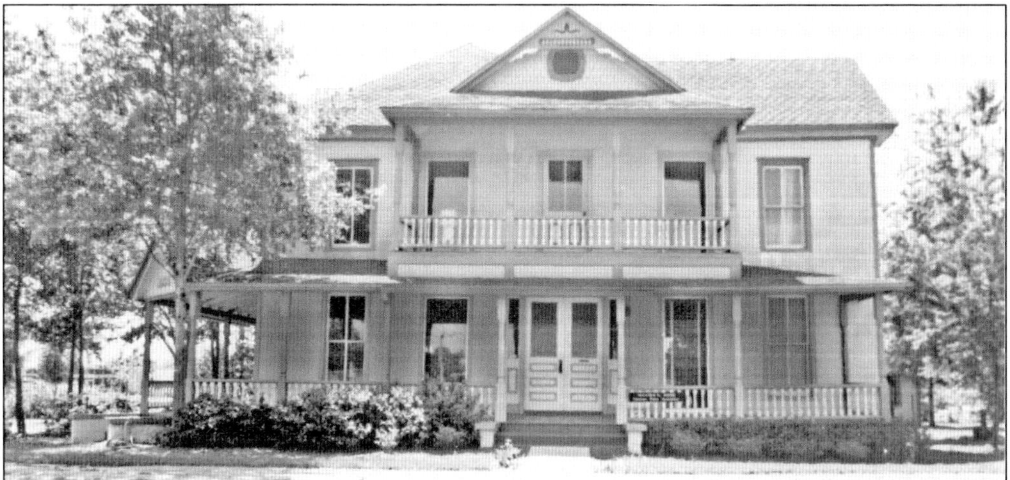

Allen-Lowry Home, South Drane Street. This large, newly constructed Queen Anne–style home was purchased by Mrs. Frances L. Allen when she moved her family to Plant City in 1884. Her daughter Mary Allen and William Lee Lowry, one of Plant City's first mayors, were married in this home in 1889. Mary was a charter member of the First Presbyterian Church and the UDC. Before her marriage, she was a teacher in Plant City's first school. Mary and William's daughter, Mary Elizabeth (Madie) Lowry, was the first infant baptized in the First Presbyterian Church in 1892.

Six

FAMILIES

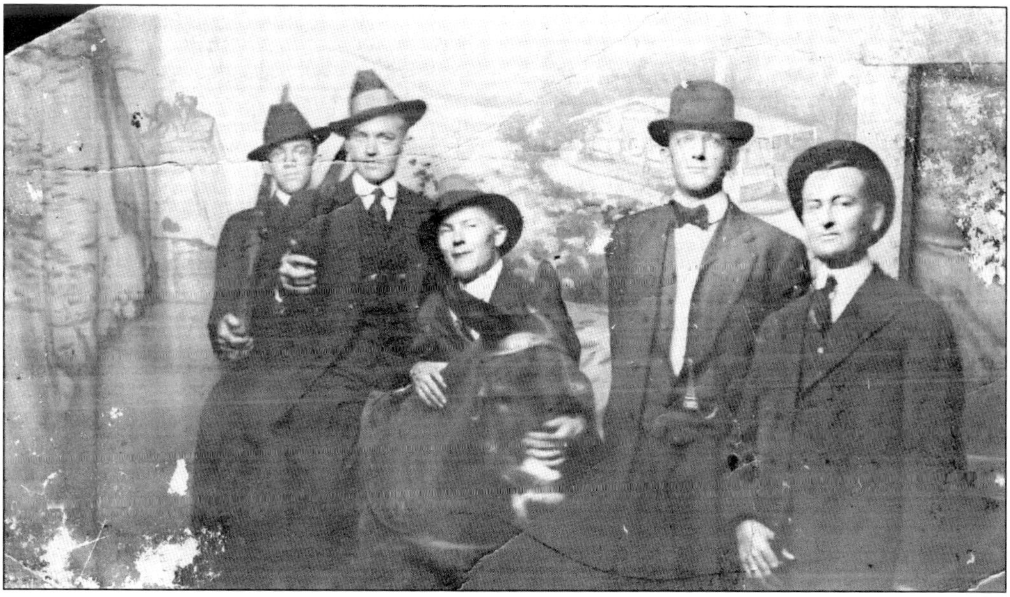

PLANT CITY'S MENFOLK. Pictured from left to right are Jack Youngblood, Bun G. Tyner, Wayland Hill, Earle Youngblood, and Bill Tyner. A donkey is in the middle!

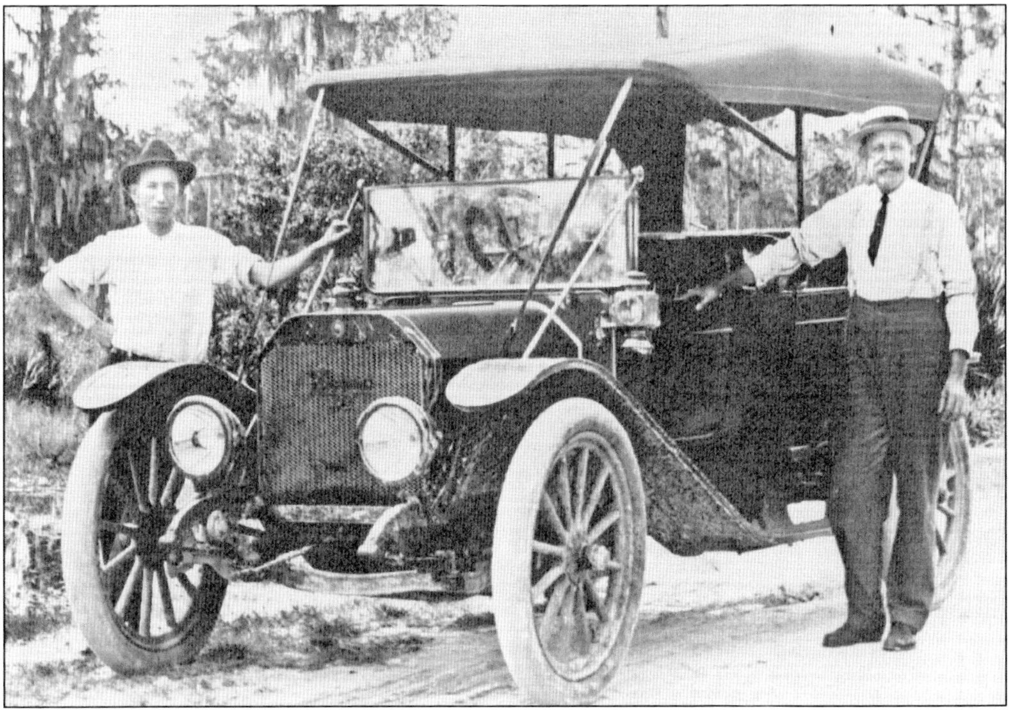

One of Plant City's First Cars. S.E. Mays, right, owned one of Plant City's first cars. The Board of County Commissioners took action in 1913 to provide the funding for paving the county roads with vitrified brick. It was determined that properly laid, vitrified brick was the best and, in the end, the cheapest material the county could use for road paving. Most of the roads were nine feet wide. (Courtesy of City Manager T.J. McCall.)

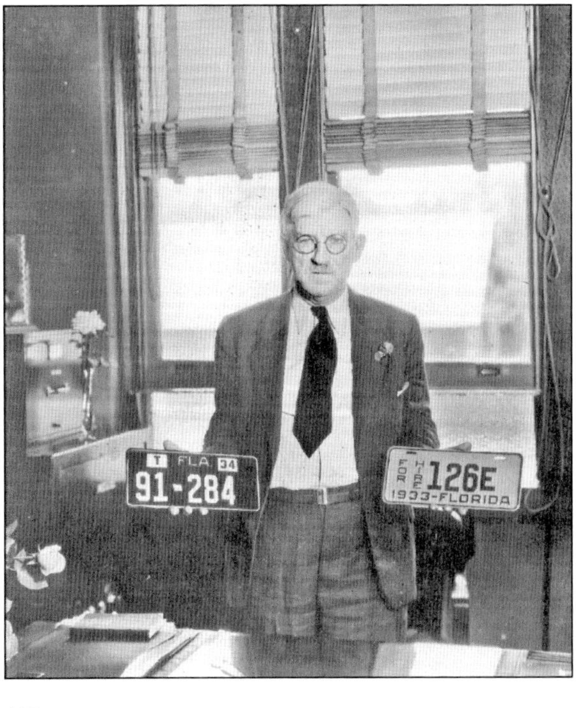

George Hamilton Wilder, 1870–1959. Born on the family homestead on February 22, 1870, in a log cabin, he attended local schools and graduated from Stetson University in Deland, Florida, in 1893. He served as an attaché to the United States Senate in Washington, D.C., from 1894 to 1896, and as the private secretary to Congressman Stephen M. Sparkman for 14 years. He was elected to the Florida State Legislature and served as Speaker of the House from 1918 to 1919. As chairman of the Public Roads and Highways Committee, he played a major role in developing the paved road system in the state and served as state motor vehicle commissioner from 1932 to 1935. An avid outdoors man, Wilder loved deer hunting and kept some of the area's finest dogs.

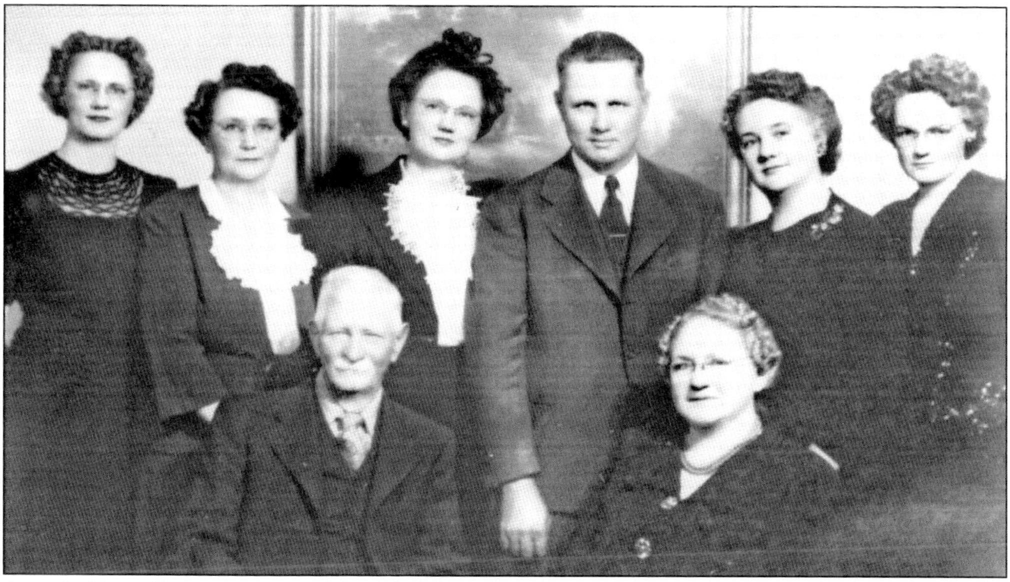

ASH A. ELLIS FAMILY. Pictured from left to right are (front row) Ash and Ola; (back row) Ollie Cunningham, Edna Ackerman, Essie Daniel, Arthur "Roy" T. Ellis Sr., Ida, and Rose. Ashley A. Ellis was the son of Thomas B. and Eliza Wiggins Ellis. Their family farm was located in the Mount Enon community on land homesteaded by Eliza's parents, William M. and Emarintha Wiggins. Members of this pioneer's family still reside on this homesteaded land.

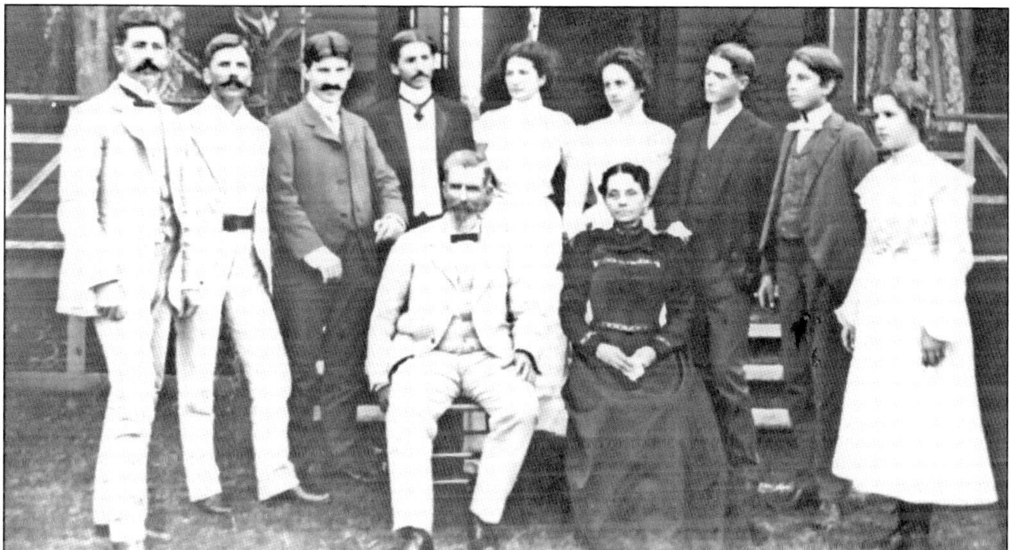

WILDER FAMILY. Pictured from left to right are (front row) Calffrey Lafayette Wilder and Joanna Singletary Wilder; (back row) Frank Badger Wilder, Samuel Henderson Wilder, George Hamilton Wilder, Irvin Hopkins Wilder, Mary Wilder (Mrs. Ed Wiggins), Mrs. Maggie Wilder Taylor, Calffrey Dana Wilder, Carney Lafayette Wilder, and Mrs. Maude Wilder Williams. Calffrey Lafayette Wilder, born in Lowndes County, Georgia, on April 18, 1843, and Joanna D. Singletary, born on July 4, 1848, were married on October 5, 1865. A Missionary Baptist, he was killed by lightning while driving cattle near his homestead on August 3, 1911. Calffrey L. Wilder was elected to serve in the state legislature for three sessions.

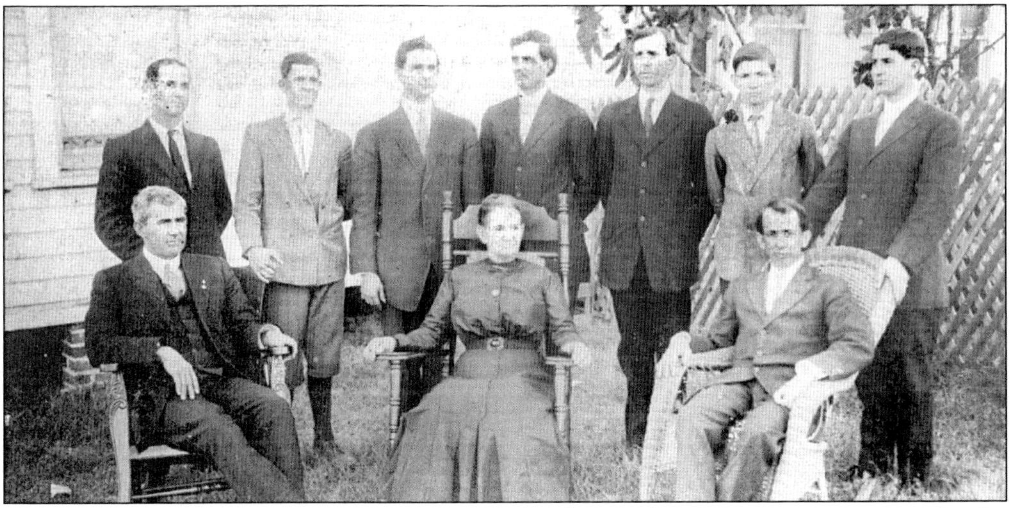

NINE ROBINSON BROTHERS. The nine Robinson brothers took a few moments to pause for the photographer with their mother, Martha Ann Roberts Robinson, wife of Daniel Frederick Robinson. Daniel moved his family of seven children to Plant City from Pavo, Georgia, in 1884, after trading his land for two wagons and two teams of horses. Six more children were born in Plant City. The nine Robinson brothers formed the first all-family baseball team in Florida. Descendants of Daniel and Martha Ann have contributed to the economic and social development of the Plant City community as educators, farmers, public servants, and merchants.

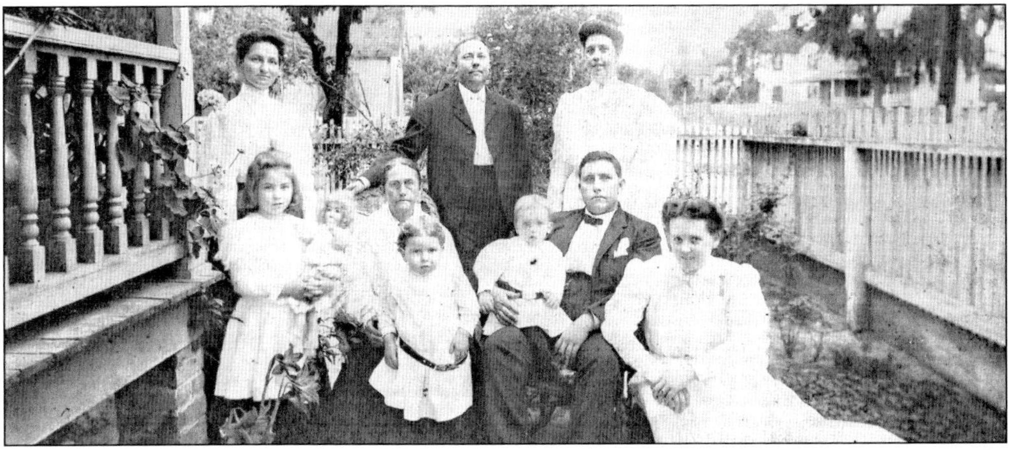

T.M. STRICKLAND FAMILY AT THEIR HOME ON PALMER STREET. Pictured from left to right are (front row) Alice Strickland, Amanda Hodges Strickland, Tommy Strickland, Willie Strickland, Johnny Strickland, and Bessie Gallagher Strickland; (back row) Fredonia Wimbish Strickland, unidentified, and Gertrude Strickland. Thomas Marion Strickland (1864–1925) was born in Homerville, Georgia, coming to Florida in 1874. When he came to Plant City in 1887, he married Fredonia Wimbish and joined in the mercantile business with his brothers. In 1910–1911, he replaced their wooden store with a brick one, which is still located downtown on the corner of Collins Street and North Drane Streets. T.M. Strickland was involved in the organization of two local banks and served on the county board of public instruction. Built in 1897, this family home transitions from Queen Anne to Colonial revival styles. The two-story, frame house was built on an L-shaped plan with clipped gables on each roof section. (Courtesy of New York Photo Co., Geo. Lemire, Mgr.)

Thomas Marion Strickland Jr. He was the son of Thomas Marion Strickland of Homerville, Clinch County, Georgia, and Fredonia Wimbish, who were married in Palmetto, Florida, on February 14, 1895. The Strickland family were early Plant City merchants, leaders of local government,and members of the First United Methodist Church of Plant City.

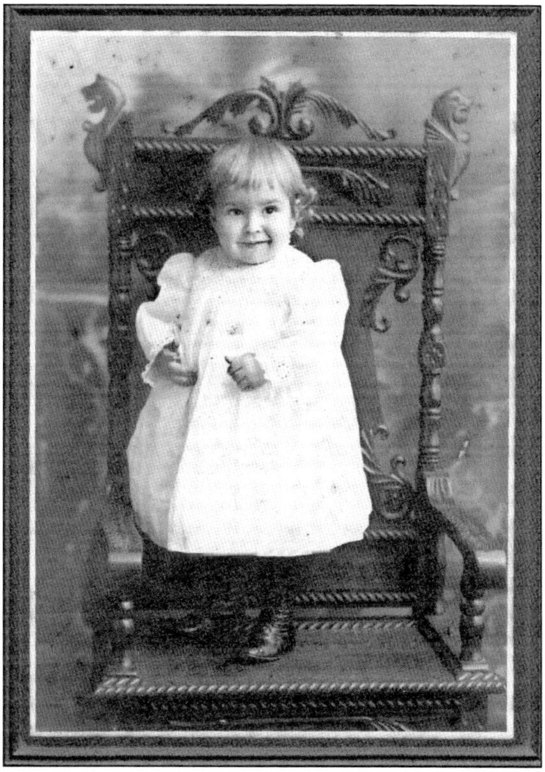

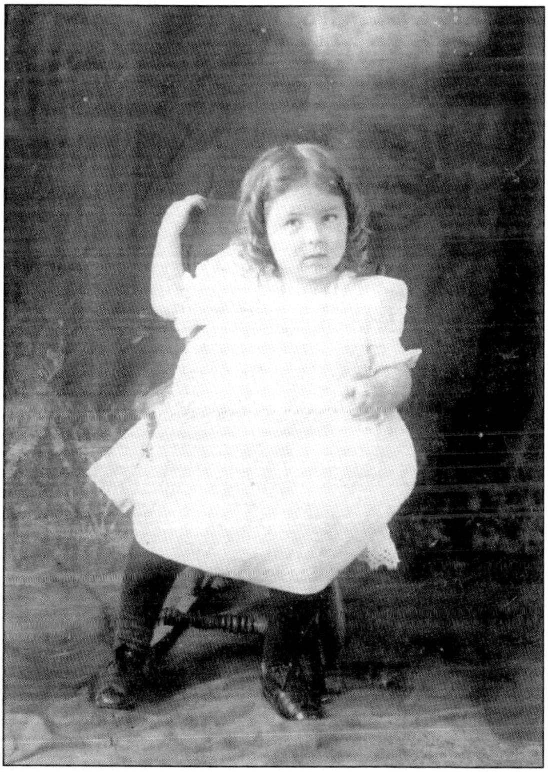

Alice Fredonia Strickland. The daughter of Thomas Marion Strickland and Fredonia Wimbish Strickland, Alice was educated in Plant City schools and was a graduate of the 1914 Plant City High School. She married Howard E. Baughman. She lived in her family home on Herring Street and is well remembered for driving her Volkswagen Bug down Plant City's brick streets.

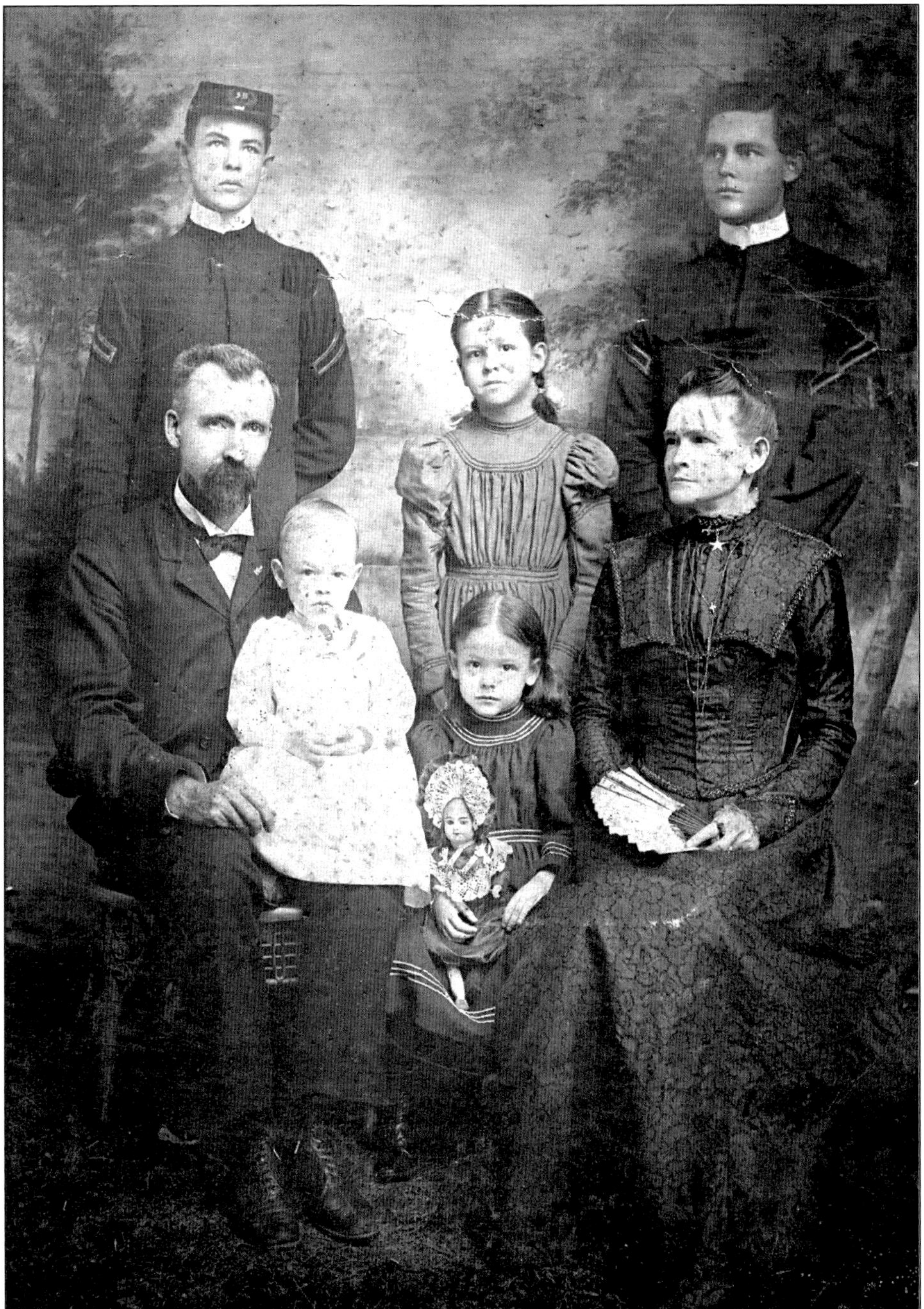

WRIGHT FAMILY. Olin Seymour Wright Sr., M.D., married Palestine Hamilton Collins on September 5, 1888. His lineage can be traced to Revolutionary soldier Silas Wright and to passengers on the *Mayflower*. Pictured from left to right are (front row) Dr. Olin S. Wright, baby Victor, daughter Pallas, and Mrs. Palestine Hamilton Wright; (back row) Vivian Collins, Juno Wright, and Tom Calmes. Vivian Collins and Tom Calmes were Mrs. Wright's sons from previous marriages. Vivian Collins became the adjutant general of Florida and state director of Selective Service.

OLIN S. WRIGHT, M.D. Olin Seymour Wright, for whom the local Masonic lodge was named, was born in Covington, Pennsylvania, on December 1, 1852. He studied medicine at the University of Michigan and received his M.D. from there in 1875. He moved to Florida early in his life and practiced medicine in Manatee County before coming to Plant City. He was made a Mason in Pine Level (now Arcadia) in 1884 and came to Plant City Lodge No. 79 in 1888. He received the Scottish Rite Degrees by communication from the Sovereign Grand Inspector General from 1884 through 1887. Dr. Wright died December 17, 1923, in Plant City and was buried in Oaklawn Cemetery, Plant City, with full Masonic honors. In his memory, in 1925, Plant City Lodge No. 79 changed its name to Olin S. Wright Lodge No. 79. (Courtesy of Juno Wright Coleman.)

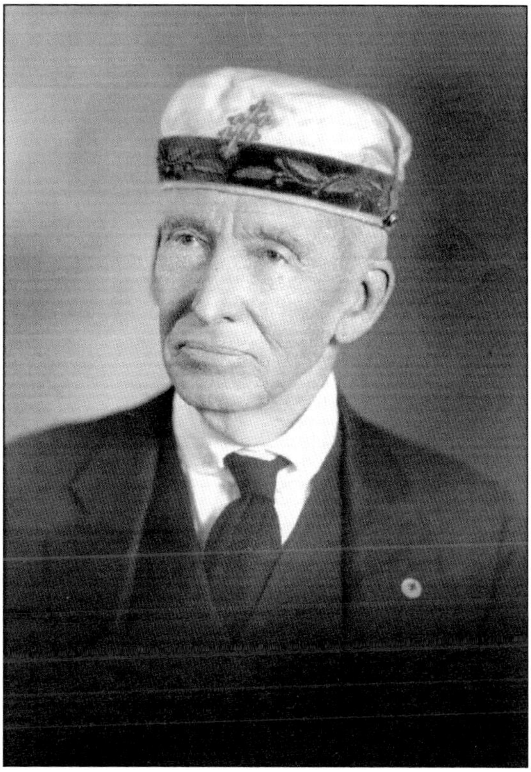

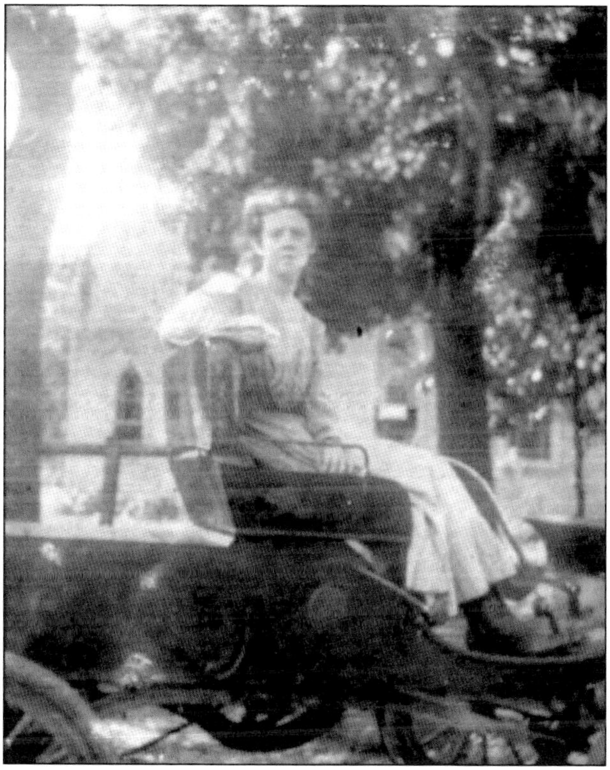

PLANT CITY'S FIRST CAR. Daughter Juno poses in Dr. O.S. Wright's Oldsmobile, Plant City's first car. The only place gas could be bought was at his Magnolia Pharmacy. The original, wooden-structure First Baptist Church is seen in the background.

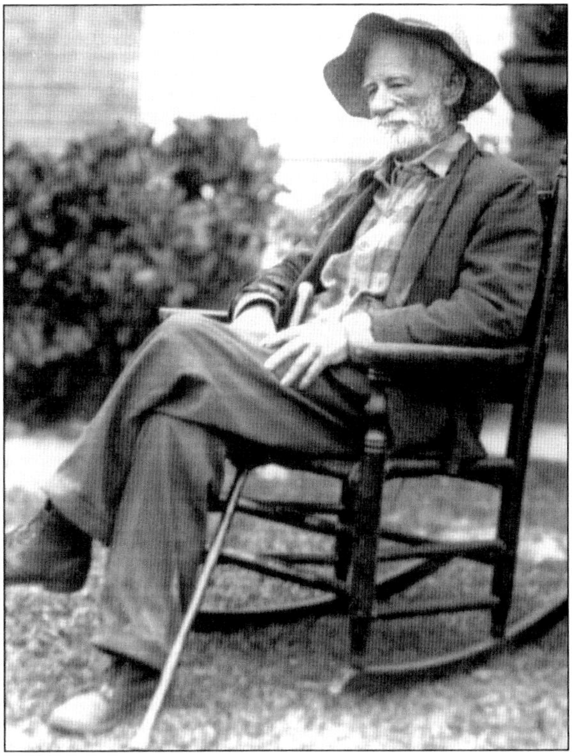

Simeon E. Sparkman. Simeon was born August 9, 1851, the son of pioneer settler Elijah Byrd Sparkman and Sarah Ann Mizell. Simeon was an educator and engaged in farming in the Dover area. He was elected a county tax collector in 1876. His public service record, which spanned some 36 years, included a term in the Florida House of Representatives. Simeon E. Sparkman was married to Mary Hackney of Hillsborough County. They had six children—Lovick Bascom, James Marvin, Walter Byrd, William Simeon, Amos Lamar, and Mrs. Sarah Rebecca Sparkman McKinney.

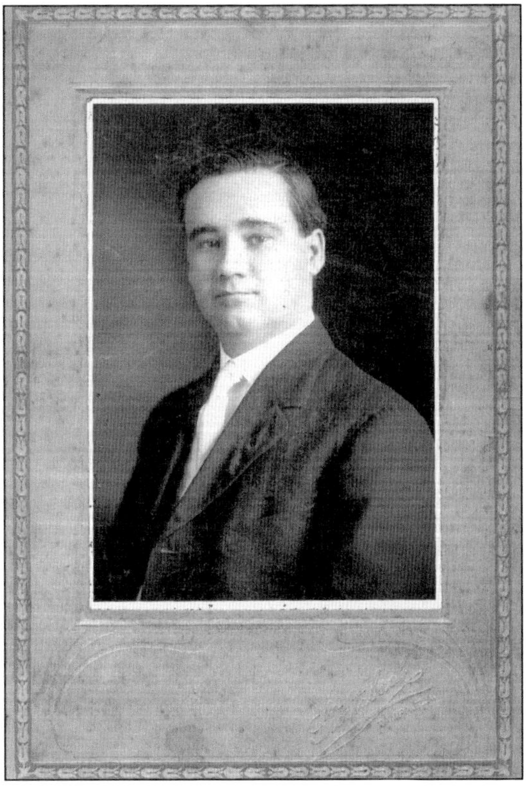

Lovick Sparkman. Lovick was a son of Simeon Elijah and Mary Hackney Sparkman. The Sparkman family descendants lived in the Dover area and were of the Methodist faith. Lovick's grandfather, Elijah Byrd Sparkman, gave two acres of land for the relocation of the Methodist Church of Dover from its original site near the Bethlehem Cemetery. It was customary for the men to sit on the right side of the church while the women and children sat on the left.

Gerald Herbert Bates. Bates was mayor-commissioner in 1931, 1933, and 1935–1937. The son of Luther and Lottie Yost Bates, he was born on March 18, 1889, in Springfield, Missouri. Mr. Bates operated Plant City's Chevrolet Agency and was married to Lorene Waver, the only child of L.R. and Minnie Evers Waver. Gerald "Jerry" and Lorene Bates' daughters are Geraldine Long Demming and Lorene McCall. Mr. Bates was a member of the Masonic Lodge, the York Rite Temple, the Shriners, and the American Legion.

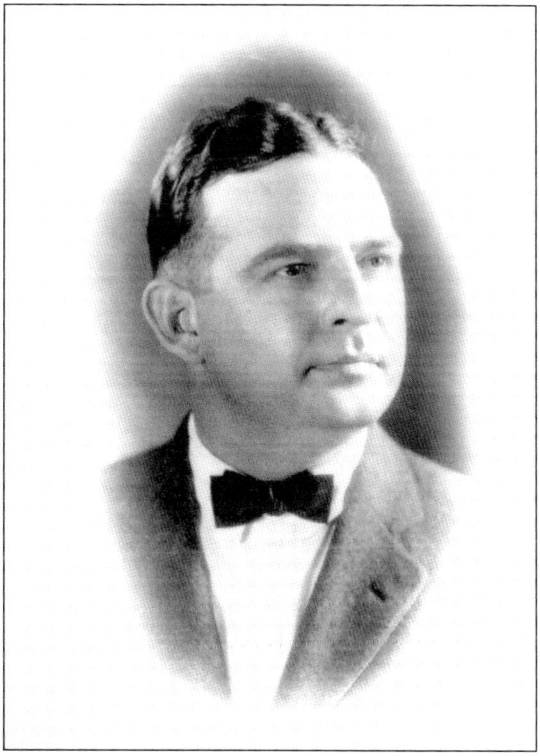

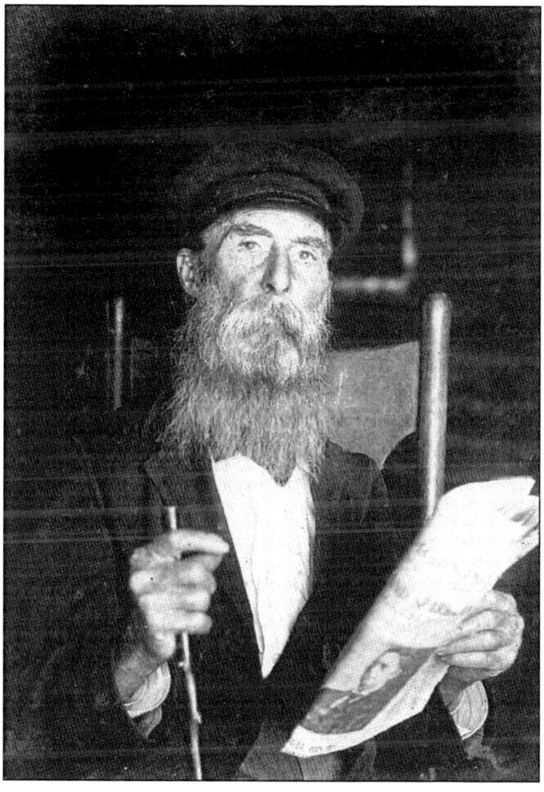

Dr. Augustus Mitchell Barns (1831–1919), Dentist. Dr. Barns was born in Beaufort, South Carolina, on February 11, 1831. He was the son of Paul and Sarah Pope Barns. He received his early schooling in South Carolina, and his medical and dental studies were at Philadelphia. He served as captain with the 6th Arkansas Regiment during the War between the States and was a member of the Hillsborough County No. 1 Confederate Veterans camp at Plant City. He was Plant City's first dentist listed in the *Florida Gazetteer, 1886-87.*

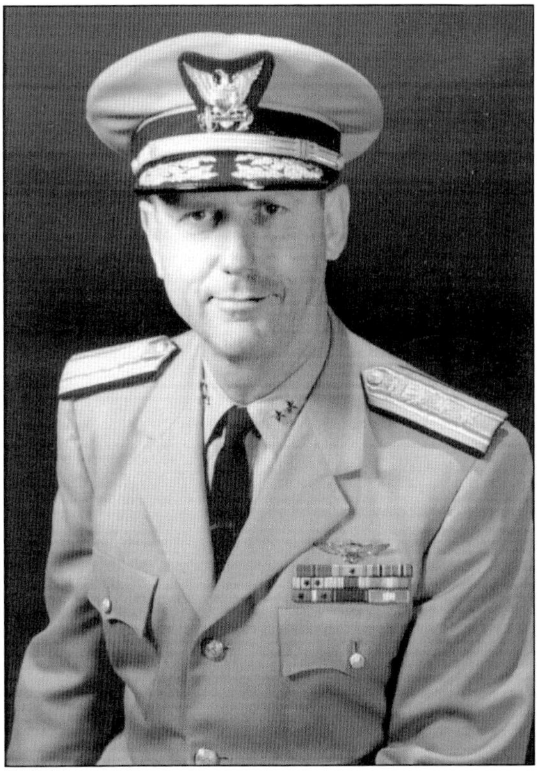

ADM. CHESTER R. BENDER, U.S. COAST GUARD COMMANDANT. Born March 19, 1914, in Burnsville, West Virginia, Bender moved with his family to Plant City in 1925. He graduated from Plant City High School and entered the Coast Guard Academy in 1932. In 1936, he became the first Floridian to graduate from the academy. Admiral Bender died on July 20, 1996, in Moraga, California, and was buried in Arlington National Cemetery with full military honors.

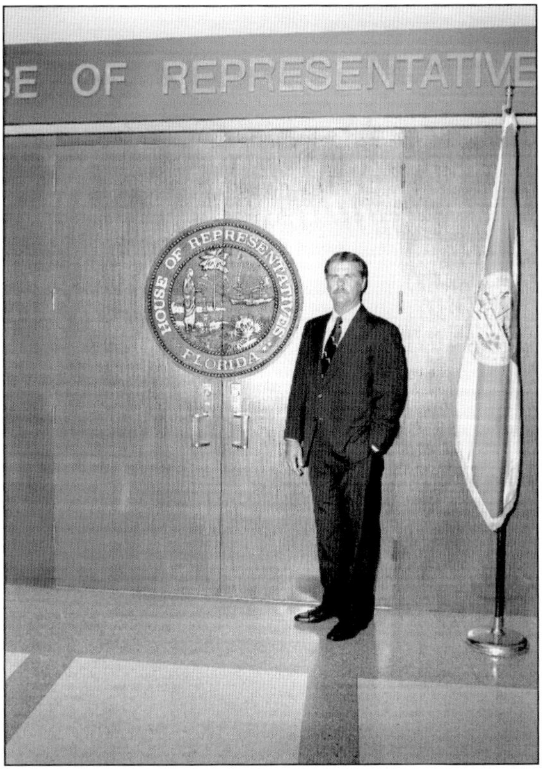

THE HONORABLE CARL CARPENTER JR., FLORIDA STATE HOUSE OF REPRESENTATIVES. Plant City native Carl Carpenter Jr. was elected to the Florida House of Representatives in 1978. He served on the Hillsborough County Commission and the School Board of Hillsborough County. A devoted family person, he has proven his effectiveness in community leadership. He is a graduate of the University of Florida.

JUANITA BRANCH HOLMES. Juanita is the daughter of John L. Branch and Jemmie Collins Branch, from two of Plant City's pioneering families. Juanita was the granddaughter of John Laurence Branch, who was born in Laurens County, Georgia, on February 1, 1820. John Laurens Branch died in Plant City on March 22, 1885, and is buried in the old Shiloh Cemetery, just north of Plant City.

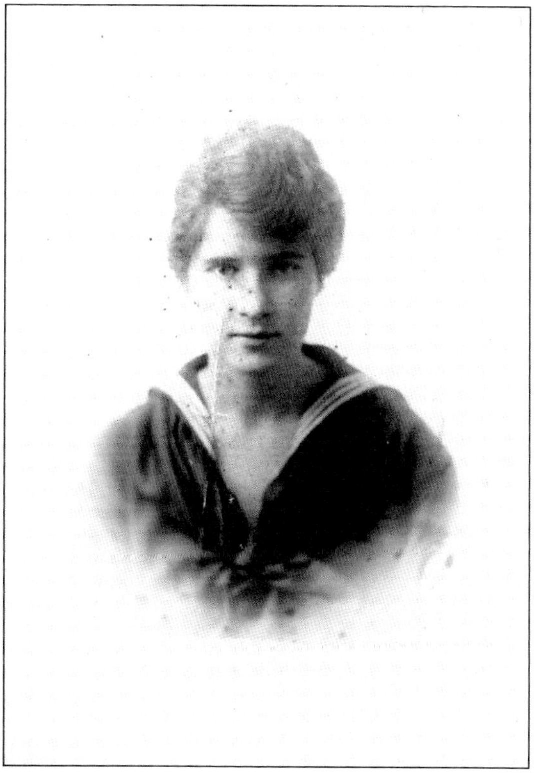

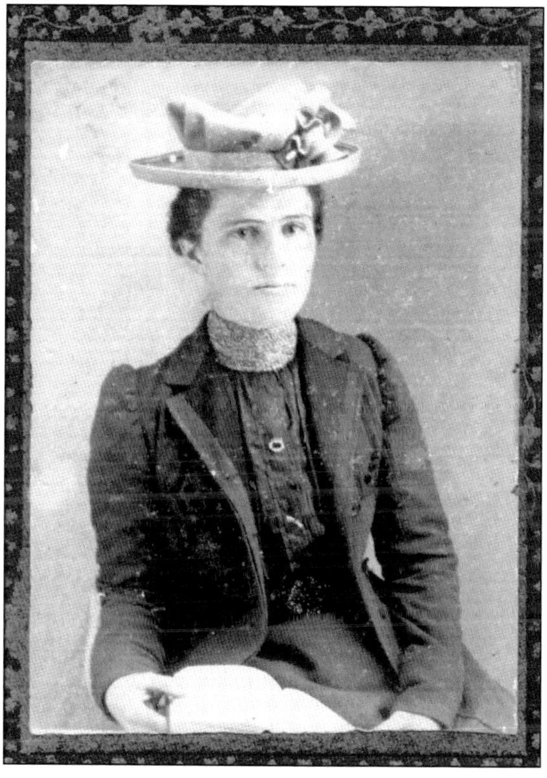

IDA BRANCH WILLIAMS. Williams was a daughter of John Laurence Branch and Eliza Basheba Wilder Branch. John Branch was born in Laurens County, Georgia, on February 1, 1820, and traveled to Florida with an uncle. He married Eliza Wilder, a daughter of Hopkins M. Wilder, and they lived for a while near Lake Thonotosassa on family land. He was the first postmaster at Silver Springs and built the first hotel there. He owned a general merchandise store in Hyde Park, Tampa, at the present site of the University of Tampa. Ida Williams was Juanita Holmes's aunt.

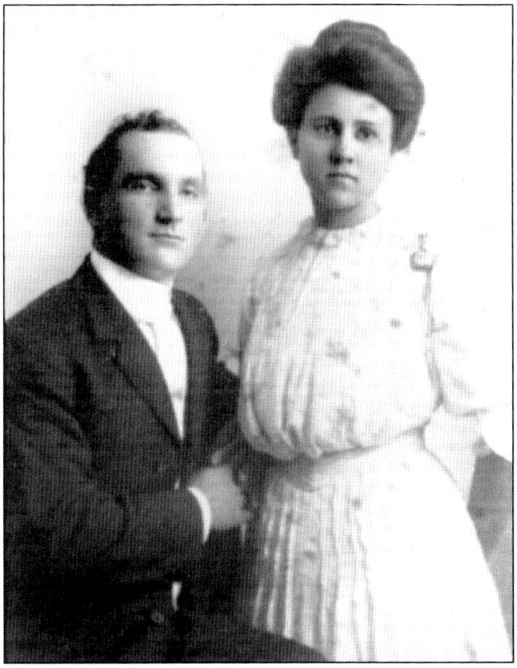

SAM AND MAE COLLINS BOONE, 1908. Mae was the granddaughter of local pioneer Enoch Collins and a descendant of Enoch Collins Sr., a successful cattleman and farmer of the Collinstown (Cork) community northwest of Plant City. Enoch Collins Sr. was born in Effingham County, Georgia, on October 13, 1807, the son of Jesse Collins of North Carolina. Enoch was the father of 29 children. Many Plant City families share connections to the Collins family lineage.

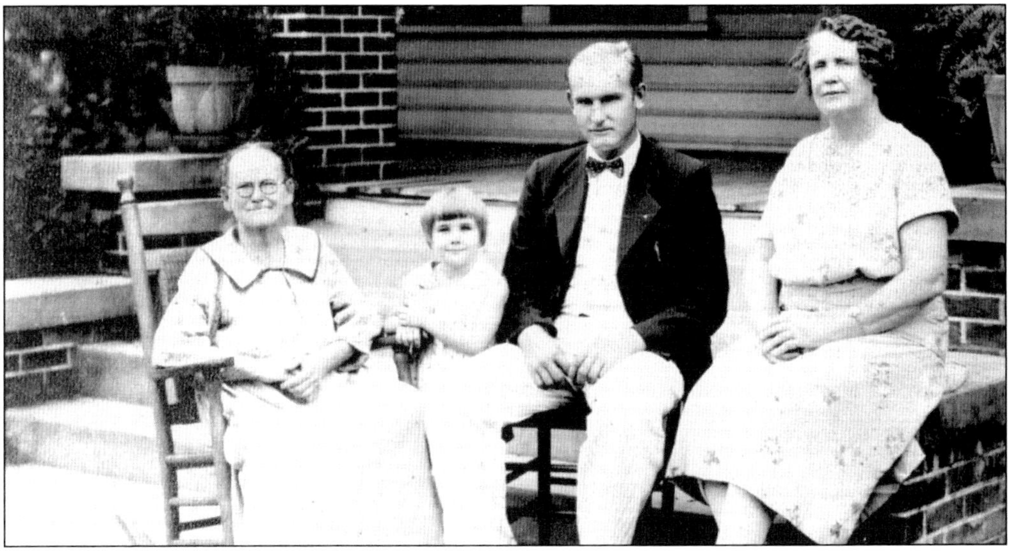

FOUR GENERATIONS. Shown here from left to right are Arrincy Harrell; Margaret Mitchell, Arrincy's great granddaughter; Omar C. Mitchell, Arrincy's grandson; and Ruby Mitchell Emmons, Arrincy's daughter. This family gathered for their photo in the early 1930s on West Reynolds Street. Omar Mitchell was a citrus grower, writer, teacher, and principal for 42 years in Hillsborough County. His great-grandfather, George Hamilton Sr., came to settle in what was then Hillsborough County in the 1840s. Hamilton and his wife, Mary Knight, had five sons and three daughters. Their oldest daughter, Arrincy, married Benjamin T. Harrell. Omar Mitchell attended school in Plant City and then worked his way through Florida Southern College by running a coal chute and pumping water for Seaboard railroad locomotives. He later earned a master's degree in education from Western State at Gunnison, Colorado, and worked on his doctorate at several other universities, including the University of Florida.

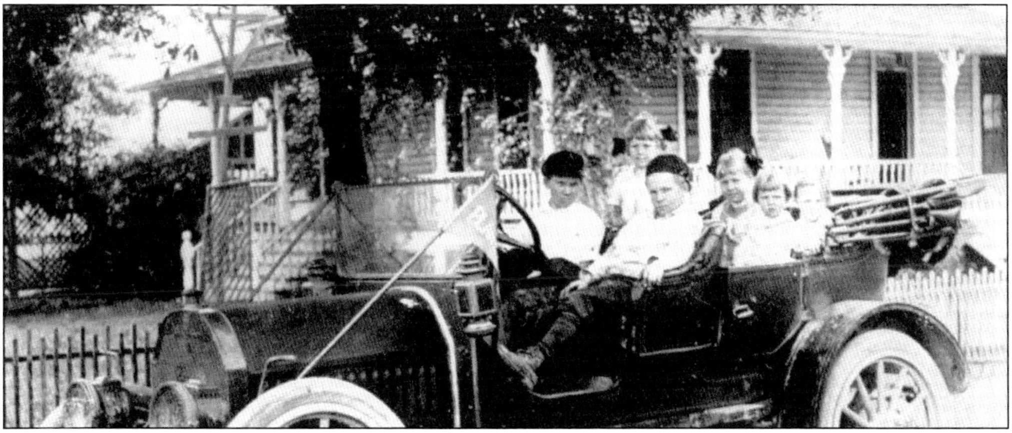

GRAHAM/SIMMONS HOME, WEST REYNOLDS STREET. Located in the heart of Plant City's Downtown Residential Historic District, this Queen Anne/Folk Victorian–style home was built in 1906 by John R. Graham and his wife, Ida Belle Causey Graham. Prominent local businessman Jesse Wright Simmons purchased the home for his family in 1912 and occupied the home for many years. The gracious foyer features high ceilings with built-in displays. Ornate woodwork surrounds the fireplace in the formal sitting room. The Victorian-style wrap-around porch features decorative tapered, turned wood posts with scrolled brackets that lead to the formal entryway of the home. Mr. Simmons stored his Warren car in the "tin" carriage garage. For years, the front lawn of this home has been the gathering spot for many of Plant City's prominent citizens as they view the processional of the Florida Strawberry Festival Parade and enjoy their annual picnic luncheon.

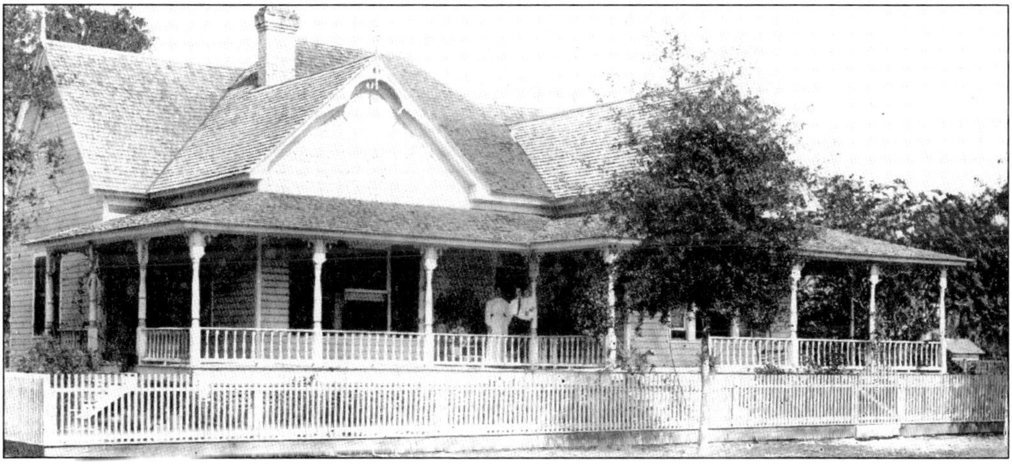

D.M. GRIFFIN HOME, CALHOUN STREET. This picturesque Queen Anne house was built in 1905 for Dr. David Mitchell Griffin, a traveling dentist who practiced his profession throughout South Florida. David came to the Plant City area by horse and buggy from South Georgia and worked for Alonzo and Alma Robertson on their homestead. In 1884, he married their daughter Clara. The couple was given 40 acres of land from her family, which they lived on and farmed until 1905. The one-story frame house has a hip roof with multiple gables featuring scalloped and pierced barge boards, sash windows, and turned posts as roof supports with balustrades between them. At the time of his death at the age 83, Dr. Griffin was survived by his widow; three daughters, Mrs. Mabel Sweat, Mrs. J.D. (Maude) Carlton, and Aldine Griffin, all of Plant City; one sister, Mrs. C.N. Isom, Plant City; and two brothers, W.O. Griffin of Turkey Creek and S.L. Griffin of Wauchula.

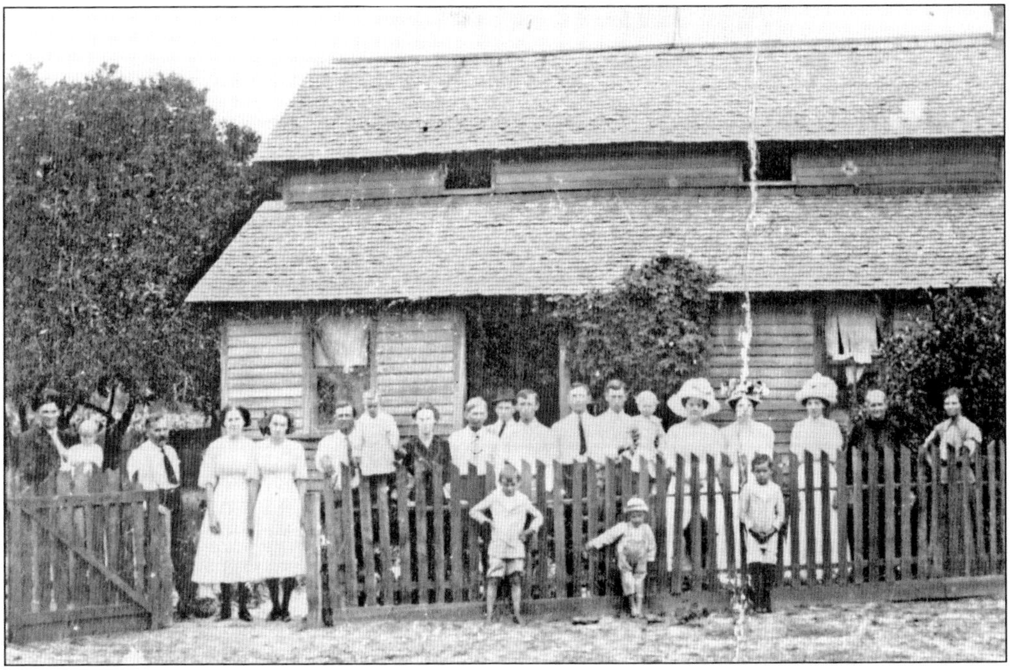

HOWELL HOME, CORONET. Pictured here is the family of Tom Howell in Coronet in 1910. The Howell family homesteaded land in the Springhead area, on a section of land known as Howell Creek. This area later became known as Howell Hammock. His homestead included a double-pen log home, smoke house, and detached kitchen. Water was drawn from a well located near the home. Howell family members continue to live in the areas of their early pioneer ancestors.

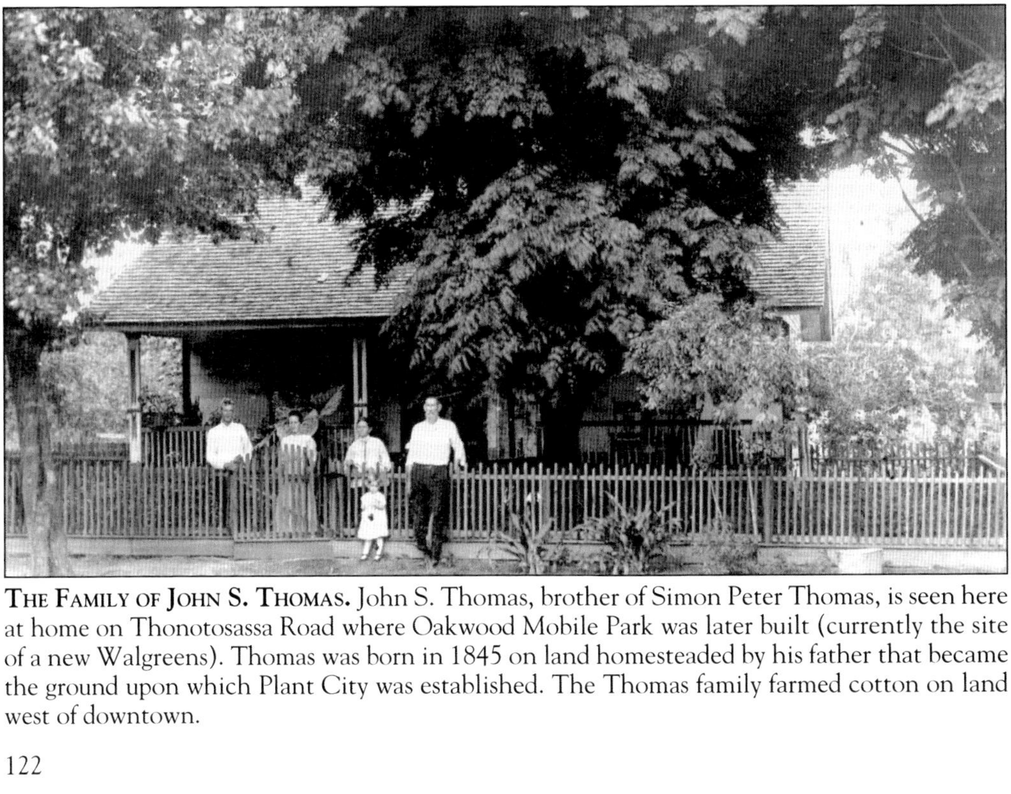

THE FAMILY OF JOHN S. THOMAS. John S. Thomas, brother of Simon Peter Thomas, is seen here at home on Thonotosassa Road where Oakwood Mobile Park was later built (currently the site of a new Walgreens). Thomas was born in 1845 on land homesteaded by his father that became the ground upon which Plant City was established. The Thomas family farmed cotton on land west of downtown.

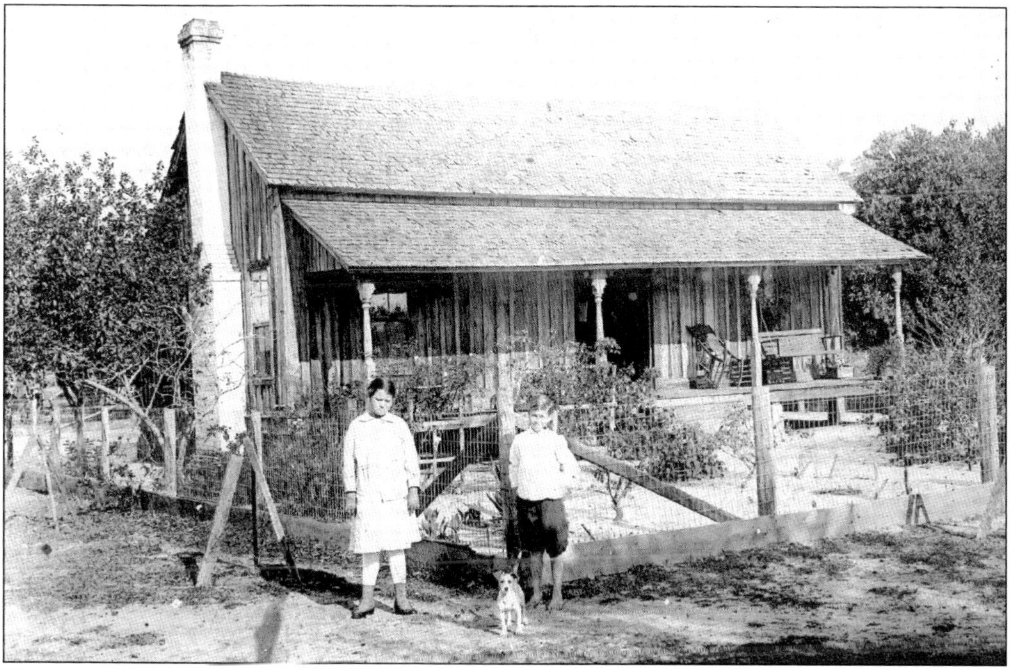

HAWKINS FAMILY HOME. The home of Stephen and Ellen Tomberlin Hawkins in 1915 was located on Highway 39 South (James Redman Parkway) at Trapnell Road. Pictured from left to right are the Hawkins' daughter Lois and son Ellis. (Courtesy of Martha Sue Hawkins Skinner; Union Photo Co. Tampa, Florida.)

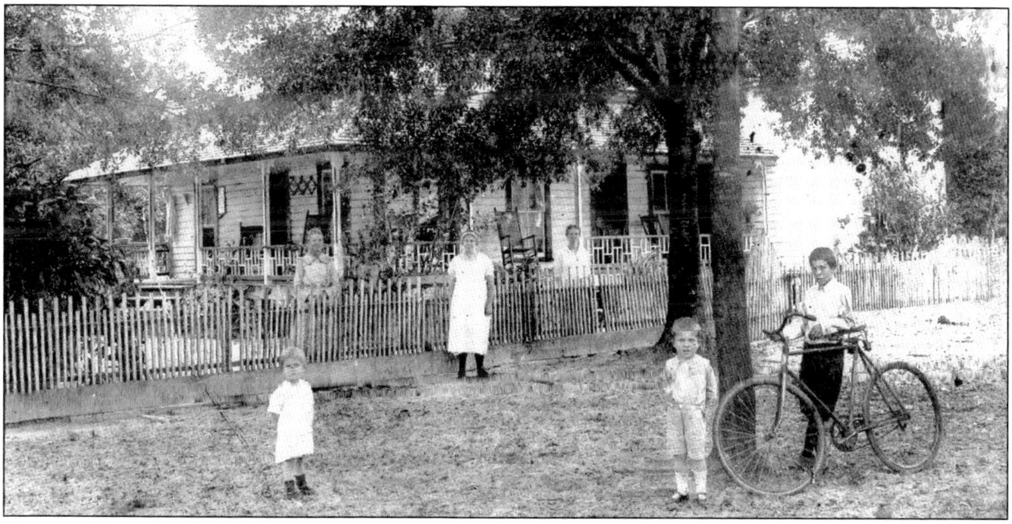

DANIEL POLLARD HOME, SPRINGHEAD, 1915 OR 1916. Shown here from left to right are (front row) Eloise DuBois (Mrs. D.E. Bailey), J.D. DuBois, and Roy V. Pollard; (back row) Mrs. Daniel P. Pollard, Mabel Pollard (Mrs. Wilmer McDonald), and Lela Pollard (Mrs. J.C. DuBois). Daniel Pugh Pollard was born on October 22, 1861, near the town of Boston, Thomas County, Georgia. His parents were Allison B. Pollard and Margaret Lamon Pollard. He and his sisters, Mary, Sarah, Laura, and Amanda, were orphaned when their parents and Daniel's twin, James, died of smallpox during the epidemic of 1864–1865. The Pollard family was of the Primitive Baptist faith and traveled by ox-cart to the Polk County area of Fort Meade.

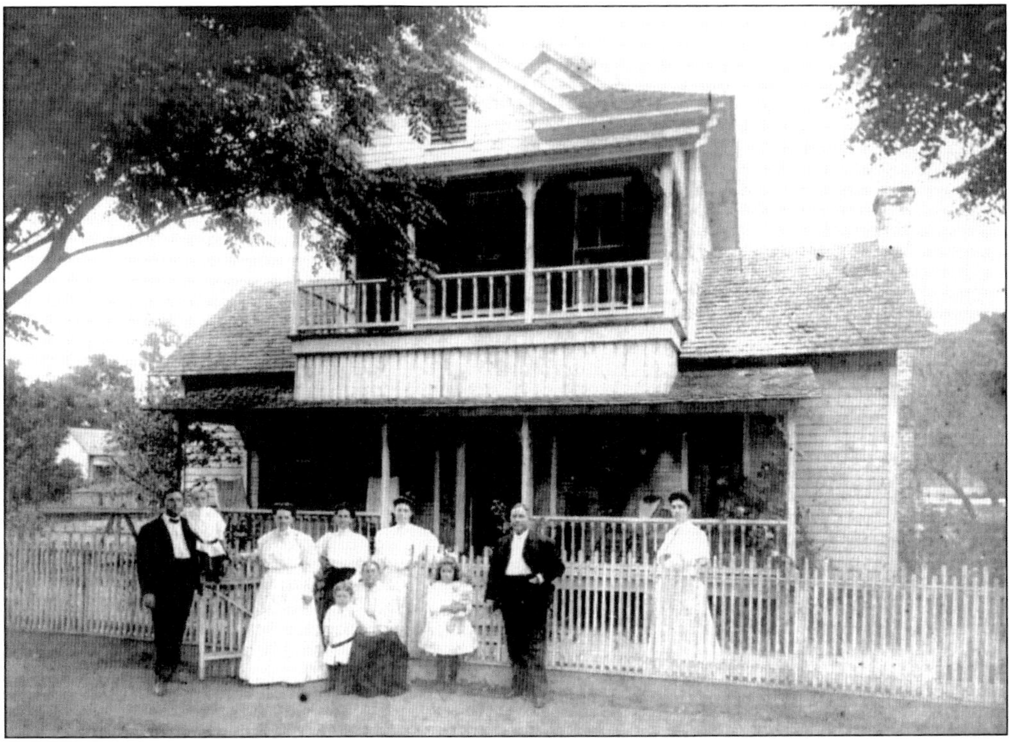

Oscar Strickland House, North Collins Street. This 1890s frame vernacular house is an eclectic combination of the Victorian architectural style and the later bungalow. It was built for Oscar Strickland, a merchant who owned a retail business with his brothers. The house has a gable roof and a three-bay porch, which spans the front and is supported by battered wood posts atop brick piers. A smaller porch atop the lower conveys the more decorative Victorian styling with its slender posts and balustrade. The house was demolished for parking.

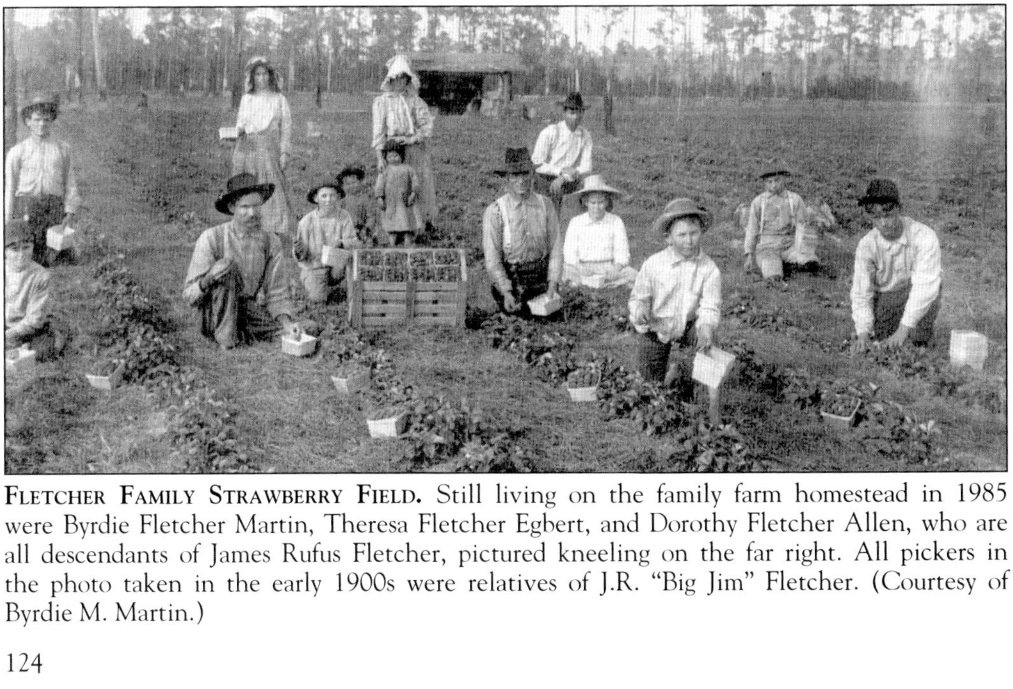

Fletcher Family Strawberry Field. Still living on the family farm homestead in 1985 were Byrdie Fletcher Martin, Theresa Fletcher Egbert, and Dorothy Fletcher Allen, who are all descendants of James Rufus Fletcher, pictured kneeling on the far right. All pickers in the photo taken in the early 1900s were relatives of J.R. "Big Jim" Fletcher. (Courtesy of Byrdie M. Martin.)

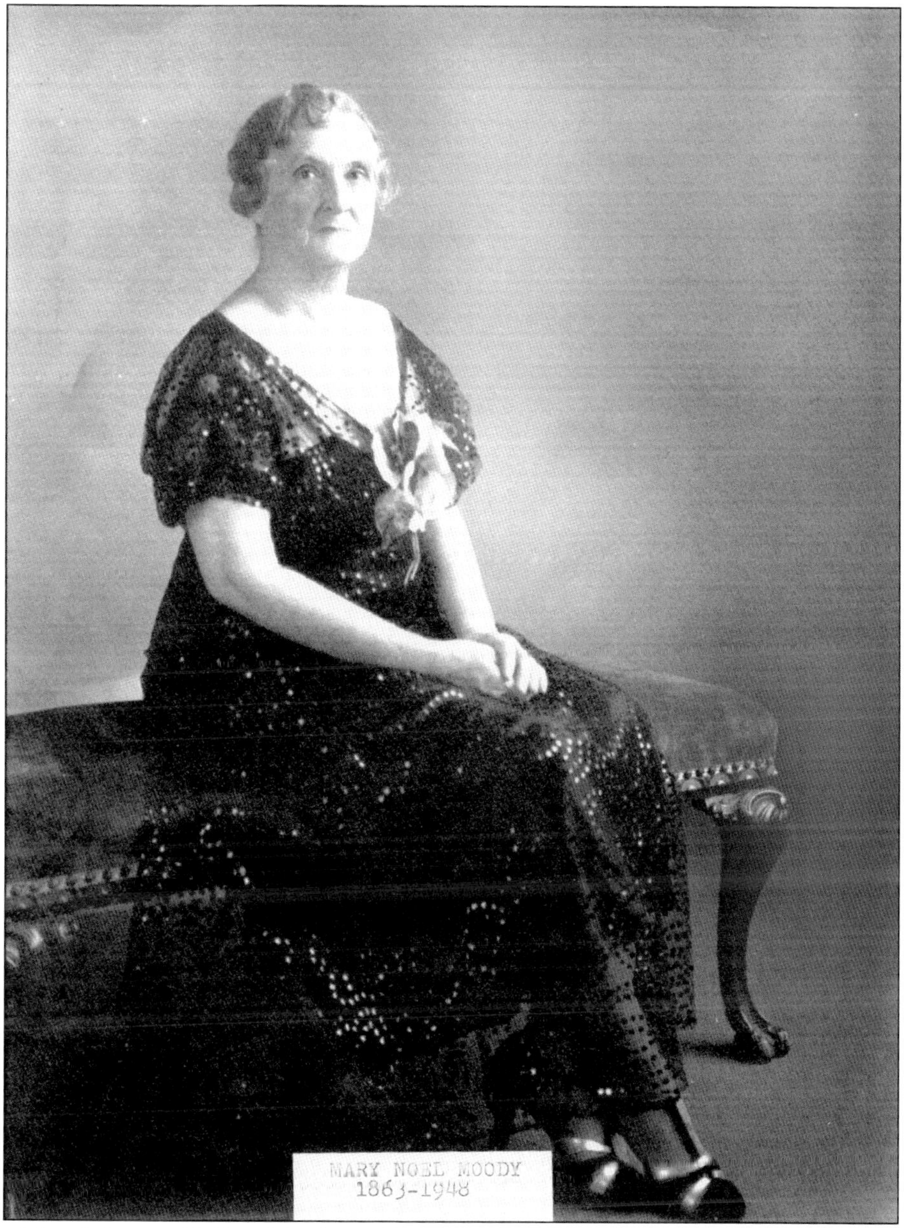

MARY NOEL MOODY, 1863–1948. Mary Noel Estes was married to Thomas Edwin Moody Sr. of Athens, Tennessee, in 1883. She was active in her church life at First Baptist Church and was the president of the Women's Missionary Society. She served the Woman's Club of Plant City as president for two two-year terms. During her tenure, she re-organized the Junior Woman's Club in 1940 and was active in the Woman's Club's work to create and operate a public library for Plant City. The Mary Noel Moody Community Room at the Bruton Memorial Library in Plant City is named in her honor. Her exemplary leadership led to a greater recognition by the community for the worthy work that the Woman's Club contributes. She was elected president at the state convention of the UDC during their 1938 annual meeting in Orlando. She also served as vice-president of the Hillsborough County Women's Club Federation. Her descendants continue her commitment to the betterment of our community.

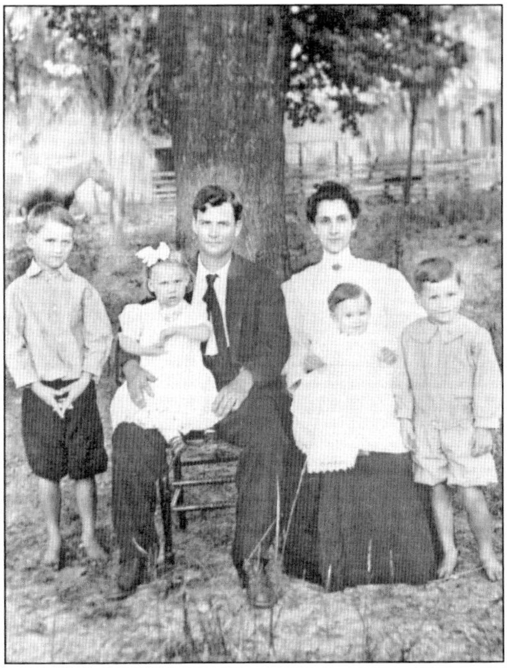

FAMILY OF JAMES MARVIN SPARKMAN AND AGNES DESHONG WALDEN SPARKMAN. Pictured from left to right are Seymour M., Mary, James Marvin, Agnes, Bascom, and Emory. Agnes was the daughter of Larry G. and Catherine DeShong Walden. Their fifth child, not pictured, was Simeon C. Sparkman. The Sparkman, DeShong, and Walden families have many descendants still living in the East Hillsborough County area.

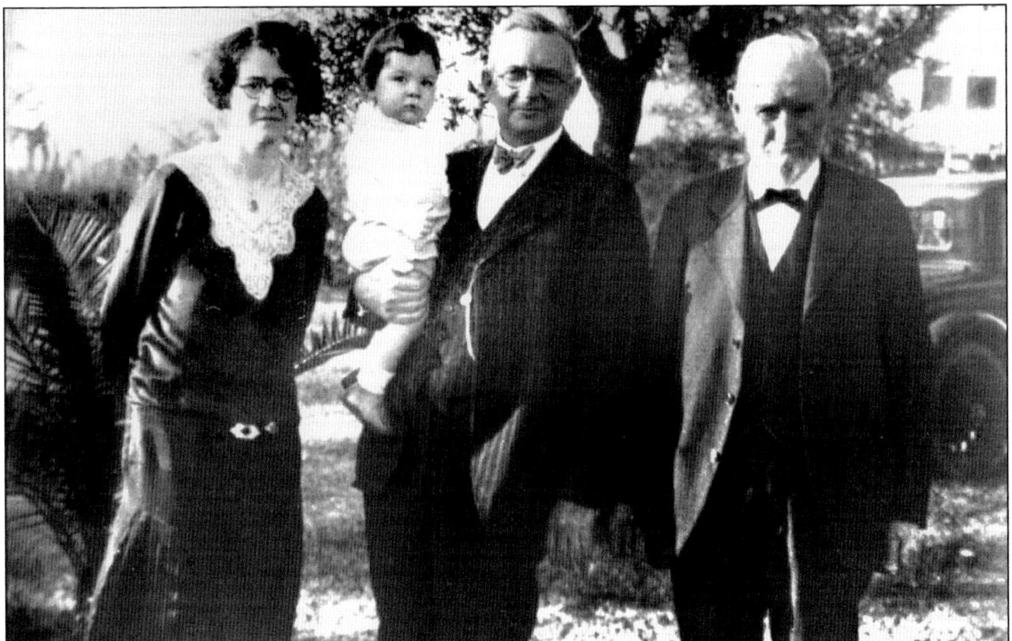

EDWIN TIMANUS ROUX FAMILY. Pictured from left to right are Mary Collins Roux Thompson, Edwin Alexander Thompson, Edwin Timanus Roux, and Edwin Theodore Roux—four generations of the Roux family. Edwin Timanus Roux was born in Fernandina, Florida. He built the Roux home, located on West Calhoun Street, in 1904. His daughter, Mary Collins Roux, married Clarence Gene Thompson from Corryton, Tennessee, in Plant City in 1928. The Roux family was involved in the lumber and sawmill businesses in Hillsborough, Polk, Hernando, and Manatee Counties.

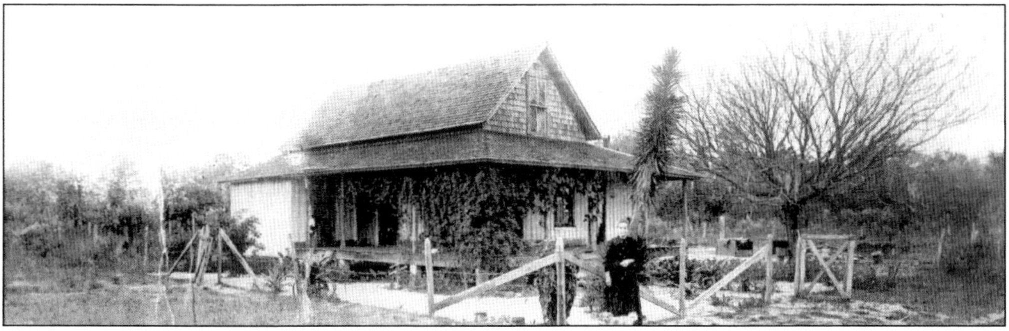

Lizzie Berry and Poodle. Mary Elizabeth Berry is pictured with her poodle at their home on East Tomlin (west of the railroad tracks). This small wood-frame home is on the eastern boundary of the local and National Register Historic Districts and is a contributing structure. (Courtesy of Frances Hayes.)

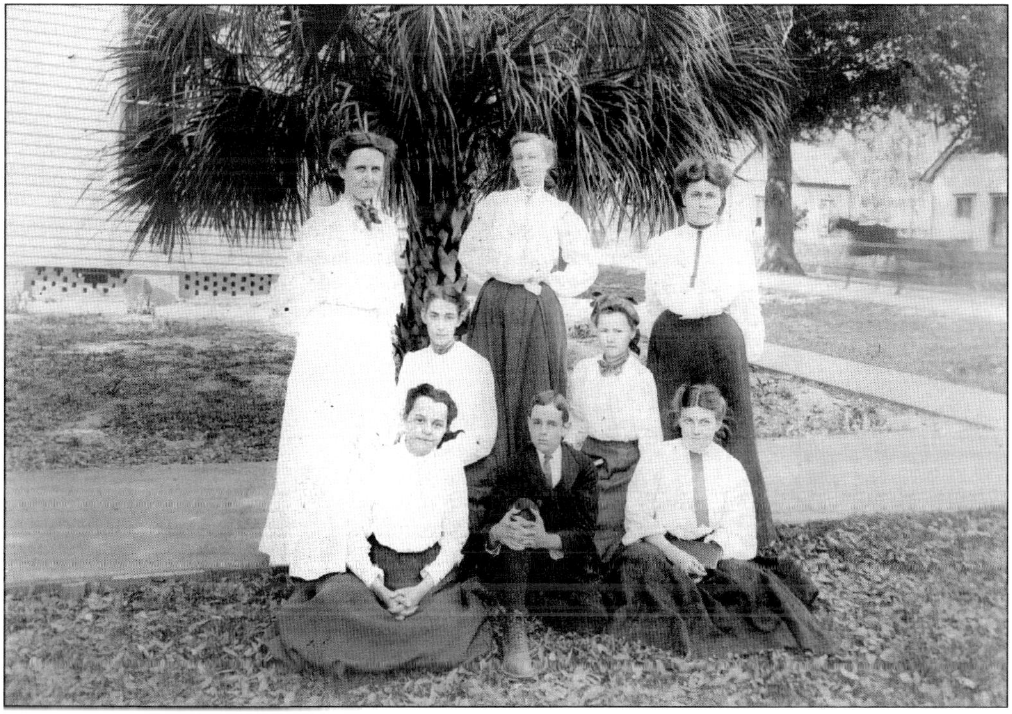

Plant City's Young Pioneers. Plant City, Florida young people gather for a photo in 1907. Pictured from left to right are (front row) Josephine Schneider Land, Walter Griffin, and Florence Smith Root; (middle row) Mamie Ray Walker and Ellen Vining Swindell; (back row) Maud DeVane Hays, Berta Platt, and Mae Collins Boone. Pictured in the background is the First Baptist Church at the northwest corner of Collins and Mahoney Streets. (Courtesy of New York Photo Company, Plant City, Florida.)

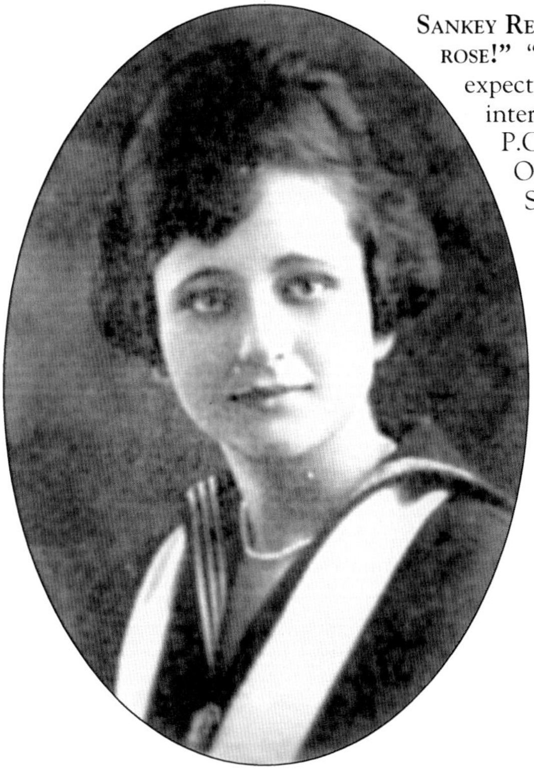

SANKEY REGISTER. "JOYOUS AND GAY AS A LOVE TINTED ROSE!" "A livelier girl we've never seen. We are expecting great things from Sankey. She is very interested in athletics and a player in particular. P.C.H.S., 1,2,3,4; Secretary and Treasurer Orchestra, 3; President Orchestra, 4; Secretary Spanish Club, 4; Assistant Cheer Leader, 4; Local Editor Spokesman, 4; Captain Basket Ball Team, 4; Art Editor *Kanyuksaw*, 4; Charter Club." Artwork featured in the 1920 PCHS yearbook, *The Kanyuksaw*, was contributed by a member of the senior class. As seen in her profile, Sankey was an active participant in academics and extracurricular activities.

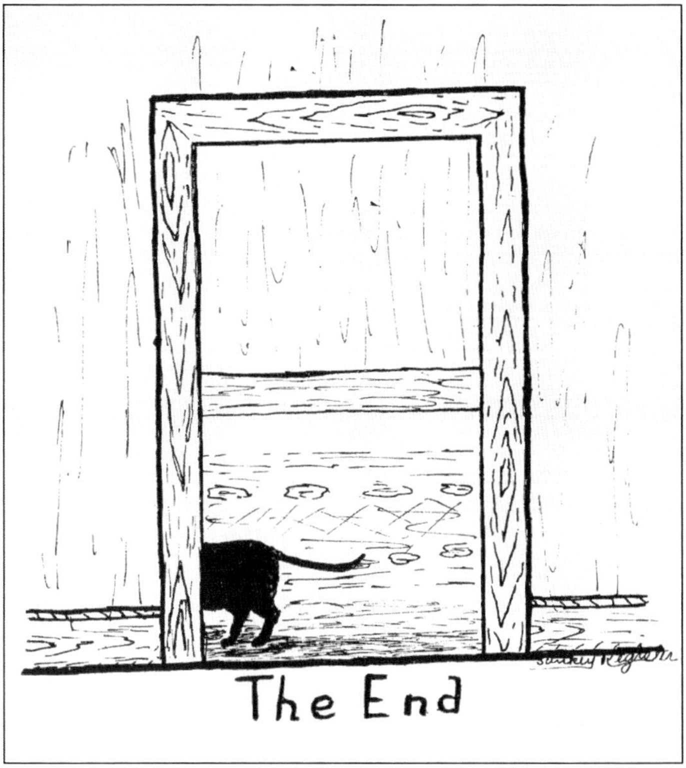

THE END.